FOOD MARGINS

FOOD MARGINS

Lessons from an Unlikely Grocer

CATHY STANTON

University of Massachusetts Press

Amherst and Boston

ISBN 978-1-62534-805-0 (paper); 806-7 (hardcover)

Designed by Sally Nichols
Set in Freight Text
Printed and bound by Books International, Inc.

Cover design by Sally Nichols
Cover photo by Cathy Stanton, 2023

Library of Congress Cataloging-in-Publication Data

Names: Stanton, Cathy, author.
Title: Food margins : lessons from an unlikely grocer / Cathy Stanton.
Description: Amherst : University of Massachusetts Press, [2024] | Includes
    bibliographical references and index. |
Identifiers: LCCN 2023046521 (print) | LCCN 2023046522 (ebook) | ISBN
    9781625348050 (paperback) | ISBN 9781625348067 (hardcover) | ISBN
    9781685750763 (ebook)
Subjects: LCSH: Food industry and trade. | Agriculture—Economic aspects.
Classification: LCC HD9000.5 .S676 2024 (print) | LCC HD9000.5 (ebook) |
    DDC 338.1/9—dc23/eng/20240117
LC record available at https://lccn.loc.gov/2023046521
LC ebook record available at https://lccn.loc.gov/2023046522

British Library Cataloguing-in-Publication Data
A catalog record for this book is available from the British Library.

CONTENTS

ILLUSTRATIONS

ACKNOWLEDGMENTS

M ANY OF THESE acknowledgments reiterate what the chapters try to convey in much more depth: that this story, and the little store at its center, reflect the sum total of the knowledge, skill, dedication, and wonderful stubbornness of many, many people, not all of whom are named in the book. I'm grateful to all those who took time to share their part of the co-op's trajectory with me and to read an earlier version of the manuscript, especially Karl Bittenbender, Amy Borezo, Julie Davis, Nalini Goordial, MaryEllen Kennedy, Pat Larson, Robin Shtulman, and Nina Wellen, and to all those who were part of the ups and downs chronicled here, including Ricky Baruch, Kelsey Cass, Craig Chernov, Dean Cycon, Siobhan Davis, the extended clan at Diemand Farm, Jared Duval, Ben Feldman, Max Feldman, Marcia Gagliardi, Cristina Garcia and others at the Farm School, Deb Habib, Frank Hains, Rick Innes, Seth Isman, Mimi Hellen Jones, Janice and Steve Kurkoski, Noelle Landry, Willie Lane, Zach LeBlanc, Mark Maynard, John and Laura Moore and their family, Diane Nassif, Marti Nover, Margot Parrot, Ingrid Schatz, Bruce and Rachel Scherer, Laura Wolfe, and Mary Wolfe. This narrative ends in 2021, and I'm also appreciative of those who have stepped into crucial positions since then, especially Ramona Hamblin and Pam Harty. Ruth Martin Curry helped us find the right title for the book, after much debate. To the many other volunteers, staff members, supporters, and friends who have played vital roles in the store's survival: there are far too many of you to name individually, but your contributions are present between the lines throughout, and I hope you see yourselves there.

One of the most challenging and enlivening facets of being an anthropologist in a grocery store is that I've often felt simultaneously like a participant in the food business and a scholar trying to figure out the big questions that our modern food system presents us with. Fortunately this work of untangling histories, reshaping systems, and envisioning futures is shared across many people and organizations who comprise the diffuse "food movement." It has been a true privilege to encounter and collaborate with some of those in my part of the world over the past several years. At Mount Grace Land Conservation Trust, David Graham Wolf, David Kotker, and Leigh Youngblood were staunch early advocates for the co-op, and Emma Ellsworth has continued their commitment. I'm particularly indebted to Jamie Pottern for her breadth of vision, awesome organizing skills, and friendship; our conversations and shared projects were an invaluable space for figuring out how to meld my academic knowledge about food systems with active engagement (while having a really good time). Amine Benali at the Local Enterprise Assistance Fund; Rebecca Fletcher at the Cooperative Fund of the Northeast; and Amy Shapiro, Alan Singer, and John Waite at Franklin County Community Development Corporation have all played key roles in supporting local food ventures, and I learned a great deal from my exchanges with them. I'm grateful to Jeff Cole, Frank Martinez Nocito, Becca Miller, and Winton Pitcoff for sharing their knowledge about the Healthy Incentives Program with me, and to all of the elected representatives who have been champions of the program and the local food sector, including State Senator Jo Comerford, former State Senator (now Director of Rural Affairs) Anne Gobi, and especially State Representative Susannah Whipps.

Others around the North Quabbin region and beyond have contributed to the telling of this story, including Deb Kent, who took me backstage in the town hall to see the stage curtains; Janice Lanou, who shared her wealth of knowledge about Orange's history; and Jim Meehan, who filled some gaps in the local Market Basket story. Al Rose at Red Apple Farm and Sean Nolan at Honest Weight Artisan Brewers were both generous with their time and knowledge. Their stories appear in this version of the book in a very scaled-down form but the experience of thinking about their work has been invaluable in putting together the bigger picture I'm working toward here. And it was a comment in a 2018 Valley Advocate podcast by Liz Wills-O'Gilvie of the Springfield Food Policy Council that sparked an "aha" moment for me and helped me see how the legacies of racism and dispossession in the food system continue to manifest in different but related ways in the Connecticut River Valley and the rural North Quabbin towns.

At the other end of the state and the more academic side of my life, I've been blessed with colleagues and students who have supported and challenged me in innumerable ways. The professional development leave granted by the Dean's Office of the School of Arts and Sciences at Tufts University in spring 2021 gave me a chance to rethink rural and urban relationships around food from the ground up. This book is something of a byproduct of that rethinking, as I came to realize how the story of the town of Orange, the Minute Tapioca Company, and Quabbin Harvest Food Co-op contained and reflected the whole trajectory of the modern food system coming into being. Students in my classes and in the Food Systems and Nutrition minor have been eager and critical interlocutors as I've unpacked that trajectory in courses and projects over the past several years; their questions and insistence on integrity and clarity have helped refine my own sense of purpose and my ability to navigate the intractable puzzles of the food system. I hope I have helped them develop some stronger navigational tools in turn as they move into an unsettled future. I deeply value the collegiality of the Tufts Anthropology Department and conversations over the years with Amahl Bishara, Tatiana Chudakova, Craig Cipolla, Jamie Gorman, Sarah Luna, Zarin Machanda, Sarah Pinto, Nick Seaver, Lauren Sullivan, Lynn Wiles, and especially Alex Blanchette, whose insights and scholarship continue to enlarge and enrich my own thinking in ways that are reflected throughout the pages of this book. In the Environmental Studies Program, Julian Agyeman, Coco Gomez, Colin Orians, and Ninian Stein have also been stimulating and valued colleagues. Beyond Tufts, Anna Duhon at the Farmscape Ecology Program of Hawthorne Valley Farm has been a dear friend and conversation partner since my first deep dive into food system politics at Martin Van Buren National Historic Site in 2010. That project, and much of my subsequent thinking about food and farming, was also greatly strengthened by engagement with the work of Brandeis University professor emeritus Brian Donahue, an exemplary scholar-practitioner and an important voice in food systems thinking and planning around New England and well beyond. And I'm appreciative of the good counsel of Matthew Goodman and Marla Miller as I was finishing the manuscript and considering where it might find a home.

It has been a delight to work with the University of Massachusetts Press again after many years. Editor in Chief Matt Becker has shepherded the project with true care from the beginning, helping to plot a course through the inexact borderlands between scholarly and trade publishing. Managing Editor Rachael DeShano, Marketing and Sales Manager Chelsey Harris, copyeditor Margaret Hogan, and Editorial, Design, and Production Manager Sally Nichols have all been thorough, quick, and supportive. Comments from the two anonymous readers helped me to sharpen the book's sense of purpose tremendously, especially the suggestion that it needed to go beyond just tracing legacies of the past and struggles in the present, to articulate more clearly where a small local venture like this one fits within the larger effort of building toward a particular vision of a better world. I assume that such a world will include mission-driven presses as well as mission-driven grocery stores, and I have more admiration than ever for those who do the good work of this kind of publishing in a world of blockbusters.

Finally, and always, I am thankful for Fred Holmgren, who has been wise enough to volunteer for the less complicated tasks at the co-op and patient enough to listen to me talking interminably about all the other ones. He reminds me continually that sometimes we all need to stop talking and thinking and just make or fix something.

FOOD MARGINS

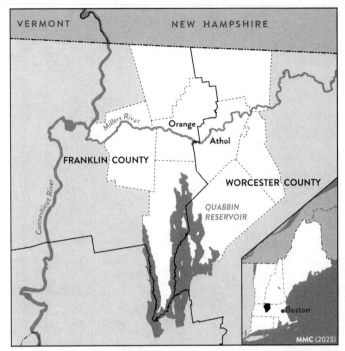

FIGURE 1. The nine North Quabbin towns in their regional context. —Created by Muncie Map Company

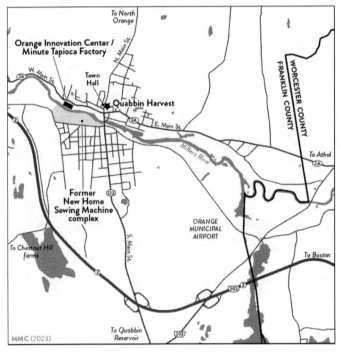

FIGURE 2. Orange, Massachusetts. —Created by Muncie Map Company

MAGIC

IT'S FRIDAY AFTERNOON and I'm sitting on the back of a palomino stallion gliding across an open plain. Its blond mane flows in the breeze. I feel powerful and exhilarated above the thunder of its hooves.

The rest of my family is shopping. There is no actual thunder of hooves; the horse is made of fiberglass and sits at the entrance to our local Dominion supermarket. At age nine, I'm not interested in groceries but I'm very passionate about horses. So I spend the time during our weekly family shopping trips imagining myself into expansive spaces far beyond suburban southern Ontario. None of us ever puts in a coin to set the horse going, but I don't mind that it moves only in my imagination.

The supermarket is part of a national chain, anchoring one end of a low strip-mall that is the first of its kind in the town. We refer to it simply as "the plaza." The Dominion store has a space-age look, with a tall, plate-glass front and bright rows of overhead lights. It seems all of a piece with the mechanical horse: smooth, shiny, and safe yet connected to far-off wonders.

We don't get all of our groceries at the supermarket. There's a little bakery in the plaza where we often buy bread. Despite Dominion's famous tagline—"Mainly because of the meat"—we sometimes go to the butcher on Main Street, aptly named Mr. Cutting. The town still has some small dairy farms. If it were as possible as it seems to ride through the towering transparent facade of the supermarket, my fiberglass steed and I wouldn't have to go very far to reach hayfields and pastureland.

The farms and the little stores don't feel like the past. But the supermarket definitely feels to me like the future. That's partly because of its actual newness and also because I am that kind of child, given to staying off to one side of whatever scene I'm part of, imagining alternatives and wondering about everyday things that other people take for granted. In the mid-1960s, the supermarket is still a little bit strange, and I am strange inside it.

I'm writing now from several decades into that future, decades in which I managed to find my way into an actual profession for people who like to stay off to the side pondering the strangeness of everyday life. In those same decades, the supermarket has become entirely normal, and like most people in the so-called developed world I came to rely on it for most of my food provisioning.

But like a lot of people, I also had a fondness for the alternatives. In the 1970s I caught the earthy-crunchy wave. I made my own granola. My housemates and I rotated our shopping between another Dominion store at one end of our Toronto street and the lively, polyglot outdoor market at the other. In the early 1980s I married an American and moved to Boston, where I sometimes trundled my shopping cart to the nearest supermarket but also enjoyed shopping for cheap end-of-the-week fruits and vegetables at the city's beloved Haymarket.

By the 1990s we had moved to rural Massachusetts, drawn by real estate that was affordable on two freelance incomes (musician and writer). I went back to school and found my way into anthropology, which is the field that's so well suited to instinctive observers and wonderers. As the twenty-first century got underway, I was finishing a PhD and starting to think more deeply about what I ate and where it came from, who produced it and how, and how all of that connected to fossil fuels and the way the planet was heating up and how my gut felt. Along with others caught up in the "locavore" trend, I read books and watched films that were starting to expose the deep problems with industrialized food.[1] I helped put together an annual brochure of local farmstands and markets and bought a membership in a little food co-op that opened in 2009 in the town next to mine. I was still freelancing, doing the kinds of academic odd jobs that you do off the tenure track. When I got a contract to do an anthropological study of farming as a way of life in the area around a national park in eastern New York State, I jumped at the opportunity to explore my own questions about how the modern food system came to be and how it had become so taken for granted over my own fifty-plus-year lifespan.[2] Eventually I found my way into a regular teaching job at the other end of the state, where I started to teach some classes about food. By then I felt pretty knowledgeable and well-informed.

And then I sort of accidentally became a grocer and everything changed. And that's what this book is about.

I say "sort of" and "accidentally" because it was never my intention to get into the grocery business per se. In the fall of 2016 I shared the collective shock on the political left after the election of Donald Trump. I was trying to think of something I could do in the next four years that would feel positive in the face of what was pretty obviously going to be a concerted attack on a lot of the fragile recent changes in American conversations about race, energy, health, environment, and all the complicated linkages among them. I knew the little food co-op was already struggling to survive, only two years after opening a storefront operation. I thought maybe I could do something to help keep it going.

I volunteered to join the board of directors and started figuring out what my niche might be. Like nearly all of my fellow co-op members, I now realize, I thought of the actual business part as something that someone else knew how to run. I certainly didn't want to try running it myself.

I had never run a business. I flirted with the idea of starting a bookstore after I finished my PhD because it seemed like a cultural project that might actually pay its own way instead of constantly scrambling for funding within what some have termed the nonprofit-industrial complex.[3] But I got far enough into developing a business plan to realize that trying to make a living selling books in our rural area would be a good way to go broke fast. When I started to get involved at the co-op I envisioned helping with communications, building organizational capacity, things I actually knew how to do. I was perfectly happy to leave the nuts and bolts of running the business to someone, anyone else. I knew my limits and planned to stay well within them.

It's hard to pinpoint exactly when that changed. It was like the proverbial ton of bricks fell on me, but not all at once: The day we didn't have enough in the bank account to cover a demand notice from the power company, and I realized it was now partly my responsibility to figure out how to keep the lights on—one big brick. The first time the freezers broke and we had to throw out all the food—another brick. The dawning awareness of just how many unpaid bills were piling up, including to local farmers and small businesses who didn't have the leverage of threatening to turn off the power—a whole cascade of bricks.

By that point, I'd been pushed over the sidelines into a hundred contradictory conversations. It was the first time I realized how being an eater and a shopper can give you a highly exaggerated sense of actually understanding anything about the grocery business. That's even truer at food co-ops, which are all about giving shoppers more control over how they get their food.

There were countless ideas but nothing resembling consensus. We should expand into a bigger space or a bigger town; we should go back to being a part-time, volunteer-run store; we should merge with a larger food co-op; radically rethink our product mix; sell only things that no one else in the area carried; lower our prices; raise our prices; try to keep up with the latest trends in the grocery sector; stay true to our health-food roots; rent part of our space to other businesses; focus on a more affluent shopper demographic; reach more low-income people; cut our losses and just declare bankruptcy.

"Meanwhile," our beleaguered treasurer Karl Bittenbender wrote in an email one day, "everyone wants to get paid with the money we don't have." Few of these conversations connected to the day-to-day struggle to keep the store open and the freezers functioning. For the whole first year I felt like I was trying to put a puzzle together without having all the pieces, and when I did manage to find a missing one, the dog had chewed it so it didn't quite fit.

The thing that helped me find some kind of footing was that this kind of disorientation is very familiar to anthropologists. In fact, it's what we do.

It's called "participant-observation" and it's an actual methodology, honed over a century or so, for studying humans' interactions in and with our environments. We ask the very broadest questions about human life, and while we know we can't possibly study everything at once, we also resist putting things too neatly into boxes (language in one, economics in another, biology in another) as many scholarly disciplines do. We reach into deep time—that's the archeological "stones and bones" part that many people think of when they hear the word "anthropology"— and across and into every imaginable space, including the spaces of the imagination itself. We explore the countless (yet patterned) ways that people make meaning out of the world around them, how they act on those meanings, and how those efforts in turn shape physical and social worlds. Lately we've been revisiting the whole question of what it even means to be human. What is "human being" now that we know that everyone's gut is home to trillions of microbial fellow-travelers whose aggregated DNA far outweighs our own? You could say this is the Western intellectual tradition finally starting to catch up to the kinds of Indigenous knowledge that European anthropologists set out to study a hundred years ago.

Food has always been interesting to anthropologists, as something material that comes to us from outside of ourselves but is thickly braided with meanings that can literally tell us who we are. And our methods work whether you're studying exchanges of yams in Indigenous communities in Papua New Guinea (a staple of old-school anthropology) or food provisioning with the touch of fingertips on a phone screen to get someone to bring you a burrito at three in the morning. Those methods consist largely of making yourself a part of whatever setting you're studying and hanging out there for a while. "Hanging out" may not sound very rigorous, but there's a solid rationale to it. You always miss something if you keep your distance and try to be more objective and scientific. In fact, the whole notion of being scientific about studying everyday human life depends on staying at arm's length and not letting reality mess up your own toolkit.

Anthropologists wade in, intentionally letting ourselves be tugged and tossed by all the contradictory evidence and agendas and ideas and experiences we find ourselves in the midst of. To a large extent, that *is* our toolkit.

What we're ultimately trying to do is to make translations—in one of the catchphrases of the discipline, to make the strange familiar and the familiar strange. We try to carry experience across gaps and communicate it in a way that honors as much as possible what we saw and heard and felt and what people told us, in all its fascinating and unsettled complexity. It's never a perfect translation, but what is? That's our point.

It's a method that seems to suit people who are constitutionally given to standing off to one side, watching and pondering. It's also deeply unsettling, because it means that eventually you do have to cross that line and start talking to people and getting pulled into their lives and work and ideas and agendas. You become implicated. Usually you become confused. At some point you extricate yourself again, at least far enough to write about what you learned. Often you aren't sure what you learned *until* you write about it.

That's what I'm doing now. I'm writing this to share what I learned from getting much farther inside the food business than most shoppers ever go. It's a dispatch from one small node within the widespread effort to reshape and resize the systems that feed us, an account of how things look and feel as that initial wave of enthusiasm for more local food runs into the realization that fixing things isn't going to be nearly as simple as just knowing and caring more about where our food comes from. It's an argument for going deeper—into the economic and political guts of the system and the mystery of how it acts on us and through us, especially those of us who have had the luxury of using or rejecting the mainstream model, as we choose. It's a view from inside a different model, within a still-emerging larger wave of change necessitated by an ever more unstable planetary climate.

I had no idea how far the supermarket-centered status quo had gotten inside my head—inside everyone's head—until I started helping to run a grocery store. I didn't realize how convenient I expected food shopping to be until I had to help make it convenient for other people or explain why it wasn't as convenient as they were used to. It took time to shift my own thinking about value, from simply looking for the best price to trying to spend as much money as I could in the co-op every week, which helped put a little more into our coffers but didn't change the fact that most people were still looking for the best price. It took a while to come to grips with what that meant for the store's ability to survive. We couldn't charge more for food—people already thought we were too expensive. We couldn't cut costs—they were already slashed to the bone and below. The challenges were economic and emotional, personal and systemic. They felt inexorable, insoluble. And from the outside, it's hard even to understand why.

After several years of trying to find succinct ways to explain it, this is as close as I've gotten.

Our food system is built on a kind of koan, a Zen riddle that has no actual answer. The riddle is, "What happens when you bring together the need for food with the logic of a market?"

Markets have been around in one form or another for millennia. They're a way to facilitate trade and generate wealth and—very often, and very sensibly—stabilize food supplies. But they also have a tendency to take on a momentum of their own. And they don't actually care whether everyone gets fed. Food-as-sustenance and food-as-commodity are not only different but can be fundamentally at odds. That's what started to happen in Europe—specifically in the parts of England that sent most of the first settlers to what's now called New England—several hundred years ago.[4]

The incompatibilities are harder to see at first. But once the system gets really entrenched and the logic of profit starts to be at odds with the need for food, the fault lines start to become clearer. Means become ends, the initial logic of the pairing gets skewed, and big problems start to push through the cracks.

There's a long history of workarounds and Band-Aids and compromises and deals to try to address those problems. In fact, the Europeans who settled here have been tinkering with and propping up this system for almost as long as they've been using it.

There's still no solution to that original koan. But more than a century ago, Americans figured out a wonderful magic trick that *seemed* like a solution. This trick made food permanently cheap by producing and selling it at very large scales, using the new wizardry of industrial production.

In fact, this turned out to be yet another workaround that caused another whole tangle of problems. But it's become a staple part of the magic act that feeds us, continually refined and added to over the past century. It's different from other workarounds because of how it changed the basic rules of the game. Once food was cheap and abundant, it became all but impossible to do anything that might limit it or make it more expensive again. The real trick was to create a food system that couldn't be changed, one that could *only* be tinkered with—one that everyone from the most impoverished eaters to the most powerful politicians would line up to defend. The more people there are who don't grow or catch their own food, the more reliant we become on those large-scale, long-distance supply chains. This cycle is still gaining momentum, especially where cities are growing and rural, food-producing people are leaving their land—often reluctantly or involuntarily—in search of livelihoods. Ironically, many of those people provide the labor in fields, slaughterhouses, fishing fleets, anywhere food is being produced on an industrial scale.

When you try to find simple, clear ways to explain this, as I often have to do in my classes, it can feel as though the system itself is resisting clarity. This actually makes perfect sense, if you think of it as a magic trick resting on top of an insoluble paradox. And if you're idealistic enough to try to find ways to change it, you tend to run into the same few blind alleyways over and over again, the way those initial conversations at our co-op did when I first started trying to understand the trouble we were in.

In fact, the problem at the core of things is very simple: by now it's become nearly impossible to make money selling food except at the very largest of scales. That's because food has been made cheap. And there are a lot of reasons—some good, some not—why we can't just make it more expensive again.

In 2016 I was still naive about what it was like—what it *felt* like—to try to operate inside the magical and crushing logic of the food business, in a space where it doesn't make any economic sense to do things differently. And yet the whole point is to do something different, something fairer and more transparent and ecologically rational.

In the same essay where farmer-activist Wendell Berry famously said "eating is an agricultural act," he exhorted eaters to "learn, in self-defense, as much as you can of the economy and technology of industrial food production."[5] The spate of exposés that began in the 1990s started us down that road, and this book heads in that direction too, telling a localized story that incorporates the interwoven and always global trajectories of the plantation, the factory, and the supermarket, those essential building blocks of the modern food system.

But it also asks where we go from here, from first-blush enthusiasms for farm-to-table eating and individual epiphanies to something more collective and structural. The next steps are far from clear, especially for eaters who are a very long way from either the day-to-day realities of operating within the food business or the day-to-day exigencies of providing enough food for themselves.

And let's be honest—most of us get more pleasure from being astonished by a magic show than from unpacking its technical workings. Who wouldn't want to ride an enchanted mechanical horse that would take you wherever you wanted to go, especially if the other option was to spend endless hours sitting on the floor tinkering with its grimy inner workings trying to get it to move even just a little bit? Like any magic show, our modern food system depends on the complicity of the audience. It relies on us not to want to get into the financial nitty-gritty where we might actually start to understand the powerful whammy that's been worked on us by making food cheap, or to wade in to the complications of trying to work collectively on visions and projects that feel like moving targets, still just coming into view and often on the verge of falling apart even as they take shape.

Another farmer-activist, Chris Newman, has put things in starker terms: "We have so far to go, it could be argued we haven't really begun."[6] In the sense of making deep and lasting change in the mainstream food system, that's probably fair. And yet we *have* begun. Some of the beginnings have deep roots and long track records. Some are very new. Many are isolated, hyperlocal. But many are not. And the connections and networks become stronger and denser all the time. It's happening in ways that are unique to particular places, and in the chapters that follow I trace some of how it's happening in Massachusetts and New England, from the vantage point of one small, local enterprise that has found ways to knit itself into relationships with the state, with partners in the non-profit world, with other food businesses working toward a vision of a fairer and more resilient food system for the region and beyond.

An anthropological eye is useful for looking at what is inchoate and emergent. It also helps when seeing yourself as part of whatever setting or community you're looking at. It prompts me to ask what it means to be a well-educated, middle-class, white woman—a core demographic of the locavore movement over the past twenty years—doing this work. As important, what does it mean to be doing it *now*, in a moment of racial and environmental and economic reckoning and a growing acceptance of the fact that none of the big problems we face can be solved in isolation from the others? What does it mean to be doing it in a part of the United States that has been inhabited mostly by white people of European ancestry since the original Pocumtuck and Nipmuc residents were pushed far to the margins more than three centuries ago? This is where the personal and local layers of this story merge with broader reachings toward racial self-awareness and a sense of what it would actually take to undo the damages inherent in how the current system came to be.

All of this brings me to Orange, Massachusetts, population 7,800.

Orange is one of the poorest towns in one of the wealthiest U.S. states. In its heyday it was a little industrial dynamo. Now it's part of the nine-town North Quabbin region, which is almost literally a backwater. (Quabbin rhymes with bobbin; it's a Nipmuc word meaning "many waters.") The term "North Quabbin" is fairly recent, but the region's backwaterishness was created in the 1930s when the city of Boston, seventy miles to the east, decided to secure an adequate drinking water supply once and for all by flooding four small towns and creating a gigantic reservoir in the middle of the state. The presence of the reservoir and the reminder of the city's demand for water press against people's awareness here, not constant but never quite absent either. We're in a hinterland, moved aside, left behind (that's what "hinter" means in the original German). It's one of many places where the kinds of people who have historically benefited most from the modern food system and the society that created it now find themselves up against the kinds of barriers that people in less-buffered settings, especially communities of color, have struggled against for a very long time.

Orange is the place where I've been moving into a more active role in the system that feeds me, coming to understand more about how the food business actually works and why it's so opaque and intractable. These chapters follow my own often unwelcome and uncomfortable learning and unlearning, alongside the long history of the mainstream system growing into taken-for-granted ubiquity and the shorter timeline of people trying to take some or all of it apart again. I'm tracking global routes and local landings, turning my anthropological eye—the one that's always looking into time and across space, alert to what's still just taking shape and attentive to who is doing the looking from where—onto one small node in a wide, uneven, lively landscape. The connections are fluid and ephemeral, purposeful and glancing, adding up to something that often seems less like an actual movement and more like a shared intuition, a conviction that food should be better, that many things should be better, and that food is a productive starting point for working to make them so. Ultimately, I'm tracing the contours of what the sociologist Michael Carolan calls "adventurous food futures"—projects that weave together vivid imaginings of a changed relationship to food provisioning with active, practical participation in building something new.[7]

It's been a process of continual discovery, a way of engaging that both refuses and reshapes the underlying premises of how most of us get our food. Climate catastrophe is reason enough to do that, but it's far from the only reason. Becoming more active in our own food provisioning is a way of being more fully alive, not just as eaters or consumers but as decision-makers, relationship-builders, problem-solvers, dwellers in place, nurturers of community. It's as easy to idealize those words as it is to romanticize our relationship to the natural world that all of this ultimately rests on, and just as hard to approach them with true integrity. But the grocery store has given me my counterintuitive starting point. There are others if you look for them. There's a lot to learn, and much of it is still just being created. The moment is frighteningly, urgently, perfectly right for more of us in still-comfortable places to step across the line and wade more deeply into the questions.

CHAPTER 1

SETTLING

N OTHING SAYS "LOCAL" like a pop-up tent. Farmers markets, craft fairs, outdoor festivals—all of them take shape as brief mosaics of ten-by-ten canopies sheltering vendors and their wares from sun and rain.

On an August day in 2009 a lone canopy popped up on the scrap of lawn outside the Orange Innovation Center (OIC), formerly the Minute Tapioca Company. Minute Tapioca, which left town in the 1960s, always prided itself on its tidy groundskeeping. The bit of grass was still neatly edged and trimmed, one vestige of a lost era of corporate paternalism.

There aren't a lot of other vestiges. The top of the yellow brick chimney has been truncated, removing the "MT" and leaving only "Co." A faded sign for the Bedroom Factory runs across one exterior wall, recalling one of the site's post-Tapioca uses. The complex sidles along West Main Street just outside the center of Orange; on the other side is the railroad track, and just beyond that the Millers River. It's a very familiar pattern in older industrial areas: road, factory, tracks, river.

Underneath a blue tent in 2009, a small group of women set out cucumbers, summer squash, basil, blackberries, potatoes, and garlic, all of it grown within a few miles. It was the first share distribution of a new venture named the North Quabbin Community Co-operative. The founders were adapting the Community Supported Agriculture (CSA) model used by farmers who presell their harvest to be shared out in installments, giving the farmer working capital and shareholders a season's worth of eating. The women in Orange had decided to go by week rather than by season, and they'd taken orders for the first week's share of the food on the tables. As the afternoon went on, people who had placed orders came to pick up their bounty.

Most of the volunteers under the tent that day were fairly new to the North Quabbin area. Newness is relative here; it's the kind of place you can live for decades and remain very aware that you'll never fully belong.

FIGURE 3. The first share distribution on August 12, 2009, at the Orange Innovation Center. Left to right, Amy Borezo, Mary Hakkinen, Nina Wellen, Julie Davis, Zita Rasid.
—Photo: North Quabbin Community Co-operative

One of the reasons for that is that not everyone who moves here *does* stay. Newness tends to cling to you until you've proven that you aren't planning to leave anytime soon.

There's a low barrier to entry—real estate is cheaper than in most of the rest of the state. Especially when times are good, there's always spillover from the more affluent and expensive parts of the Connecticut River Valley, just to the west, and the even more expensive Boston area to the east. A lot of people move here because it's affordable and beautiful and quiet. Some of them move away again within a few years when they discover the other sides of affordability: fewer restaurants, slower internet, more gaps and problems and fewer resources for fixing them. And, well, it's quiet. Not everyone actually wants quiet when they find themselves in the middle of it.

People with a longer history here often have a complicated reaction to newcomers. In a place where resources are thin, there's an urgent need for new energy and ideas to fill some of the gaps. But a lot of those gaps were left by previous people and projects that didn't stay or didn't deliver the lasting benefits they promised.

Industry was the biggest of those, but there were others too. Route 2, which spans the northern part of Massachusetts, used to be Main Street in Orange and dozens of other towns. In the late 1950s a series of bypasses moved the highway outside the town centers, and Main Street became Route 2A. The hope was that shortening and smoothing out the trip would bring more people and businesses to the area, and to some extent that has happened. But it also turned the little mill towns into fly-over country. When my husband and I told people in 1988 that we were moving to Athol, most of our friends knew it well but only as that funny name they saw on the sign when zipping past on the way to the Berkshire Mountains or Vermont.

People in hinterlands are often very ready to grab at new possibilities but also quick to say "I told you so" if something doesn't work out. It's how you get when you've been overlooked or abandoned or discounted. People hold their parochial and familial networks close because those are the resources you can count on when you need them. Coming in from the outside means you're never going to have those, not really.

Many of the women under the tent on the OIC lawn in August 2009 were a lot like we'd been when we first arrived—part of a patchwork of educators, librarians, writers and artists and musicians, people in social and municipal services, some with deep roots in the area but mostly more recent migrants. Some had regular jobs; others, like me, were piecing together contingent livelihoods and careers.

Amy Borezo was an artist, graphic designer, and bookbinder. She and her librarian husband had moved from a larger Massachusetts mill town to the east in search of something more rural as they raised their daughter. Orange wasn't rural exactly but it was close. Robin Shtulman started out as a historical archeologist and found her way into library work. She moved to Orange when she fell in love with an artist who already owned a big house there (they met at a community contradance—"a classic New England story," Robin calls it). Nina Wellen was an art teacher who had lived in the area for twenty years but spent the first decade in the smaller hill towns to the west, "full of hippies and artists and musicians." Her friends never came to Orange. Like the Borezos, Nina and her husband only discovered the town after their son was born and they were finding the few available properties in the hill towns too expensive. Despite the grueling commute to her job in Boston, Nina liked what she calls the "realness" of the area, meaning that you don't get a sense of being buffered from real-world problems the way you often do in the college and college-adjacent towns of the Connecticut River Valley (known to many people as Happy Valley for exactly this reason).

All three were in Orange because real estate was cheap. They all lived within a block of the old Tapioca factory, and all had young children, part of a nearby cohort of kids. Along with their own networks outside of Orange they quickly formed one of their own, "a network of people who had no built-in local network," Nina calls it.

It turned out that they also shared an interest in local food. Robin and Nina had seen each other around the neighborhood but didn't actually meet in person until one day at the customer service desk of the local Hannaford supermarket, where they were both trying to find out why Dean's Beans, a coffee roasted in Orange, had recently disappeared from the shelves. When they learned it was a corporate decision and that the formerly regional Hannaford chain, based in Maine, had recently become part of a global grocery conglomerate headquartered in Europe, they bonded over dismay at the corporatization of food.

No one can quite remember when the notion of starting a food co-op first came up. It was around the time of the worldwide economic crash of 2008, when a lot of globally scaled systems were looking less and less reliable. Amy recalls "a conversation in someone's backyard." Nina thinks it might have been in "one of our corner hangouts" while she was walking her dog around the neighborhood.

The idea simmered until there was enough interest to warrant an actual meeting. People brought in other people. The woman who ran the little café in the OIC was interested, and Nina Wellen knew some farmers on the edge of town who were excited about the idea of having a new outlet for selling their products. The group included the couple who were transforming the former Minute Tapioca property from a furniture factory into an incubator hub.

Julie Davis was another newcomer who attended that first meeting. Against the advice of their nonlocal realtor, who saw real estate in Orange as a bad investment, Julie and her husband had recently bought one of the big Victorian houses perched at the top of a steep hill overlooking the town. In their previous home in a nearby town, Julie had discovered local food, mainly through visiting farms and farmstands in the valley with her two toddlers. It was an easy, low-cost outing that entertained the kids and tired them out. In the process she'd learned a lot about area farms and foods.

Unlike most of the other people at the meeting, Julie also knew a lot about the grocery business. She'd worked at her local Stop & Shop supermarket in central Massachusetts all the way through high school and college, eventually reaching a point where the company sent her out in the summers to cover for vacationing store managers around the region.

At that first meeting, as the idea of a weekly order-as-you-go CSA-style produce share began to come together, Julie volunteered to be the contact person for the farmers who would supply the fruits and vegetables. As is the way with new ideas and volunteer groups, the initial group quickly narrowed down to a smaller core who committed to doing the actual work of organizing and running the project. Conversations continued through the winter and spring, and the first shares were distributed that summer.

Busy doing freelance research and teaching at two schools a hundred miles apart, I was only peripherally aware of the launch of the new co-op. But my commissioned study of farming as a way of life in eastern New York State was teaching me a lot about what it means that we've tied our food provisioning so tightly to an economic model driven by the central goal of making a profit. It's where I started to understand the magic trick that's been worked on all of us by industrializing food, leading to a food system resistant to change at its very deepest levels. It was also making me more aware of how many people are trying to change it for the better, or even just to operate on a small scale within it. The Hudson River Valley, where I was conducting my research, was a hotbed for those kinds of alternative projects, and the new co-op in Orange was clearly in the same vein. Some of my friends were starting to volunteer to pack the shares, and I heard secondhand reports about plans to try to keep going through the winter months, sourcing from Connecticut River Valley farms that offered winter vegetables as well as suppliers bringing organic produce from farther south along the East Coast. But I didn't have a lot of time to get involved, beyond buying a weekly share now and then.

When the pop-up tent reappeared for a second summer in 2010, my husband and I were in the process of moving from mill town to hill town, from a rickety, two-family clapboard house built for tool factory workers to a house in the midst of woods crisscrossed by old stone walls and long-disused farm roads. By the time the dust settled, I was down to just one full-time teaching job. It was still a long way from where I lived but steady enough that I could start to do more thinking and teaching about the food system questions I'd been pondering in the Hudson Valley. And I was finally able to become more involved in the local side of my life again.

I had a much deeper understanding of the North Quabbin area after spending a couple of years investigating what had happened to farming in this part of the world over the past couple of centuries. I could see myself and the other arrivals of the past few decades as a thin top layer of the landscape, drawn by the devalued real estate of deindustrialized places and finding reasons to stay over time. That layer included the entrepreneurial couple who turned the old Minute Tapioca factory into the OIC starting in the early 1980s. Their furniture company employed seventy people at one point, but like so many small and midsized businesses, it was increasingly pressured by competition from big-box stores that could offer something nearly as good for half the price. As the new century began, the owner, Noel Vincent, was renovating some of the sprawling interior spaces of the factory into offices and studios and workshops in a familiar pattern of reconfiguring empty mills for new uses.

Noel and his partner were excited about the food co-op, seeing it as a boost for the area's farm economy as well as a young business in itself. There was a widespread feeling in the town, common in economically depressed places, that Orange needed to be more business-friendly if it were going to climb out of its doldrums. But there wasn't any agreement about what that meant—attracting traditional manufacturing? chasing trends like biotechnology? grabbing whatever presented itself? In the 1980s Orange residents had fought off—and fought over—proposals for a heavy metal recycling plant and a drag-racing strip that many people thought would hurt more than help the town. In the rancorous aftermath of those and other fights, any encouragement of new enterprise seemed positive and potentially unifying.

Amy Borezo had moved her bookbinding and artist studio into a third-floor space in the OIC a couple of years earlier, alongside other artists and artisans, a scattering of small service businesses, and some public-sector and social service offices. There was also still some light manufacturing of things like plastic trash bags, plus a handful of food ventures.

In addition to the tiny café inside the complex, Laura Moore, who lived on a farm north of the center of Orange, was opening a small bakery on the river side of the building, where she made breads and pies that her family sold at area farmers markets. Like Julie Davis, Laura had worked in supermarkets, honing her production skills in their in-house bakeries.

The little swirl of new activity inside the Tapioca factory was in contrast to the downtown area a quarter-mile to the east, where a lot of the storefronts sat empty and efforts at revitalization never quite seemed to get traction. This is also a familiar pattern in places where industry has been and left. Athol is still home to one major tool-making company, but others there had closed or moved away by the time we moved to the town in the late 1980s, some of them after bitterly fought battles between corporations and unions. Orange's losses have been more gradual, more than a century of them now. The biggest buildings in town—factories, foundries, offices—were built by the New Home Sewing Machine Company, once the county's largest employer.[1] An elderly friend told me once that he remembered older people in town describing the day in the 1920s when they heard that New Home would be closing its plant for good. "They talked about it as though the world was ending," my friend said. Most of the big brick buildings that remain still stand empty, a hollow place at the town's heart.

The sense of not only loss but abandonment, even betrayal, lingers in the built environment of most old mill towns. Sometimes there are efforts just to wipe away the past. North Adams, in Massachusetts's northwest corner, tore down one whole side of its ornate Main Street in the 1960s in a spasm of attempted modernization. Larger places like Worcester and Hartford obliterated older neighborhoods with multilane highways, convention centers, and malls. Mostly the process is more sporadic, a fire here, a demolition there.

In places that have managed to find the new vitality that everyone is searching for, business incubators and waterfront districts and lofts and new construction can erase the past in a different, subtler way. But in Orange the losses are still very raw. You feel it in the cavities inside and between buildings. One of the town's most visible landmarks, a three-story commercial block with a corner clock tower at the central intersection, burned in the 1950s and was replaced by a nondescript, one-story structure with a flat roof. Other buildings have had their top stories lopped off and roofs flattened too, a common way for property owners to lower their tax burden. Orange is a pared-down place now, a place with scars and an uneven gait.

But you can also glimpse how prosperous and optimistic the town once was. In the hillside neighborhood where Julie Davis and her family live there's a sense of how quickly the money once flowed in, how there was enough wealth and audacity to put spacious homes on the steep rock where people could look out from their porches over the bustling little downtown, the clock tower, the mills, the river, the hills beyond.

Orange's industrialists were sons and grandsons of white farm families, men with ambitious startup ideas and varying levels of business sense. For a while in the nineteenth century they put up little factories along every stream that tumbled down a slope, capturing any waterpower that could turn a wheel and drive a machine, churning out things like wooden pails and brooms and furniture and shoes.

There are countless stone foundations along the little rivers and streams all around the North Quabbin, evidence of that manic entrepreneurial energy and of the speed with which most of the smallest mills got left behind once the logic of bigness—scale up or get left behind—really started to kick in. It helped to have built your factory on one of the larger rivers, like the Millers. That gave you enough waterpower to expand and eventually enough capital to import coal and other fuels after you hit the natural limits of how much energy the river itself could provide. It also helped if you made something that someone needed in order to make something else—tools, say, or machinery for other factories, or sewing machines that women used to make clothes at home from the cheap textiles made in the first generation of big mills in New England. Industry fed insatiably on itself and built out and out in ways that have never slowed down, expanding and contracting unevenly across landscapes that are global in scope.

For Orange and Athol and a lot of other mill towns in this part of New England, the metal industries turned out to be the foundation for nearly a century of prosperity. In Orange, besides the sewing machine giant, there were two big companies making water turbines and other large-scale metal fixings. A couple of particularly venturesome local entrepreneurs even took a shot at car manufacturing at the turn of the twentieth century. They couldn't make it work, but the factory they built still stands, fittingly used today by a tire company. Minute Tapioca came along at about the same time as the car factory, initially seeming pretty lightweight. The growing factory complexes along the Millers River drew Orange's commercial and civic life down from the old farming center to the north and injected the money that built a small and vibrant town center.

The mills also pulled in new settlers whose parochial and family connections gradually became interwoven with the older Yankee layer. Like other industrial places, New England's mill towns and cities had—and as a result still have—strikingly distinct ethnic and religious mixes, Finns here, Portuguese there, Irish and French Canadians nearly everywhere. Many people emigrated because the agrarian economies and small farms of their homeplaces no longer generated enough food or income to support their families. The Irish potato famine was the most extreme calamity, but crop failures and soil depletion and rural economic decline were all-too-common experiences for Europeans coming to the industrializing United States, sometimes overlapping with the ways that farmers in the northeastern United States too were beginning to struggle for livelihood as the nineteenth century went on.

Which brings us back to the blue pop-up tent and the older agricultural layer of the North Quabbin's landscape.

A lot of the vegetables in the first co-op share on that August day in 2009 were grown at Moore's Maple Grove Farm, owned by John and Laura Moore. Laura is the baker, John the farmer, the seventh generation in his family to farm in Orange. Someone took a picture of him making the delivery that first day, standing in the bed of his pickup truck unloading waxed boxes and bushel baskets of cucumbers and squash. In the picture, and in real life, John looks just like everyone's image of a Yankee farmer: solid, tanned, taciturn.

In the academic world that I was finding my way into in 2009, we speak very matter of factly about settler colonialism and white settlers' theft and occupation of Indigenous land. In Orange, settler colonialism means families like the Moores, who've been here for so long they've acquired a kind of nativeness of their own, like the white ranchers of the much-mythologized West. This is where white American romanticism about family farms runs headlong into white American romanticism about Indigenous peoples and makes it hard for a lot of people to really see or understand either one.

Like the Nipmucs and other Indigenous people who'd been finding and growing food in this landscape for thousands of years, the first white settlers sought out the flattest, most fertile pockets of land for their farms. Those were often in the river floodplains, where rich muddy water had spilled onto the fields at regular intervals over millennia and made it possible to grow crops like corn that need a lot of nutrients. That land was snapped up early by whatever settlers claimed land in a new town, leaving the hillier, thinner soils for those who came later.

And, of course, those river bottoms were also the best places to build factories. They were the only places where industry could really expand once expansion became a necessity. Farming itself was starting to become more industrial and therefore more profitable—in other parts of the country by the mid-nineteenth century, and the farms that remained around the outskirts of towns like Orange were by definition small, often hilly, and not suited to large-scale cultivation.

There's a too-simple story about farming in New England that says all the soils were poor and full of rocks, the farms too poky and old-fashioned, the region's population too large to really sustain agriculture after industry took over. In fact, there were—and are—still areas of outstanding soil and plenty of ingenuity and persistence among New England's farmers. And in a pre-supermarket era, all those nonfarming industrial workers and their families had to eat after all. The industrial towns and cities were eager markets for the region's farmers right into the middle of the twentieth century. But farmers also had to adapt what they grew if they wanted to take advantage of those markets.

Farms in some parts of the region—usually the flattest, most fertile parts, like the major river valleys—were able to do that in ways that mirrored the "scale up or die" logic of the newer industrial economy. They bought or leased as much land as they could, invested in new machines, specialized in particular crops that they could grow in enough quantity to satisfy scaled-up ways of processing, moving, and selling food.

But that was never an option for the smaller farms that the topography and soils around Orange would support. So longtime farm families like the Moores adapted by filling smaller niches closer to home. There may not be a lot of rich soil outside the river bottoms, but there's lots of good pastureland. Along with many other farmers in the long-settled parts of the Northeast, the Moores turned to dairying, because you could still make a living selling and delivering fresh milk to local markets. A lot of little farms went out of business as the twentieth century went on, but John Moore's parents were among the more than thirty small dairy farmers still operating in Orange at midcentury.

By the time John took over the farm at the turn of the twenty-first century, you needed to be bigger to stay in that game too. Regional dairy aggregators wanted to be able to collect milk in bulk trucks and sell it to supermarket chains and big food-processing companies, not make multiple stops at little farms all over the map. The former dairy farms that have hung on in this area, like Moore's Maple Grove, are now growing mostly hay for other farms' horses and cows and doing some small-scale food production for hyperlocal markets.

In John Moore's family tree you can also see that risk and loss were always just on the other side of industrial prosperity. His mother's family came to the area from one of the larger Connecticut River Valley towns in 1895, after a series of personal tragedies and a turbulent few decades of national economic booms and busts. They combined jobs in the mills with some small-scale farming, seemingly part of the first back-to-the-land impulse that prompts many Americans to try to keep at least one foot on a farm whenever the national economy takes one of its cyclical nose dives.[2] That impulse rests on a kind of tacit recognition that markets can't be completely trusted with the necessities of life, a sense that having access to land and the ability to grow or catch your own food was a way to insure yourself against the threat of actual famine that lurks in the very back of the settler imagination.

Noel Vincent, the furniture-maker who launched the Minute Tapioca factory's third act, also saw diversification as a form of security in a place where big companies and up-like-a-rocket industries had too often come down like the proverbial stick.

"In order to have a stable base for the community," he told an interviewer in the second summer of the pop-up co-op, "you can't have any one type of business because those businesses come and go. Having many small companies that are growing provides a lot of new employment for the community, as opposed to the big factories that are leaving all of our communities in this country to produce offshore."[3]

This strategy makes a lot of sense in one way and none at all in others. Rooting as many resources as possible close to home, nurturing what's unique about a community and its people, learning the hard lessons of a century of corporate abandonment—all good. And Orange always has its ace in the hole: affordable real estate. When the OIC opened you could rent a modest studio space with decent internet access—not exactly blazing fast but better than other options in the area—for a couple hundred dollars a month, a real enticement for artisans and would-be entrepreneurs.

But most—all?—former industrial towns and cities in the region and a lot of other parts of the country are trying to entice the same pool of artists and entrepreneurs into their own empty mills. And a lot of those other places have more inducements to offer. Even for the minority of people who prefer the quiet and realness of Orange, that's part of a further challenge, a really big one.

Staying in business at a small scale isn't easy—often isn't even possible—in an economy fueled by competition and the demands of endless growth. We're back to that Zen koan that our whole food system is built on, the one about how producing food and finding profitability are intrinsically at odds yet yoked so tightly now that most people would starve to death if we tried to untether them all of a sudden. "Grow or die" is more than just a turn of phrase: it's the foundation of our whole economic system, including the crucial part that feeds us.

So diversified local economic development sidesteps the old mistake of putting all your eggs in one basket. But it means juggling a whole lot of little eggs and hoping enough of them stay airborne that you don't end up with just a sloppy mess on the pavement.

Noel was a big supporter of the co-op in its startup moment, offering free storage space in the back of the factory and a hand with organizing. His partner Zita was one of the women helping out under the pop-up tent on that first share distribution day. But that was the easy part. Now the new egg was in the air, and someone had to keep it from going splat.

In the mix of new neighbors, long-settled farmers, and local entrepreneurs beginning to commit to that task for the North Quabbin Community Co-op there was one other strand visible on that first day under the pop-up tent: more recent back-to-the-landers who had taken up farming in the area as part of what has often been called "the food movement."[4] The greens and garlic in the first shares were grown by Ricky Baruch at Seeds of Solidarity Farm on the hilly western edge of Orange. Ricky and his wife, Deb Habib, had both been suburban East Coast kids who took the kind of latter-day hippie path in the 1980s and 1990s that a lot of my college students still follow today: short stints on farms as interns and laborers combined with a good deal of spiritual seeking, odd jobs, and some graduate school (Deb has a doctorate in education).

In the mid-1990s they fetched up in Orange, drawn by—you guessed it—affordable land. They'd been searching around western Massachusetts and the Connecticut River Valley for a place to start their own farm and were beginning to despair when a friend suggested contacting Mount Grace Land Conservation Trust, a regional land trust headquartered in Athol.

Land trusts typically focus on "natural" places and ecosystems—forests, rivers, endangered habitats—sometimes to the point of fetishizing them. But Mount Grace, whose service area covered twenty-three towns in north-central Massachusetts, was part of a move to broaden the vision of land conservation to include working agriculture.[5] When the financial value of land as real estate outpaces farmers' ability to make a living from it by selling food, selling land is often the only way a farmer has to stay solvent, unless someone—a land trust, a state government—is willing to pay them for the development rights to the land, which then essentially get locked up and the key thrown away.[6] Sometime in the mid-1990s Mount Grace was looking for its first farmland conservation project, and its executive director was glad to get the call from Ricky and Deb.

There wasn't any actual farmland to conserve at that point. The Chestnut Hill Road property that became Seeds of Solidarity Farm hadn't been cultivated for eighty years, and like a lot of old farms in the North Quabbin area it had grown up into forest. The soil had never been nearly as rich as river bottomland and it was seven miles from the center of Orange, which wasn't really the center of anywhere. Like other newcomers, Deb and Ricky heard a lot of "why would you want to move to Orange?" from their friends when they decided to settle here.

But settle they did. In the decade before the North Quabbin Community Co-op launched they literally built up fertile soil in small clearings while incubating other small and large projects: an annual garlic festival, a youth leadership program, and the kinds of gatherings and conversations about local food that helped to catalyze the new co-op when the neighbors in Orange first floated the idea in 2008.[7]

It was Deb who brought Julie Davis to the first big meeting. They met when Julie was a festival vendor with a cottage business selling reusable cloth diaper covers made from old wool sweaters. Julie had been talking about home-schooling her kids; Deb was on the Orange elementary school committee and convinced her to give the public system a try. Deb has a way of suggesting things gently, kindly, and before long you find yourself doing exactly whatever it was that she immediately saw would be the best possible outcome for you and everyone else. She recognized what a gift Julie's abundant energy and grocery experience could be for the new co-op.

At the foundation of all these layers of the North Quabbin landscape is the land itself, the soils, the rocks, the water, what was here before those white settlers showed up, when it was still Nipmuc homeland. The fact that you can still get a sense of that here—that you can hike or paddle or pick berries or fish or hunt within a few minutes' walk or drive of any of the town centers—is one big reason why a lot of present-day people come to the area, and a reason why some of us stay.

A lot of the satisfactions of those recreational or seasonal encounters come from getting a glimpse of what it must be like to move through a landscape that hasn't been completely parceled out and bounded by paper deeds and lines on map, to be able to see the food sources in it as fellow beings with whom you coexist in interdependent ways. This is the part that modern people tend to wax romantic about, the same way nonfarmers tend to fantasize about the satisfactions of working on the land. These pleasant imaginings are only possible because most of us don't directly have to depend on hunting or gathering or farming for our food or our livelihood. That horse is out of the barn, to use one of the countless agricultural metaphors that crop up (see what I did there?) in the language of people who have never hoed a row in their lives (have a cow, bet the farm, reap what you sow, put all your eggs in one basket).

Most of us, at the end of the day, get most of our food from a store. And yet growing numbers of us know, with greater clarity all the time, that the industrial food system we depend on, which both exemplifies and enables the modern world we live in, is careening toward—or maybe already over—an ecological and economic cliff and taking all of us with it.

Recognizing the foundational problems is a good start. That's essentially what I'd been doing in my deep dive into agricultural history in the

northeastern United States. In hindsight, that project was like the obligatory coursework you do before moving on to some original research
that you'll eventually write your dissertation about. I had a pretty solid
grasp of a lot of the fundamentals, in an intellectual, observer-ish way.

The people who started the food co-op in Orange in 2009 were wrestling much more actively with the insoluble riddle that has made the
modern food system so hard to understand, let alone change. Some, like
the Moores, had been at this their whole lives, finding ways to keep their
farm going despite the grinding logic of competition and expansion that
has worked against small-scale farmers in New England and so many
other places for more than two centuries now.

Others, like Amy and Robin and Nina, were brand-new to the game
and just beginning to realize how hard it was to put all the pieces together
in a way that made financial and logistical sense for everyone along even
a very short food chain. Not all of the co-op's suppliers initially grasped
the concept of the share pickup schedule, and sometimes a farmer would
fail to deliver on time. Sometimes things arrived in a form that didn't
really work, like the truck that showed up with its bed full of whole eda-
mame plants when Julie had been expecting only the bean pods. Some
things turned out to be prohibitively expensive or impossible to find, like
fully organic apples and peaches. As the co-op branched out a little more
to include things like local cheeses and Dean's Beans coffee, everything
got even more complicated. Each new step seemed to add another layer
of problems. And each solution in turn spawned new complexities, most
of which ultimately came down to money. "The economics of it just
knocked us flat every time," Nina recalls.

Right from the beginning, though, the co-op also included people like
Deb Habib and Ricky Baruch who had put themselves into a different kind
of relationship to that insoluble puzzle. They certainly weren't setting
themselves apart from the food business—Seeds of Solidarity was a working farm and they wanted to be paid for the produce they provided for the
weekly shares. But they also refused the gambit of trying to reconcile the
needs of continual economic growth with the necessity of feeding people
well and caring for the land. They were purposefully looking for ways not
to be knocked flat by the economics of a market-based food system.

Theoretically, you could also do that by simply insisting that food
shouldn't be a matter of business at all. And there's a case to be made for

that. But in the non-theoretical world, the food system we've got—the one that most people in many parts of the world depend on for survival itself—is based on that logic of profit and growth and competition. If you want to engage in the food sector in even a rudimentary way, it's something you've got to reckon with, whether you see it as subverting from within or getting to know your enemy or just dealing with what's right under your nose.

The refusal to let money drive everything has been the downfall of many a food business, including a lot of idealistic co-ops. And it's important to recognize the difference between trying to run a business that way and not really having any idea how to run a business at all. A lot of the people around the new co-op were in the latter category, just as I was when I got involved a few years later.

But from the start this little venture also included people who saw clearly that you had to both refuse *and* engage, a koan of its own and one that helped keep the co-op alive as it began to grow beyond the hyperlocal shares under the blue pop-up tent on the lawn.

CHAPTER 2

HANDHOLDS

F IVE YEARS AFTER that first pop-up season I stood in the aisle of a new grocery store in an old bank and worried that what I was seeing on the shelves was not what most people in the area were likely to buy.

The bank was quite small, just one open, ground-floor space with some offices upstairs. When it was built, in Orange's industrial prime, it was ornamental in a late Victorian, red-brick-and-shutters kind of way. But it was one of those buildings that had lost its top floor over time, maybe to reduce the tax burden or to make it look more modern as the town's fortunes declined. In 2014, when the North Quabbin Community Co-operative turned it into a grocery store called Quabbin Harvest, it was basically just a modest brick box, its exterior painted institutional green with a flat, bland facade. A faded sign above the second-story windows still said, "Workers Credit Union."

It's also worth noting that scaling from startup to storefront in five years is lightning-fast for a food co-op. The common wisdom is that you need several years to raise capital and plan a store launch. Quabbin Harvest got there in a hurry and on a shoestring.

All the steps along the way felt logical and even inevitable. After the first two summers of distributing fresh produce shares on the Orange Innovation Center lawn, the organizers thought, "Why not continue through the winter?" Winter farmers markets and CSAs were starting to be a thing around New England as growers and eaters tried to expand their commitment to local food. None of the farms in the immediate area offered winter shares, but the co-op was able to source from a couple of Connecticut River Valley farms that did. Amy Borezo's husband worked in the valley and could pick up the vegetables on his way home. The OIC was excited to see the little business starting to expand and

FIGURE 4. Karl Bittenbender hangs a banner to announce that the former bank is now home to the food co-op, 2014. —Photo: North Quabbin Community Co-operative

gladly arranged for some free storage space in the back of the factory complex where the co-op could put a couple of refrigerators.

The main problem was the cold. That and the celeriac. The free space was literally an unheated closet. "It was very cold!" Amy remembers. "We were very dedicated!" But even the most committed locavores began to balk when the same limited rotation of local winter vegetables kept turning up in their shares week after week after week. Julie Davis, who still does the ordering for the co-op's produce share program, says, "I haven't put celeriac in a share in years. I have a little PTSD about it."

The next steps were obvious. If they were going to continue, they needed to move into a heated space. There was a small office available on the second floor of the OIC complex, with enough room for a cooler and freezer and a few shelves. "But getting out of the cold meant paying rent," Amy says. "And if we had to pay rent, we had to sell more stuff."

They'd already formed a little buying club so members could get bulk items from a regional natural foods distributor, but not everyone wanted twenty-five-pound bags of things, especially when foods that were once available only through co-operative buying were now on the shelves of every supermarket. Having a store space meant the co-op could offer those items in bulk bins and members could buy however much they wanted.

Getting beyond the glut of local celeriac required another change: a partnership with a produce distributor called Squash Inc., based in the Connecticut River Valley. Squash got its start in the early 1970s supplying vegetables from big-city wholesale markets to valley food co-ops. One of those was known as the Amherst Food Conspiracy, which tells you all you need to know about the political leanings of a lot of those early co-ops.

Squash's founders had definite far-left leanings of their own. A hand-drawn early T-shirt design shows a happy bearded driver with a truck full of giant squash above a sign, "Squash Capitalism," and a banner along the bumper reading, "Live Right, Eat Right, Squash the State."

But in the intervening decades the little trucking company created a niche for itself somewhere between east and west, left and right, capitalist and collectivist. At the valley co-ops, eyebrows were sometimes raised over Squash's association with the real world of business and profit-seeking, while the old-school produce wholesalers in Boston and Springfield were amused by the presence of a hippie company on the fringes of the cut-throat grocery sector. Eric Stocker, who owned Squash for many years, remembers that drivers would sometimes ponder the strangeness of this on their way back and forth across the state. "Both sides think we're on their team!" they would laugh, capturing the uneasy positioning of a small, intermediary business somewhere between the mainstream and the alternative.

Sourcing produce from Squash moved the co-op in Orange a little closer to the mainstream. Now they could offer fruits and vegetables outside the growing season, although they stayed with all-organic produce and Julie specified that she wanted things grown along the East Coast, not trucked from California.

The North Quabbin Community Co-operative formally incorporated in 2011. As in all co-operative businesses, members elected a board of directors, which in this case consisted largely of the core organizers who had already been functioning essentially as a board. The same year, they opened a tiny store upstairs in the OIC for a few hours a week, staffed by volunteers.

The limitations of the new space quickly made themselves felt. The cramped space was hard to ventilate, so things went from too cold to too hot. With limited funds, the co-op opted for used freezers and coolers that didn't always stand up well to the heat. Sometimes a unit would just quit; sometimes the power went out or a volunteer didn't notice a too-high temperature in the freezer when closing up the store for the day. When that happened, all the food inside had to be thrown away. It was cold comfort—or maybe warm—that the members included farmers, backyard chicken-keepers, and the owner of a local compost company, all of whom would gladly take the food rather than sending it to the landfill.

The moment you even think about selling perishable foods in the United States—the moment you go beyond that farmer with a box of freshly picked cucumbers in the back of a truck—you have to intersect with what's known as the "cold chain." It's part of the invisible lifeblood coursing through the modern industrial food system, along with the petroleum that fuels everything from the farmer's tractor to Squash's delivery vehicles to the giant semi-trailers disgorging pallets of food at supermarket loading docks. The cold chain runs from field or sea to plate, through a thick tangle of regulation and inspection. It's not something you can opt out of if you want to get into the modern food business and stay there, even for a minute.[1]

So the discussions at the North Quabbin Community Co-op quite quickly started to circle around getting more reliable equipment. Doing that meant having a bigger space. To pay for a bigger space, they needed to sell more food. And to do that they needed to be in a much more visible location. Robin Shtulman remembers, "The conversations that we had before we moved to the storefront were that we couldn't grow any more and we weren't going to be able to keep doing what we were doing unless we grew. We had to grow in order to keep going."

The little co-op in Orange was teetering on the edge of the cycle that helped create the modern supermarket system, where small stores have gradually—or sometimes suddenly—scaled up and larger ones have continually expanded into chains and absorbed smaller ones in their own pursuit of growth. Every step can be a logical and often a purely logistical one—freezers, sales, visibility, more sales. But eventually it takes on its own momentum. Like the cold chain, it pulls you into something far beyond what any individual store can control. And once you're in it, you're in.

The corollary is that when you're out, you're out. The food business is a famously hard place to get a handhold and hang on, something you can glimpse between the lines of even the biggest successes.

Minute Tapioca was once one of those. Its story gives a sense of why those handholds are so hard to find and so slippery when you do grab hold of one.

Like most industrially processed foods, Minute Tapioca had a carefully crafted origin narrative designed to transform a commodity into something that customers can identify with on a personal level. Its founding tale goes like this: A Boston landlady named Susan Stavers served some tapioca pudding to a boarder who complained that it wasn't as smooth as he was used to from his years as a sailor in the South Seas. In some versions of the tale, the sailor was ill and wanted comfort food. In others, he gave the landlady a cassava tuber brought home from his most recent voyage. The common thread is that she figured out how to run tapioca flakes through her coffee grinder to make a much smoother pudding. Voilà—a new product was born. Stavers named it "Tapioca Superlative" and started selling it door to door in little bags. The business grew and was bought out by an enterprising newspaperman in Orange, John Whitman, who started it on its road to becoming a national brand.[2]

Inevitably, there's much more to it, as I found when I started tracking Stavers and Whitman through bits and pieces of archival and genealogical data.[3] It's not just that Quabbin Harvest started out in the old Minute Tapioca factory or that the company was part of the memories that haunt empty factories and storefronts of Orange. In Minute Tapioca's story we can trace the whole arc of the industrialized food system in all its perplexing abundance, its reliance on cheap raw materials and cheap labor, and its efficiencies and concentrations that eventually combined to inoculate the whole system against change. This story shows just how perilous the economic terrain was at the turn of the twentieth century, when the system was really being put in place. Everyone was looking for moonshots but (spoiler alert) the people who came out ahead tended to be the ones who'd gotten into it with some capital and property and experience to begin with. And even then, there were no sure things.

Susan Stavers seemed at first to be one of those who might be poised to succeed. Her parents' families were well-to-do. But her father died when Susan and her sister, Clara, were infants. At some point they migrated from coastal New Hampshire to Boston with their mother and brother. In 1865 they were living in a boardinghouse, but in the 1870 U.S. Census the two girls, still in their early twenties, jointly owned a town-house in downtown Boston. Had they inherited some money? Susan was listed as a music teacher and Clara as a store clerk, so they didn't seem to be independently wealthy. But somehow they'd managed to acquire property and buy in to Boston's booming real-estate market at an auspi-cious moment. Their building, home to half a dozen lodgers, was in one of the substantial blocks of four-story residences that were absorbing the city's mushrooming population. (Boston added the equivalent of its entire 1840 population every decade between 1860 and 1920.)[4]

Susan and Clara's 1870 boarders were a motley bunch, with hard-to-trace names and no listed occupations. It's hard to know if this was where the encounter with the sailor happened, if it ever did. It's possible it was in the following decade, an eventful one in Susan Stavers's young life.

First came the Great Fire. In 1872 a huge swath of downtown Boston burned in half a day. The fire started a block from the Staverses' board-inghouse, which was reduced to rubble, probably along with Susan and Clara's wealth. There's no evidence they ever owned property again. In the 1880 U.S. Census they show up a few blocks away as lodgers in another downtown boardinghouse inhabited by another highly miscel-laneous group of clerks, factory workers, students, and businesspeople.

Interestingly, they were living directly across from the makeshift laboratory where Alexander Graham Bell invented the first telephone in 1876.[5] And they seemed to have caught the inventing bug that was going around at the time. That same year, several patents were filed in their names for improved methods of sifting ash from coal stoves and fire-places, using mechanisms not unlike a coffee grinder.

There's no sign that their patented ash-sifter ever made it onto the market. And just a couple of years later their whole side of the street was demolished as developers continued to remake the downtown as a cen-ter for finance and commerce. Even if they'd still had money, Susan and

Clara Stavers probably would have been priced well out of the Boston real-estate market by that point. There's a sense of the family gradually sliding down the socioeconomic ladder as the 1880s went on. But Susan seemed to keep on searching for ways to recoup her lost capital, hoping to find investors, dreaming about success in the manufacturing economy that was surging all around her.

Seventy-five miles to the west in Orange, John Whitman was entertaining similar dreams. Whitman had learned the newspaper trade in Orange and then moved to Boston, working his way up in city newspapers. But his time in the city was as unlucky for him as it had been for Susan Stavers. In 1892 he fell down an elevator shaft and injured his spine so badly that he was immobilized for a year. He returned home to recuperate, married his sweetheart, and became the manager of a local paper.

Perhaps while lying flat on his back, he came up with the idea of starting a company to manufacture and sell instant tapioca and other specialty groceries. Tapioca was a trendy new food, the açaí berry or quinoa of its day, with similar overtones of healthfulness and naturalness. An 1889 article in an Orange newspaper noted that "Florida housewives have used it for making bread, puddings, custards, fritters, jellies, &c.; also as a vegetable it is used in all ways in which Irish potatoes are used," as well as being useful in feed for all kinds of livestock.[6] The tapioca craze dovetailed neatly with both refinements in industrial processing and the changing habits of U.S. housewives, who were starting to look for convenience, novelty, and value when they shopped.[7] Sometime in early 1894 John Whitman set up the Whitman Grocery Company as a side hustle, keeping his main job at the newspaper.

It's not clear how he knew about Susan Stavers—perhaps from his days as a reporter in Boston. He reached out to her in 1894 with a proposal that she merge her one-woman business with the company he was envisioning, which would follow her model of making and selling ground tapioca door to door. As Stavers later described it, he offered her a chunk of company stock and said she would continue to represent the venture in the Boston area, with a salary plus commission on sales. It must have seemed like the big break she was looking for. She signed a document relinquishing her rights to the product and promising to keep the processing method a secret. The written contract mentioned the stock but not the other parts of the deal, which, according to Stavers, Whitman promptly reneged on.

To be fair, he may simply have been unable to honor his promise. It turned out that running a food business was very different from running a newspaper, and Whitman struggled right from the beginning. It wasn't all bad news—within a year he had a dozen employees and a small cadre of traveling salesmen in central and western Massachusetts. The Orange Historical Society still has the big hand-turned coffee-grinder that the company's first workers used, following Stavers's method.

But getting raw materials was a problem. Whitman started out importing flake tapioca from small, British-owned factories scattered throughout Malaysia, but both quality and quantity were inconsistent, and there weren't a lot of other sources for bulk tapioca flakes at that point.[8] At home in Orange, it was hard to find the right kind of production space and even harder to recruit a board of directors to guide things toward profitability. One board member quit at the second meeting; at the next one, the board president followed. Whitman stepped in to replace him, but then the treasurer left. The next treasurer lasted only a couple of months.[9]

Not all of this was because of the food business. Some of it was timing. The country was still reeling from the Panic of 1893, which prefigured the Great Depression and spurred a backlash against the concentrated wealth and political power of the so-called Gilded Age. A lot of local businessmen were feeling the pinch, and barely a year after its founding, the Whitman Grocery Company, like many of the town's smaller businesses, was in a very shaky state.

But convenience foods were getting more popular all the time, and that got the attention of executives at Orange's better-capitalized businesses like the New Home Sewing Machine Company and the Grout Brothers Automobile Company. The Grouts even got as far as launching their own competing food brand, Lightning Tapioca.[10] But Frank Ewing at New Home saw a shorter route. Over lunch one day at a downtown diner, he found himself sitting next to a despondent twenty-year-old who was one of Whitman's remaining directors. Despite an impressive-sounding title—vice president and assistant general manager—the young man had nothing good to say about the company's prospects, and he jumped at Ewing's offer to buy out his 250 shares of stock. Ewing finished his lunch and went to talk with the Grouts about consolidating their efforts into one company that could actually capitalize on the growing demand for tapioca products.

Then as now, success in the processed-food industry rested not only on cheap raw materials and up-to-date technologies but also on the knowledge of how to combine them in a way that could result in profit. Even John

Whitman knew that, and he'd taken steps to secure his intellectual property through his written contract with Stavers. (When the company bought a big new safe, Whitman's paper reported that "a gentleman who seldom cracks a joke says he thinks the company got it to put their secret in.")[11]

The new management went further. They didn't want Stavers operating as a semi-free agent in Boston, going door to door and telling people how she'd invented the product. They didn't want anybody going door to door, period; they could see that the future of processed food was in mass markets, spurred by advertising in national media. There was poor Susan Stavers thinking she was catching the wave in the food industry when in fact she represented something that probably seemed painfully backward to the ambitious men now in charge. She was small-scale craft; they were industrial production, and industrial production was the future.

So they hired an elite Boston law firm to file a complaint against her with the state's Supreme Judicial Court in April 1895. By June they'd secured a ruling in their favor, enjoining her from ever selling her tapioca again or breathing a word about how it was made. They claimed she was continuing with her business activities in the interim, although she insisted through her lawyer that she wasn't. The company went ahead with a petition to find her in contempt of court, and Oliver Wendell Holmes, later chief justice of the U.S. Supreme Court, signed the order. Susan Stavers was effectively out of the picture and out of the food business.

And out of options, apparently. She and Clara, then in their mid-forties, both died in December of that year in facilities for women without means of their own, Clara in what was then called the Taunton State Lunatic Hospital and Susan in a hospital for indigent women on Long Island in Boston Harbor. Clara was buried in a pauper's grave with a little generic metal marker, now badly rusted. I wasn't able to discover Susan's burial place, and her death certificate lists her cause of death as unknown. But it does mention her occupation: "Domestic"—that is, a domestic servant. In the sad ending of this story you get a sense of two enterprising single women from a once-prosperous white Yankee family trying and failing to hang on to some kind of financial security in the tumultuous turn-of-the-century industrial economy.

In July 1895 the rest of the original tapioca company directors, including John Whitman himself, resigned, probably with huge sighs of relief. The business was now in the hands of those who had both the capital and the skills to scale it up.

FIGURE 5. In this 1944 *Life Magazine* advertisement, the sad and complex story of Susan Stavers's invention of Minute Tapioca has become a fable of American enterprise supporting business leaders' vision for the coming postwar order. —Photo from *Life Magazine*, Vol. 17, No. 5, 1944, p. 57.

By then it was really starting to take off. Whitman had already changed the name of the product from Tapioca Superlative to Minute Tapioca, using the image of the famous Minute Man statue in Lexington, Massachusetts, to remind consumers that the new product, like the revolutionaries of 1775, could be ready at a minute's notice. Over time the patriotic messaging faded; it was the convenience that really mattered. Ironically, Susan Stavers's own story—or a carefully crafted version of it—was put to promotional use. A full-page ad in a 1944 issue of *Life Magazine* ascribed the invention of Minute Tapioca to Stavers's "Yankee gumption," spurred by the sailor's complaint about lumps in her pudding. That same gumption, the ad copy went on to make clear, was behind the growth of American industry and the nation's success in both the war then being fought and the peace that would follow. Stavers's struggles were transformed into an affirmation of the American Dream.[12]

The new owners changed the name from Whitman Grocery Company to Minute Tapioca and bought a large factory along the riverside—the same one where Quabbin Harvest got its start a century later. The factory had been built by a group of local businessmen as a way to promote industrial development and job growth in the town. (Does this sound familiar?) It was obvious, one of these civic leaders said at the dedication of a later addition to the building, that "as an agricultural section the interests of Orange must always be restricted"—that is, by its farms' limited size and fertility. "Neither is this town likely to become famous as an educational centre, or to be known as a health or pleasure resort."[13] No, attracting more industry was the town's best hope for prosperity, and to that end they lured a shoe manufacturer with labor problems to Orange to set up shop in the new factory building. As is usually the case, the sweetener was financial: five years of free rent and a ten-year exemption from taxes.

The shoe company threw 250 people out of work when it closed in 1901, barely ten years later. The local newspapers didn't seem to want to talk about it, and it's tempting to imagine the same hurt-and-betrayed reaction to industrial abandonment that became more pervasive as time went on. But in 1901, New Englanders could still be optimistic. The following year, Minute Tapioca moved into the empty space. Not that everyone agreed it was a step in the right direction—the paper noted that some local people were dismayed to see "the little 'puddin' factory' mov[ing] into that 'fine, great building'," suggesting that the new craze for convenience foods wasn't universally seen as a *real* industry like metal-working or shoemaking.[14] But move the company did. And it stayed for sixty years.

During those sixty years the industrial food system as we know it was cemented firmly in place. The basic building blocks were companies that figured out how to deliver a particular product efficiently and affordably and get it onto the national stage through aggressive advertising. Countless iconic American brands—Heinz Ketchup, Oscar Mayer Wieners, Campbell's Soup, Quaker Oats, the list goes on and on—followed this model, either bringing new products to market or more fully industrializing existing ones around the turn of the twentieth century.

And then there was Postum.

Invented by a health-conscious entrepreneur named C. W. Post in 1895, Postum was the cornerstone of what quickly became the Post Cereal empire and later General Foods. Postum was a grain-based coffee substitute that responded to widespread American anxieties about health and nutrition (including, ironically, the effects of processed and industrialized food). It was also an important harbinger of what was coming next in the food business.

Post was a master marketer who approached marketing as a zero-sum game with room for only so many brands to become household names. There were a lot of coffee alternatives on the market, including a short-lived offering from Minute Tapioca called Malta Coffeena, and once Postum started to feel the effects of all the competition, Post set out to corner the market. He started packaging Postum under a second company name, Monk's Brew, and instigated a vicious race to the bottom by selling it at a loss. This sowed public confusion and suspicion about *all* coffee substitutes and had the effect of driving most people back to the familiar Postum brand, which they saw as the most consistent and reliable.[15] It was one way to come out ahead in the increasingly fierce competition for market share.

You could also take the route that Postum started to follow in the 1920s: scaling up by buying other companies. And that's when the current, highly concentrated state of the corporate food system really got underway.

Minute Tapioca was one of Postum's first acquisitions, bought for cash in 1926. Over the course of the wildly speculative "roaring twenties," dozens of other well-known brands became part of the "Postum family," foods like Baker's chocolate and Hellmann's mayonnaise and Log Cabin maple syrup. In a big step beyond Postum's origins as a healthful alternative to coffee, the company also acquired both Maxwell House and Sanka, which quickly became the leading national coffee brands in a sector formerly filled by smaller, more regional importers.

An even bigger step came in 1929 when Postum bought the General Seafoods Company, based on the Massachusetts coast. Its founder, Clarence Birdseye, had patented a quick-freezing method that was the cold chain on steroids—a whole new horizon of convenience and transportability. By the end of the 1920s Postum had gone public and was listed on the Dow Jones under its new name, General Foods.[16]

In Orange, the acquisition was hailed as good news. Minute Tapioca was now a national brand but its executives recognized that on its own it was vulnerable to both competitive pressures (remember Monk's Brew) and the kinds of macroeconomic shakeups that made the company's early days so shaky. Postum assured them it had no plans to move the manufacturing of Minute Tapioca anywhere else—Frank Ewing and his team had created a cutting-edge facility, a production method hedged around with detailed patents, and a smooth supply chain for the factory's major raw material, tapioca flour from Java. Why mess with success? Alignment with a growing corporate giant offered more security for the many people in Orange who owned Minute Tapioca stock as well as opportunities for ambitious local men to climb the company hierarchy. For a long time—long when reckoned against the tight boom-and-bust cycles of industrial markets—this felt like a good thing for Orange.[17]

And then it came to an end. In the early 1960s rumors appeared that General Foods was planning to consolidate the production of Minute Tapioca and other foods at a new plant in Delaware. In 1963 it came to pass. The Orange plant was kept open a while longer with a skeleton staff testing new products like Jello Cheesecake Mix and something called Mr. Wiggle. But in 1967 the 115,000-square-foot factory was emptied out and the few remaining employees either moved or started looking for other jobs. Older people in town remember students suddenly being taken out of school and houses going on the market overnight.

This time the newspaper didn't bother to hide its feelings. "No True New Englander Will Like Delaware" was the headline of an editorial after the news of the impending move went public: "Anyone used to the beauty of nearby hills and distant mountains of New England will miss having something to lean their eyes against." The editor insisted he wasn't trying to make the people leaving Orange feel bad. He was trying to make those staying in Orange feel better about being left behind.[18] Between the lines you could hear, "Fine, go then, see if we care," a message no doubt conditioned by the recollection of that end-of-the-world moment four decades earlier when the New Home Sewing Machine Company had also abandoned Orange. Worlds, as people who have been conquered or colonized could tell you, can end more than once. Remaking them gets a little harder every time.

The same questions drive all of the present-day revitalization efforts in all of the places like Orange. How can we get people to come here? And how can we get them to *stay*? Cheap real estate and nice hills to lean your eyes against may help with the first part, but the second one is more of a challenge.

In 1926 Minute Tapioca's executives believed the answer was to align themselves with a much larger entity that could give them stability in turbulent times. They'd been watching the New Home Company struggle with the pressures of expansion and a heavy debt load. They were proud of what they'd accomplished and aware of their company's economic and social importance to the town.

After doing their due diligence, the Minute Tapioca leadership found they weren't alone in believing there could be a better way: "Disinterested bankers and economists have told us that the Postum theory is right and the prospects of success certain," the company's vice president assured his employees in a letter about the Postum acquisition, adding rather grandiloquently, "The least we owe to Minute Tapioca is to do what we can to insure its life and growth for so long as the people of this and foreign countries shall continue to eat desserts."[19] The company's leaders were hedging their own bets in an economy where it was increasingly obvious that you had to either buy or be bought.

There wasn't—and still isn't—any end point to all this consolidation, unless you count the unfolding ecological catastrophes set in motion by the past two centuries of industrialization and scaling up and up and up. Within the food system itself, the process continues just as feverishly as ever. In 1985 the tobacco giant Philip Morris bought General Foods as part of its own image makeover and rebranding as a food company.

Three years later Philip Morris acquired Kraft and put the two together as Kraft General Foods. In 2000 Nabisco was added to the mix and everything was consolidated under the Kraft name. But then Philip Morris spun off many of its food holdings, at which point the mega-giant Kraft merged with Heinz, itself owned by a couple of global-scale holding corporations.

By that time the beverage that launched the whole empire was so old it could start to be new again. Kraft stopped making Postum in 2007, but the product still had a devoted following, especially among faith communities that avoid caffeine on principle. In 2012, the same year the North Quabbin Community Co-operative started planning for its storefront expansion, a Mormon couple created their own company to buy the secret Postum formula and began manufacturing it in North Carolina.[20] Like the co-op in Orange, they were looking for entry points into a food market now dominated by giants, but with sometimes surprising opportunities for alternatives—if they could find a way to get a grip and then hang on.

TARGET MARKET

J UST LIKE THE Minute Tapioca executives when Postum came calling, the Orange co-op's leaders did their due diligence. They commissioned a feasibility study from a firm of consultants who took stock of the local grocery landscape and concluded that there was enough demand within the North Quabbin area for the kinds of foods the co-op was proposing to sell. The key would be to target a specific kind of consumer and keep staffing costs as low as possible.

The study did note that there were already two large chain grocery stores in the area and a third on its way. A couple of miles east of the center of Orange was a recently opened Walmart Supercenter, a mile beyond that a Hannaford supermarket. Walmart was on the brink of becoming the world's largest corporation, devouring or outcompeting its rivals, while the regional Hannaford chain had already been gobbled up by another pinnacle player, the Belgian supermarket behemoth Delhaize. Delhaize had been starting to make a move on the U.S. market at that point, going head to head with its Dutch rival Ahold, which had recently bought the popular New England–based chain Stop & Shop. There's a striking sameness to all of these grocery histories: they usually start with a single modest store (Delhaize in Belgium in 1867; Hannaford in Maine in 1883; Ahold in the Netherlands in 1887; Stop & Shop in the Boston area in 1914) and proceed along the growth continuum. Along the way, countless other smaller stores close their doors when they can't match the lower prices and larger selections of the giants.

The other smaller grocery stores in Orange and Athol were gone by the time the co-op did its feasibility study. Despite the presence of full-service supermarkets in the area, the centers of both towns were considered "food deserts" in U.S. Department of Agriculture (USDA) parlance, reflecting the distances that low-income residents, especially those without a car, had to travel to get food. That was one argument in favor of putting a new grocery store in downtown Orange.

The study data showed that many local shoppers were traveling twenty or thirty miles to the Connecticut River Valley to shop at Whole Foods, Trader Joe's, and the larger food co-ops there, and the consultants identified these people as the core customers for the co-op's new store. Obviously, if the same kinds of products were available closer to where those shoppers lived, they reasoned, people would come to Orange instead. They did a ten-year cash-flow projection that showed the business reaching profitability just three years after the move.

With these numbers in hand, the co-op's leaders set about raising capital and finding an affordable space. They turned up at every local event for a couple of years, talking to people, signing up members, getting the word out about their plans.

Finding a storefront was more of a challenge than they'd expected. Nothing inside the Orange Innovation Center quite fit the bill. And although Orange had a lot of empty buildings, once you looked more closely there weren't many that would work as a grocery store. The space needed to be big enough to stock enough inventory to hit the target sales numbers while also having room for the crucial cold-chain apparatus—coolers, freezers, a walk-in unit for storage. Ideally it would be in a visible location. The renovation and startup costs needed to be manageable, so it couldn't be too much of a fixer-upper. Oh, and parking. After decades of supermarket conditioning, most people won't shop for groceries unless they can park right outside.

There was precisely one available storefront in the center of Orange that met all of these criteria: the former Workers Credit Union on North Main Street. There was something particularly fitting about this, because credit unions are also co-ops, in this case banks where people without substantial resources pool what they have and help each other out with loans and other kinds of credit. Launched in 1911 by socialist Finns in a central Massachusetts mill town, Workers had very solid co-op cred. But by the time it took over the smaller Orange Credit Union in 1980 it was already on the growth continuum, trying to keep up with the consolidation in the banking industry spurred by the loosening of regulations on financial institutions. While the food co-op was shopping for storefront space in Orange, Workers Credit Union was building a much larger new space on the far edge of town as part of an eastward growth spurt.

If the trend for a lot of businesses at the turn of the twenty-first century continued to be in the direction of bigness, the "alternatives" were also alive and well, especially in the more politically progressive segments of the Connecticut River Valley. The larger co-operative grocery stores that seemed to prove the existence of a market for the Orange venture were part of a dense weave of co-ops up and down the valley, including several dedicated to providing funding and technical assistance. Those were an obvious early stop in the North Quabbin Community Co-op's capital campaign. Co-ops also raise money by asking their own members for small loans, and that was part of the campaign too.

But the old bank on North Main Street wasn't for rent, it was for sale. The man who'd bought the building from the credit union was an entrepreneur from the Boston area with ambitious plans to turn it into a boutique dinner-movie theater.[1] People in Orange, always ready to roll out the welcome mat for new business, were provisionally excited about the idea, despite its inherent unlikelihood in an era when everyone's big-screen TV and coffee table had become dinner-movie theaters in themselves.

Enthusiasm cooled when the entrepreneur got into disputes with neighbors over their right of way across his parking lot. He put up a chain-link fence that sent a very un-neighborly message, and things deteriorated further when the bank's still-functional, hair-trigger alarm system kept going off for hours or even days at a time. There was something metaphorically apt about a loud alarm bell ringing locally that could only be turned off by an unreachable absentee landowner.

The entrepreneur was open to selling by the time the food co-op was looking for space. The problem was that without collateral, the co-op wasn't going to get a mortgage from even the friendliest lender. And it didn't make economic sense to put a lot of money into coolers and other equipment in a space where the store would be at the mercy of a short-term lease.

Part of the answer to this and a lot of other questions came in the form of an energetic retired minister, farmer, banker, and economic developer named Karl Bittenbender. Like the truckers at Squash, he was a pragmatic altruist, hovering somewhere between the economic mainstream and the radical fringes. Because of that, people on both the pro- and con- sides of the redevelopment projects he championed in the North Quabbin sometimes viewed him with suspicion or even hostility. The corollary was that he knew everybody and was audacious about making connections. It was hard to stay hostile to him for long, especially once you realized how completely free of ego his efforts were. Karl's banking and business development experience were a gift to the group of artists and educators at the core of the young co-op.

One of the connections he made was with Mount Grace Land Conservation Trust, which had been continuing to work with farmers since its first project with Seeds of Solidarity in the 1990s. It wasn't immediately obvious why Mount Grace might want to own a grocery store, but some in the organization argued that they should be moving beyond just conserving farmland toward more holistic support for the farm sector, and that the new grocery store, with its mission of supporting local agriculture, could be a natural fit.

Mount Grace's interest in buying the building made the whole project much more feasible, although it didn't answer all the questions. All that cheap land around the North Quabbin is only *relatively* cheap, after all. It's not cheap on the same magnitude that food is cheap, which meant that even with help and the best will in the world, the numbers might still not add up for small farmers and a little grocery store trying to turn a profit in an area that was far from wealthy. But it was a big step.

By early 2014 the sale was completed and the partners had worked out a ten-year lease. Volunteers got to work, turning the vault into an office with a walk-in cooler in the back, adding sinks and shelving, getting rid of the chain-link fence in the parking lot. The faded Workers Credit Union sign still hung at the top of the facade and the whole building still said "bank" rather than "grocery store," but new hand-painted signs on the first-floor windows invited people in with the message that Quabbin Harvest wasn't an exclusive buying club but a store open to everyone in the community.

Deb Habib and other volunteers made a garden at the front edge of the parking lot; another hand-painted sign encouraged passers-by to help themselves to whatever produce was growing there. Karl, who could turn his hand to an astonishing range of tasks, was part of the building crew, along with members and friends who were also carpenters and electricians and just generally handy. One corollary of being a rural place where resources are thin is that people tend to know, or learn, how to do things for themselves. This goes double for farmers, who have to be their own problem-solvers most of the time. Bruce Scherer, who with his wife, Rachel, ran a goat dairy farm near Seeds of Solidarity on the Chestnut Hill side of Orange, was king of the problem-solvers, showing up with trailers and jacks and a little front-end loader that he could do almost anything with. When all else failed, he applied sheer muscle when something had to be lifted or moved or shoved into place.

The next big step was to hire a store manager. And that's where things really started to diverge from the plan set out in the feasibility study.

The consultants and planners had envisioned that the store could be run with a minimum of paid help and a lot of volunteer hours. But by the time the fundraising and membership campaigns and lease negotiations and building renovations were finished, the core volunteers were getting a clearer sense of just how much they'd taken on. They were more than ready to hand over the reins to someone with actual experience running a grocery store. The manager they hired, who had worked at one of the big valley food co-ops, argued that operating with a skeleton staff and a lot of volunteers was impractical. Right away, the staffing costs were doubled.

The new manager also brought old freezers. Great big ones.

They'd been free for the taking from the larger co-op, which was in the process of upgrading its own building. They took up the whole middle of the store, changing the floor plan radically. Installing them required a lot of carpentry and wiring and plumbing work that wasn't in the budget. And that was before they even got turned on.

At that point it became clear how much it was going to cost to run equipment that was both oversized and inefficient. Grants were quickly written, energy conservation experts consulted, additional equipment installed to try to decrease the electric usage. But there was no getting around the fact that the freezers had been near (or maybe past) their prime even before they came in the door. The recurring problem of old and unreliable equipment had followed the co-op into its new home.

The first inventory too reflected something much larger in scale than the co-op had initially planned for. That's what struck me when I came into the store for the first time during its soft launch in October 2014. I hadn't expected to see quite so many national natural-food brands and upscale nonlocal products. There were local foods too: Dean's Beans coffee was prominently featured, and there was late season produce from some of the area farms and beef from John Moore's cows and goat cheese from Bruce and Rachel Scherer's dairy. But overall, the store gave the impression that it was trying to be a smaller version of Whole Foods, a scaled-down premium supermarket rather than a scaled-up farmstand.

It was pretty clear that I was precisely the consumer being targeted with this selection of food, and I probably should have been happier to see so many items I typically bought myself at larger stores. But even as I was putting things into my shopping basket—the gluten-free pasta from Italy, the organic corn cakes from Australia—I felt uneasy rather than pleased.

Part of the unease stemmed from thinking about logistics. Just because people like me could now buy some of what we wanted in Orange, there was a lot that such a small store couldn't possibly carry. If we still had to drive twenty or thirty miles to get some things, why wouldn't we just get everything else while we were there, especially since the price would probably be lower? The ambitious stocking plan didn't do anything to change the fact that the center of Orange hadn't been anyone's shopping destination for a long time now.

But logistics were only one piece of the problem. There were also subtle—or maybe not so subtle—class overtones to what was on the shelves on opening day, and they raised the kind of questions about disparity that haunt a lot of well-meaning food-movement projects and businesses and spaces.[2] Those disparities often fall along lines of race, but class comes into it in a big way too.

It's not that every longtime resident of the North Quabbin is blue-collar or working-class, not by a long shot. But overall there's a working-class sensibility in the area, especially in the mill towns, a kind of conservatism that looks askance at the upscale, the pretentious, the hip. As with a lot of things about social class, it's hard to put a precise finger on this quality. Some of it has to do with cheapness and the perverse way that high-quality food has become a luxury item in the United States. A lot of it has to do with the histories of industrial growth and loss that have shaped these towns. Pride and bitterness and tenacity and resentment are all balled up in it.

After twenty-five years I was still enough of a newcomer to sense the class distinction in how a lot of people saw me. My husband and I were anything but wealthy when we moved to the area, but there was never any question that we were on the white-collar side of the line. By 2014, though, I was also enough of a local to feel some of that resentment in turn about anyone who presumed to know about the place without actually living there or committing to it for the long term—people like the consultants who produced the feasibility study for the new store. I knew that any business targeting me as its core consumer ran the risk of overlooking or actively alienating a lot of other potential local shoppers.

The same distinction had shown up in the study itself. In making a case for the existence of a niche that the new store could fill, the consultants had quickly dismissed the existing Orange Farmers Market as not sufficiently supportive of truly local food because it was, in their words, "one of the only local farmer's markets that allow vendors who do not grow their own food, which results in food from unknown origins in competition with locally grown sustainable produce."[3]

In fact, none of that was quite accurate.

The farmers market in Orange had been created in the 1980s by a group of civic planners, part of that long succession of efforts to generate economic development in the town. They took a hard look at the available vendors from the immediate area and concluded that the market stood a better chance if it cast a slightly wider net around the idea of localness. So they wrote the bylaws to allow for one specific vendor to resell produce that he purchased at wholesale from farms in the Connecticut River Valley, the same midsized commercial produce sellers that Squash's trucking business drew from. Far from being of unknown origin, this was food that a lot of North Quabbin shoppers knew and valued. The nonlocal vendor reliably had the earliest asparagus and strawberries and corn, the biggest raspberries and tomatoes, and often the lowest prices because the larger and more fertile valley farms could reach economies of scale by growing and selling things in bigger quantities. Moreover, the food was healthy, it was arguably sustainable, it was even more or less local, depending on how you cast that net.

The popularity of the nonlocal vendor inevitably caused some tensions with the truly local farmers selling at the market. But it also attracted a wider range of customers, just as the planners had intended. And it proved that there were lots of people in the area who did appreciate fresh local produce and understood about seasonal eating. They just weren't on any kind of mission about it. When the growing season ended, they weren't driving down to the valley to shop at Whole Foods or one of the larger co-ops; they were more likely to go back to buying their fruits and vegetables at Hannaford or maybe driving in the opposite direction to shop at lower-priced chains. This was class and taste and localness manifesting at the point of sale.

The co-op's feasibility study targeted a market segment that wasn't typical—in fact, in a lot of ways was just the opposite—of the area overall. It betrayed an assumption about who the "real" customers for a locally oriented market would be: those who *were* on a mission to support local foods but who also wanted—and could and would pay for—a wider range of "natural" products, literally buying into the vision of a food system where everything you eat is healthy, every choice you make is ethical, and every link in the supply chain is transparent.

There are a few places and people in the United States that can sustain this fantasy, and a lot of businesses doing their best to uphold it. Whole Foods is built around it. But in places where resources are scarcer, the gaps in the fantasy are easier to see. The "realness" of the North Quabbin—the scrappy, sinewy quality that attracts some people and puts others off—marks it as being on the scarcer-resource side of the line. That's what set off an alarm bell for me as I was filling my basket on opening day.

At the same time, it was exciting—and pretty astonishing—to see the store actually in existence. Launching a small grocery store in downtown Orange might be only slightly more practical than trying to make an upscale dinner-movie theater there, but it had happened, and that put Quabbin Harvest far ahead of a lot of other business ideas that had failed to launch.

It was fun to attend the official ribbon-cutting celebration the following May. The inevitable bevy of pop-up tents filled the parking lot and gave a sense of the diffuse and tenacious network of people and businesses that had come together to make the new store. There were farmers selling seedlings and root vegetables, young gardeners from Seeds of Solidarity's youth program serving up salad, volunteers offering samples of local cheese and bread and pickles. Dean's Beans had a tent. So did Mount Grace. There was free ice cream from a popular company in the valley. Deb Habib showed people around the little garden. Robin Shtulman's husband, professionally known as Ed the Wizard, made balloon animals. There was live music. There was an inaugural procession with kids carrying big stars on sticks, borrowed from the committee that organized the town's annual New Year's celebration. It was a combination of hippie craft festival and rural fall fair, earnest and homegrown and hopeful in all the ways that a lot of alternative food ventures are.

I still worried that it wasn't going to resonate with enough shoppers in the North Quabbin and that going from zero to storefront in five years was recklessly fast. But in an area where people had good reason to be disillusioned about promises that don't pan out and businesses that don't stay, I could also see that spending six or seven years being sensible, raising more money, and signing up more members might be a mistake in the other direction.

"If we hadn't done it then," Amy Borezo says now, "I think it wouldn't have happened at all." They'd seized the moment, the building, the opportunity for a partnership with Mount Grace, even the oversized freezers, and brought the new store into being. The old bank was built like a bunker and there was something reassuring about that, despite its bland exterior and the fact that it really didn't look anything like a grocery store.

I felt that if I was the target consumer I'd better start acting that way, and I resolved to shop there as often as I could. At that point in my education about the grocery business, "as often as I could" meant "when I can find things here that I was going to buy somewhere else anyway." Like most people in Quabbin Harvest's target demographic, I was still going to other stores while starting to figure out what it meant to make more of a commitment to the new store in Orange.

Before I'd figured it out, I noticed that a lot of the things I wanted to buy weren't there anymore. Eventually I bought all six packages of the Australian organic corn cakes. But they were never restocked. And other gaps were opening up on the shelves. Before long I was finding that I *wanted* to spend money in the store but couldn't find much to spend it on.

My commitment already felt more complicated than I'd expected or wanted it to be. Beyond spending money, the only other way I could think of to honor it was to make more use of the skills I had in education and research and communication. So shortly after the gala opening, I partnered with Mount Grace on a project about the history of small farms and food production in the area. I got my own pop-up tent and prepared to hit the summer circuit of fairs and festivals and farmers markets. If I couldn't shop, at least I could talk.

CHAPTER 4

DECONSTRUCTED BURGER

A s SOON AS classes were over in the spring of 2015 I visited our three local supermarkets, trying to compare apples and oranges. Or rather, burgers and buns.

The farm history project had been a tough sell to both Mount Grace and the state humanities council that funded it. The land trust was mostly focused on protecting more farmland for agricultural use and supporting related food system projects like the co-op. It wasn't particularly interested in history per se. The humanities council *was* interested in history, including how reflecting on the past might play a part in civically engaged projects. But land trusts and grocery stores were far outside its usual network. It worried that it was being asked for money to support advocacy, which nonprofits aren't supposed to do. There was a very fine line between talking about real-world issues and engaging in them, and I was trying to position myself right on that line.

I still thought history was a good way to take a step sideways and gain some more perspective on issues of the day. The land trust was doing a pilot inventory of farmland and other food and farm resources in six contiguous towns, including Orange and Athol. We decided to try to bring some of the big questions about land and food and economics and power down to earth by developing a microhistory of one farm in each town and using those as conversation-starters with people at public events.

I had a pretty good idea that people strolling through a festival field or shopping at a farmers market might not be immediately drawn to someone asking if they wanted to learn more about history. We needed hooks. And they needed to be fun. So we had a life-sized American Gothic cutout that people could stand behind and have their pictures taken. I made little trivia contests and puzzles and timelines that people could try to match events to.

We also made wooden build-your-own burgers, similar to the stacking cones of colored rings that you give to babies to encourage manual dexterity. Our burgers had a circular base with a post in the middle, onto which people could slide a disc for the patty and then various toppings (cheese, tomato, lettuce, all cut out of craft foam sheets), with a rounded bun that slid onto the top. All the pieces had prices and names on them, reflecting what they would cost from different sources: fifty cents for a slice of organic tomato from Market Basket, grown in Mexico, or seventy cents for an organic slice from one of the six local farms we were highlighting.

We didn't plan this as a kids' activity but it quickly became one, which turned out to be a great strategy for drawing in adults without being too pedantic about the history part. Sometimes people just built burgers and glanced at my poster with the pictures and locations of our six farms and that was enough. Many people didn't get beyond noticing a simple price comparison: the nineteen-cent bun from Walmart versus the fifty-cent hamburger roll made by Laura Moore in her bakery at the back of the old Minute Tapioca factory.

Then there were those—kids more often than adults—who took the time to reflect on every single slice of cheese and tomato, meticulously adding up the total on the calculator we put out on the table. We were surprised at how thoughtful and purposeful these burger-builders often were. Some made the cheapest burger they could, some went for the most truly local burger. (I'd chosen burgers because it actually was possible to make a 100 percent local burger, including the grain for the flour in the bun.) One girl opted for the cheapest of everything else so she could splurge on a slice of organic cheddar from a farm in the town just north of Orange, saying that she wanted to support local farmers but knew she had to economize elsewhere to be able to do it—clearly a child being raised by locavores. We had conversations about the complexities of organic labeling and the ethics and practicalities of eating meat at all. It turned out that the organic ground beef from Hannaford and Market Basket started out on the hoof in Australia and flew to Colorado to be processed, yet it cost about the same as the beef from Stillman Quality Meats in Hardwick, the southernmost of our six towns. Both were quite a lot more expensive than John Moore's grass-fed organic beef. We talked about why that was: Kate Stillman ran a larger-scale operation with more employees, a recently built abattoir that was giving her more control over her own processing, and a booth at the newly launched Boston Public Market on a piece of high-priced real estate in downtown Boston. John Moore managed his farm with some help from his family and sold what he produced at the most local of farmers markets and now at Quabbin Harvest. The meat from his small herd of cows on North Main Street in Orange cost just a little more than the nonorganic stuff from Hannaford and Market Basket, although it couldn't touch the absurdly cheap bulk beef in giant plastic tubes at Walmart, which came from God knows where.

I got pretty good at sneaking in historical factoids and provocative questions, and I was struck—and heartened—by how many people paused to think about what they knew, or didn't know, about the past and present of farming in New England and how that related to their own shopping habits. But pretty soon I realized that I hadn't begun to figure out how to talk about food prices. And that that had everything to do with what I hadn't figured out yet about supermarkets.

Part of this had to do with how I'd been thinking about history itself. I'd been attaching the historical part of the project only to the six farms, trying to show how small-scale farmers in this part of New England had struggled with the demands of commercial markets for over two centuries, constantly adapting, sometimes getting out of farming, sometimes getting back in, occasionally resisting and refusing to let the market dictate terms. For all the famed independence and contrariness of Yankee farmers, there hadn't actually been that much direct resistance. You had to go all the way back to Daniel Shays's Rebellion in 1786 to find a case of people who farmed in the European tradition banding together to fight back against the way the interests of financiers were being put over those of people whose wealth was tied up in land and livestock.

Those farmers hadn't been opposed to the market per se. They just wanted a fair shot at prospering within it.[1] Since then, farmers in New England have sometimes raised questions about whether that kind of fairness is actually a possibility within markets built on the profit principle. But mostly, in agriculture as in other sectors, New Englanders have tended to keep their sights on getting a share of the wealth rather than undermining the entire system.

When I framed out this big narrative, I put supermarkets right at the end, as a kind of present-day coda to the long story of farmers struggling with markets. The supermarkets and the build-a-burger exercise were a way to get people thinking about how we'd ended up with the food system we have today. It worked pretty well as a hook. But there were also two big problems with it.

One was that supermarkets have a lot of history too. In tacking them onto my timeline at the very end, I'd slipped right back into the mindset molded by my own childhood experiences of shopping with my family and being entranced by the space-age architecture of our local Dominion store. Supermarkets were *now*, and the fact that the Dominion of my 1960s childhood would now seem quaint and cramped only proved it. Supermarkets continually move with the times, pulling all of us into the future with them.

It turned out, though, that grocery stores had actually been doing that for a very long time—almost exactly a hundred years, as I discovered when I started to think about them more seriously.

Chain grocery stores had existed before the 1910s, but they were small, with limited selections. Shopping there was a lot like going to the butcher or baker or fishmonger, where you asked a person behind a counter for the items you wanted. At precisely the same early twentieth-century moment when Henry Ford was figuring out how to manufacture cars more efficiently on an assembly line (an idea he copied from the slaughterhouse "disassembly" lines of Chicago's meatpacking industry), the grocery store chains—first A&P, then others—were making the same discovery about shopping.[2] In 1916 the Piggly Wiggly chain in Tennessee opened the first self-serve store where everything was on open shelves and customers picked out their own groceries. That seems perfectly natural today, but at the time it was a drastic change. On a practical level, it cut down on labor costs for the store, which is one of the ways chain grocery stores made food cheaper. But much more important, it gave customers an exhilarating new feeling: they could simply reach out and take whatever they wanted from an abundant and ever-expanding universe of food. Maybe they'd seen a magazine ad for Maxwell House coffee or Minute Tapioca—and there it was on the shelves in their local store! And so cheap! Who could possibly resist?

A lot of farmers and smaller retailers and their allies *did* resist, because this new concentration of market power in the food sector was already starting to make it harder for smaller businesses to survive. A&P alone went from 650 stores in 1914 to more than 4,000 in 1919 and 8,000 in 1923.[3] They did it by building big, centralized warehouses; standardizing their inventory; and starting to buy foods in huge quantities, which also let them lower their prices.

There was a spate of antitrust legislation in the 1930s, but by then that exhilarating feeling was starting to seem normal, and most people didn't want to go back.[4] The word "commodity," after all, stems from the French *commodité*, which means convenience. When the first true supermarket came along in Queens, New York, in 1930, bringing the butcher and baker and greengrocer and fishmonger and everything else together under one big roof, it was a way to keep the dream going. There's a lot more to this story, but basically you can boil it down to the fact that most Americans got hooked on convenience and haven't looked back since.

I started to weave this history into my project as the summer of 2015 went on. I looked at old street directories and discovered that the major chains had had stores in both Athol and Orange until the 1960s—two A&Ps, two Piggly Wigglys, two First Nationals, all starting in the small downtowns and then moving gradually outward as stores got larger and people did more of their shopping by car. I made quizzes with historical pictures to see who could match present-day buildings with their earlier incarnations as supermarkets. People were fascinated by this as a kind of visual time machine.

But it didn't necessarily do anything to dent the fascination that the convenience and abundance and cheapness of the real-life supermarkets still exerted for nearly everyone I talked to. And that was the second problem I discovered as the summer and fall went on.

I knew how food had been made cheaper and more abundant by producing it industrially and then buying and selling it at huge volumes. I understood the basic principle of how the magic trick had been worked, how the lady appeared to have been sawn in half. But I hadn't really reckoned with how much people still loved those old tricks. And I hadn't started to come to terms with what it meant that the magic act itself was resting on top of that insoluble koan, a kind of compound wizardry that made it even harder to see and understand the foods that were right in front of us. I'd been trying to compare apples and oranges, but to most people it all just looked like burgers.

———

A woman helped clarify this for me at the very first event where we set up our tent. "It's interesting, isn't it," she mused, "how we're taught that saving money on food is just something you're supposed to do. It's part of how you look after your family."[5]

That's part of the trick. Basically, we're talking here about the magic of the commodity. More than a century and a half ago, Karl Marx talked about the uncanniness of commodities, how a cheap package of meat from Walmart or an organic tomato from Mexico can soak up and miraculously replace the work of all of the living entities involved in growing it and getting it to the supermarket, turning it into a kind of blank surface onto which consumers can project care or desire or fantasy.

My burger exercise did what most people do when they're trying to relate to food in a less-commodified way. I wanted to make the supply chains more visible, more transparent, more personal. The implication is that if we know more about where our food comes from, we'll opt to source from closer to home and be willing to pay the often-higher price for it. We'll be able to push back against the way commodities mess with our minds.

This feels right if you're a local-food supporter, as I already was. But in talking with people about the burgers they were building out of my wooden pieces, I started to understand more fully how many problems there were with this "know your farmer, know your food" approach.[6]

The assumption is that knowledge will translate into action—that is, that people who learn more about where their food comes from will come to care enough to resist the siren call of the commodity.[7] But that's not a given. For one thing, there's more than a whiff of moralizing in suggesting to other people that they *should* care and change their habits as a result. Financially and logistically, not everyone *can* do it, which is one of the many things that make the system so resistant to real change.

And not everything about long-distance food supply chains is bad. People in cities have relied on food transported over distances (albeit not usually the kinds of distances we can now span with ease) for thousands of years. It makes sense to grow some things in quantity and ship them in bulk. And for all its flaws, the modern industrial food system does provision immense numbers of people. You can eat very healthfully as a supermarket shopper, assuming you have the resources of time and money and knowledge. Localness isn't even a guarantee that food is more ethical or better tasting—you still have to ask who's producing it and how.[8] More complicated yet, we're living in a time when knowledge itself is increasingly commodified, when a whole industry of third-party watchdogs—many of them funded by the food sectors they're providing information about—has sprung up to help us with our transparency problem.[9]

So knowledge is good, but it's not magic. We live in a world where it's all but impossible to approach food simply as sustenance. Food-as-commodity has been around for too long and it's too tangled up with how most people live and think and feel. It goes back far beyond the making-food-cheap trick that happened with industrialism, long before the supermarket and the cold chain and organic beef that can travel from Australia to Colorado to Massachusetts and cost the same as beef from cows raised just a few towns away.

That doesn't mean you shouldn't try to do get outside the commodity mindset or that people *aren't* trying to do it, all the time and in countless creative ways. But relating to food-as-sustenance in a way that's truly free of food-as-commodity requires a lot of mental agility and a lot of knowledge about history. You can't get there with simple side-by-side comparisons, as I was trying to do with my deconstructed burgers.

If I were doing that project again, I would try to find some way to talk about the assize of bread.

The assize of bread was a medieval English law that regulated the size and weight of loaves of bread in relation to the price of wheat. By the thirteenth century, when the law was first enacted, the price of wheat was already being determined by "market forces"—supply and demand, competitive pressures, the economic effects of lean harvests and abundant ones that meant bakers sometimes had to pay more for their flour and sometimes less.

The feudal state stepped in with what was essentially a consumer protection law to make sure eaters—especially the poorer and non-grain-growing ones—didn't suffer too drastically from swings of the market. The law said that when wheat was more expensive, bakers had to make smaller loaves and keep the retail price the same. It wasn't a perfect answer—obviously you got less bread for your money when wheat prices were high. But at least you got some, and that kept people from agitating for more, or—heaven forbid—demanding more money or more land to grow their own food. The assize of bread served elites' interests as well as those of the poor.[10]

This legal concept, and a keen awareness of how social and political stability were linked to the price of food, traveled across the Atlantic with English colonization. But the very fact that these laws existed tells us that bakers chafed against the limits to how much they could charge, much as present-day laws capping the price of milk are resented by dairy farmers who often find themselves unable to recoup enough money to cover their own costs. Especially in the new United States of America, where opportunity was so closely aligned with the emerging market economy, many bakers saw the assize of bread as regulatory overreach, unfairly limiting their ability to profit by their own labor and skill.

In November 1801 bakers in New York City underscored this point with a one-day work stoppage. Shelves emptied and customers panicked, demanding that the city council force the bakers back to their ovens. There were fierce debates about rights and opportunities and responsibilities. Bakers and their allies argued that independent entrepreneurs had a right to whatever wealth they could derive from the market. Like the farmers who took up arms during Shays's Rebellion, they weren't protesting against capitalism; they just wanted their fair share of it. They pointed out that even at the very best of times it was hard to make much money selling bread. One pseudonymous letter-writer demanded to know whether anyone had ever met a "rich loaf-maker."[11]

It took twenty more years, but eventually the assize of bread law was repealed in New York. Ultimately, though, the bakers lost by winning. They were now free to charge what they wanted. But they'd been very naive about how much power small producers would be able to wield within a more wide-open market system.

They got their first inkling at the hands of the New York Bread Company, a corporation founded by Alexander Hamilton's brother-in-law and a consortium of other businessmen and bankers. These men saw the power of the old artisanal guilds like the bakers as a drag on the growth of free markets. They realized they could break the power of the trades and corner a section of the food market for themselves by capitalizing on the public's deep unease about the security of the bread supply.

And capitalize they literally did—they started selling shares of stock the day the bakers went on strike in 1801. The Bread Company launched on an entirely new scale, with cheaper bread, home delivery, and a fourteen-loaf "baker's dozen" instead of the traditional thirteen—the equivalent of a supermarket's grand opening special. Unable to compete, small bakers were reduced to asserting the supposedly inherent virtue of the artisanal classes and the potential dangers of letting one large company control so much of the food supply—pretty much exactly the same argument that gets made today about corporate overreach and the need for more local-ized food systems. Then as now, plenty of people sympathized. But many were also just happy for the lower prices and seemingly reliable supply.

That reliability, like so many of the promises of scaling up, turned out to be illusory. The New York Bread Company burned to the ground in May 1803, an occupational hazard for all bakeries in those days of wooden buildings and wood-fired ovens. It closed out a brief but telling moment in the history of food-as-commodity.

Talking about the assize of bread could have given me a useful way to compare and contrast the fresh hamburger rolls from Laura Moore's lit-tle bakery in the old Minute Tapioca Company factory with the stacks of buck-a-bag buns at Walmart. It might have sparked conversation about what happens when you make food into a commodity in the first place, and how there are both good and bad things about doing that, which is one of the reasons it's so hard to think clearly about our modern food system.

Those are the kinds of questions anthropologists love to pose. It's the "making the familiar strange" part of what we do. Anything that people take for granted is fair game. Why do we have markets anyway? What *is* a commodity, when you get right down to it?

People in our capitalist society tend to talk about "the market" as though ours was the only kind, but anthropologists know that's far from true. A market is any system that enables trade and exchange or balances supply and demand. It often involves some form of money, whether that's cowrie shells or silver or bits and bytes, as a medium for swaps that are more complex than just I-give-you-two-bushels-of-corn-you-give-me-three-sheepskins. When you start valuing anything in terms of what it's equivalent to in the market, or producing something in order to be valued and sold there, you've got a commodity.

Historically, one of the main reasons people have created markets is to help smooth out unevenness in their food supply, especially in times and places with growing numbers of people dependent on others for their food—that is, urban people, displaced rural people, impoverished people. It happened in Babylonia, in what is now Iraq, at least 1,800 years ago, and in Song-era China more than a thousand years ago. It happened in medieval Western Europe not long after that. Market creation is linked in close and complicated ways with the growth of cities and centralized states, with power struggles among nobles and traders and bankers and artisans, with innovations in transportation and technology. And it's different in every case. Markets don't take one universal form. They're always embedded in particular societies and animated by those societies' values and social structures and ideas about how the world should work.[12]

The assize of bread shows that in the particular kind of market economy that started to take shape in medieval Europe—the one that has become dominant throughout most of the world—there's also a very long history of people feeling ambivalent about the relationship between markets and food. There were a lot of interests being negotiated through the assize of bread: elites' worries about social and moral stability, city-dwellers' fear of not having enough to eat, a whole raft of concerns on the part of bakers. Many of those bakers were undoubtedly just trying to feed their neighbors and make some kind of a living. Others were probably trying to game the system by selling shoddy or underweight loaves and pocketing the difference. Those who were able to hang onto a bit more profit were better positioned to expand, hire more workers, and gain a bigger share of the market. Others quickly hit the downslope and struggled just to stay in business—the Susan Stavers and John Whitman story. Medieval accounts tended to emphasize the bad apples, but that may have been perception or legal posturing by those who resented the power of tradespeople and artisans, not only in the food supply but in the political sphere as well.[13]

And it wasn't just the bakers that both poor people and elites were anxious about. It was the morality of capitalism itself. It was complicated enough to try to balance and negotiate all these different interests through the new system. But as they did, the market was also taking on its own momentum, becoming an end in itself instead of just a means to an end. So people weren't just arguing about food and power *through* the market, they were also arguing *about* the market. And we've been doing both of these things ever since.

No wonder it's so hard to think clearly about food.

These are the kinds of things an anthropologist can sit and talk about all day. I mean, how fascinating is it that the first assize of bread was enacted eight centuries ago and it's still not clear how—or whether—you can find a fair balance between the workings of markets and the need for everyone to have adequate food? I loved the idea of talking with people about the thirteenth-century English lawmakers who understood—however imperfectly—that you couldn't just let market forces have their way with your food supply, because market forces don't actually care whether people eat or starve. I thought about ways to connect that with the New York City bakers who came to see, six hundred years later, why that law might not have been a completely bad idea in the first place.

And then I envisioned people's eyes glazing over and their kids getting antsy, wanting to move on to the next tent. Face-painting or economic and legal history? Hmm, let me think.

Even with the kinds of people who were turning up at farmers markets and festivals and local food venues, it was pretty clear that this approach was more suited to a fifteen-week semester than a stroll-by encounter at a summer festival. Being a scholar adjacent to the food system was interesting, but it didn't feel like enough. I needed to find some way to do more, especially now that Market Basket had come to town.

CHAPTER 5

(SOME) PEOPLE BEFORE PROFITS

I N THE MIDST of my build-a-burger conversations in the summer of 2015, my friend Pat Larson and I sat down one muggy morning with Amy Borezo and Karl Bittenbender to find out why we were having a hard time spending as much money as we wanted to at the store.

Pat had been volunteering to pack the co-op's weekly CSA shares almost since the very beginning in 2009, and like me she'd been trying to shop as much as possible since the store's soft opening. But it was a rare week when either of us was able to hit the fifty-dollar mark, and that had us worried. If even the people who set out to spend money there couldn't do it, what were the chances the business was going to survive?

We met in the little café at the back of the outfitter store at the main intersection in Orange, just about the only gathering place left in the center of town. Amy told us about a new program they were working on for the store, called "Basics." Like me, it turned out, co-op volunteers had been going around to the supermarkets price-checking particular items, in this case so they could put together a list of staples for the program.

"There's a perception that everything in our store is too expensive," Amy said. "We've decided to take a lower margin on some things and promote that as our affordable product line."

I wondered whether that would attract enough new customers to offset the loss of revenue from the lower profit margin, but I applauded the effort. After all, I'd had exactly the same concerns about the store's initial inventory mix seeming out of touch with the demographics of its market area. Countering both the perception and reality of those higher prices seemed important. And anyway, supermarkets did this too, with their generic, private-label items.

Karl told us about another new talking point for the co-op. He'd run the numbers and could show that out of every dollar spent at Quabbin Harvest, sixty-eight cents stayed in the North Quabbin's economy in the form of wages and purchases from local farmers and other vendors like Dean's Beans.

"Most of the businesses in this area take money *out* of the community," he said. "They're extractive, not additive. There are very few companies here that actually make a product locally and then recirculate the money here from selling that product."

Amy had taken Karl's factoid and made a little infographic out of it. They were also piloting a new tagline: "Shop Co-op First." It was a way of acknowledging that while you might not be able to find everything you wanted at Quabbin Harvest, you could still support the store by shifting your shopping route a little, rewiring the I-was-going-to-Whole-Foods-anyway impulse.

Karl admitted that it was challenging to pitch these messages so that they were upbeat without being preachy. As someone whose professional life had included time in both the pulpit and the Chamber of Commerce, he was clearly comfortable with the territory somewhere between an ad pitch and a homily. But his usual buoyancy did seem a bit dimmed as he talked about whether the messaging would work.

"You run up against real pain points in trying to get people to change their shopping habits," he said. "The question is, can we find enough customers who are willing to work past that?"

Inevitably, that got us around to talking about Market Basket.

Market Basket is iconic for a lot of New Englanders. It's a biggish regional supermarket chain—nearly 90 stores and 25,000 employees—but in the words of one pair of authors who are clearly among the true believers, it's "a $4.5 billion supermarket that retains its mom-and-pop feel."[1] And that resonates deeply with its extraordinarily faithful and very specific customer base.

The previous summer that base had spontaneously rallied alongside workers and suppliers in a way that business analysts and scholars are still puzzling over. The 2014 uprising, or strike, or maybe mutiny would be a better word, was a collective action that flew in the face of a lot of economic theory and nearly every recent trend in the supermarket sector and labor organizing and consumer activism.

It seemed, in fact, to offer a resolution to that foundational conundrum about how to have a food system that feeds everybody well while still generating profit. It showed that there are sometimes limits to how far things can be pushed in the direction of pure profit-seeking. But the resistance in this case was rooted deep in a defense of the same cheap food and corporate hierarchies that the whole system rests on, tangled up with a particular vision of America and a particular experience of mobility and work and family. And all of this had implications for the attempt to start a new little grocery store in the North Quabbin region.

Market Basket's story starts out in 1917 in the industrial city of Lowell, Massachusetts, with the familiar single store. The founders were a Greek couple named Demoulas who did their own slaughtering and sold fresh lamb and other meats to other Greek immigrants. They started out in the Acre, the city's poorest neighborhood and traditionally the landing point for nineteenth-century newcomers from Ireland, French Canada, Greece, and more recently Latin America, Southeast Asia, West Africa, and elsewhere.

The couple's two sons took over the business in the 1950s and expanded it during the postwar supermarket boom.[2] At first they stuck with the family name DeMoulas (the founding patriarch may have capitalized the "M" because he thought it had a touch more class) but switched to calling it Market Basket in the 1970s.[3] They followed the usual supermarket-expansion trajectory in some ways, adding two big central warehouses and opening new stores at a steady clip all around eastern Massachusetts and southern New Hampshire. A lot of people in the area remember working at Market Basket as their first job or shopping there with their parents when they were kids. But Market Basket's trajectory also diverged sharply by seeming to stop time at the historical juncture when food had become cheap and abundant and you could still support a family on a supermarket cashier's earnings.

The chain's tagline is "More for your dollar." But in 2014, "people before profits" was the phrase you heard most often when people talked about Market Basket.[4] And yet there have been plenty of profits too. Not only does Market Basket seem to reconcile food-as-sustenance with food-as-commodity, it seems to fulfill the promise that industrial food—and industrial capitalism more generally—can deliver benefits for everyone without exploiting anybody.

To understand why this is so amazing, really to understand anything about the food business at all, you have to grasp that once you've made food cheap and abundant, the profit margin on any individual item becomes almost nil. Zip. Zero. One joke in the grocery sector is that you actually lose money on every sale. The punchline? You have to make it up in volume. That's why supermarkets sell so many different things—why they became "super." They only work at scale. As one industry pundit put it as early as 1941, "Mass! Mass! That's the key idea and you must never lose sight of it."[5]

The grocery business generates a fantastic amount of revenue. Everybody has to eat, after all. It's one of the few truly reliable markets out there. It just doesn't generate a fantastic rate of *profit*. Net annual profits of 1 or 2 or 3 percent are the norm in the grocery sector—a very long way from unicorn level.[6] And after decades of competition and consolidation in the supermarket sector—not to mention the reality of "inelastic demand," meaning in this case that the human stomach can absorb only so much food—those excruciatingly slim profit margins are even less achievable simply through selling food.[7] Increasingly, supermarkets and the corporations that own them have made their money by selling things like pharmaceuticals, lawn furniture, space on their shelves, Prime memberships. They also learned from the big food manufacturers that they could grow by gobbling up their competitors or cornering a particular market niche or region to give them huge economies of scale. The digital era has let them gather fantastically detailed data about their customers' purchases and preferences, through point-of-sale software and loyalty programs and online ordering apps and tracking devices in carts and baskets that show how we move around stores, where we pause longest, which displays capture our valuable attention and our dollars. And they're always in search of ways to cut their costs, especially the biggest one: payroll.

Market Basket has managed to thrive without entirely following that playbook. To a striking extent, the chain has operated on a philosophy of loyalty and reciprocity. Reversing the trend of big supermarket chains abandoning low-wealth urban areas, Market Basket celebrated its eightieth birthday in 1997 by opening a brand-new, state-of-the-art store in the Acre, still an impoverished, diverse, and lively place. When I was doing my dissertation fieldwork in Lowell and living in the Acre a few years later, that store was my favorite place in the city. You could find plantains and lemongrass and longan fruit and ten different kinds of rice in fifty-pound bags. You could hear two or three languages being spoken in any given aisle, with arguments about local or transnational politics. It wasn't open late at night—Market Basket's hours are shorter than those of most big chains—but it was always bustling when it was open. It felt very porous to its surrounding neighborhood, reminding me, more than anything else, of the vibrant outdoor market district in Toronto where I used to live, which was pretty astonishing when I thought about it.

A lot of the working-class and immigrant neighborhoods where Market Basket sited their stores have changed over the decades, becoming much more affluent as the region has shifted toward a postindustrial economy. The Demoulases' insistence on buying real estate outright rather than leasing it from mall developers has paid off for the chain, reducing their overhead and giving them lots of equity to work with. But even the newest of its stores don't tend to scream "upscale." Many of them remain oddly unassuming, even when they're huge and shiny and filled with every commodity food you can imagine.

And this is the appeal of Market Basket for a lot of people. It's what creates that billion-dollar mom-and-pop feeling. Partly it's the shorter hours, the heavy emphasis on low-cost generic items, the plain-Jane architecture and fittings, the slightly old-fashioned uniforms and clean-cut staff (no hair below the collar line for male employees). Market Basket doesn't have a loyalty program because it doesn't want to create different tiers among its customers. It hasn't joined the rush toward self-serve checkout stations either because they want you to interact with actual humans in the store. For a long time the company even resisted having a website. They just didn't think their clientele needed or wanted one. A devoted but frustrated customer launched a site in 2011 (mydemoulas.com) to keep track of the weekly specials. When the corporate office finally made one of their own in 2017, the *Boston Globe* quipped, "Welcome to 1997."[8]

When we first moved to the North Quabbin there were still a couple of small supermarkets that felt like they'd stopped time in the 1960s and 1970s, respectively. One was a locally owned company that once had multiple branches but was down to just a single venue in Orange. It had a low ceiling and a small in-house butcher shop and checkout counters where the cashiers pushed your items through by hand. It was that checkout chute—wood-lined and smooth with use—that sent me straight back to the Dominion stores of my youth. I couldn't have told you exactly when moving checkout belts came along, except that they belonged to "after." This place definitely felt like "before."

The other supermarket was in downtown Athol, a branch of a small regional chain called Victory started by another immigrant family—Italian, in this case—around the same time as the Demoulas family founded their store in Lowell. Victory's 1970s vibe came from the fact that its footprint was a little smaller than a newer supermarket, its aisles a little tighter. Most of the produce was tightly wrapped in plastic. And like Market Basket, Victory's stores catered to very particular ethnic and class populations. You could buy salt herring and cans of *poutine râpée* at the Athol store, reflecting the fact that a lot of Acadian French Canadians came to this part of central Massachusetts to work in the mill towns. (If you know Quebec *poutine*, this is nothing like it. It's a gelatinous, softball-sized lump of mashed potato with salt pork in the center.)

What's radically different about Market Basket is that it has *intentionally* stopped the clock on a lot of the changes that are endlessly propelling supermarkets into the future, something that theoretically shouldn't be possible in a brutally competitive business with impossibly thin profit margins.

It's not that they're not competitive. "If you show a little bit of skin," one vendor has said about the experience of negotiating prices with the chain, "they may come after it."[9] But they seem to accept a version of capitalism that operates within limits, out of a sense that that's what's best for everyone in the longer term.

That sense of limits has kept Market Basket at a regional rather than a national or global scale. It means they haven't hoovered up smaller chains like Victory whenever they've had a chance. They've also resisted taking on debt in order to grow. As a stubbornly regional chain, Market Basket can still source at least some of its inventory from big regional suppliers, which becomes difficult or impossible once you're talking about a larger scale.[10] It has helped launch some untried regional products that have since become major brands, like Ken's Salad Dressing and

Cape Cod potato chips. And it did so without charging a fortune in the "slotting fees" that big supermarket chains demand from companies that want to get their products onto the shelves.[11]

Market Basket started an employee profit-sharing program in 1963 and has never discontinued it. Twice a year, employees get a bonus check, averaging $1,600 per person in a year. The company promotes people from within their own stores rather than parachuting in people straight out of business schools, creating a corporate structure where almost everyone has firsthand experience of working on the floor.[12] It's the most hierarchical and paternalistic structure imaginable, and people within it tend to be fiercely loyal not only because of the bonuses and the chance to rise in the ranks but because the style of management actually does encourage initiative and a sense of ownership from top to bottom.

There are things to question about all of this. And I'll get to that.

But just pause for a moment and consider how astonishing it is when someone or something is able to hold the line against the destructive tendencies inherent in the larger system that defines it—when a coach or a team in a brutal contact sport puts the wellbeing of their players ahead of the demand that they continue to run headlong into things no matter the cost to their brains, or when a city resists turning its police into soldiers even when people are fearful and dangers are real.

My analogies with other hierarchical, competitive, male-dominated domains are quite intentional. This is a particular style of cohesiveness, a specific vision of how the world should work. But sometimes it actually does seem to work in a way that feels relatively healthy and balanced. Resisting certain kinds of changes or demands says, in essence, "We're refusing the bait of these short-term gains because we can see that in the long run we'll have lost something we all value." There's a sense of being part of an "all," a place, a community, however idealized that might be.

In the summer of 2014 a family power struggle within Market Basket's board of directors put a faction in charge that *did* want shorter-term gains. The ensuing mutiny showed how quickly an idealized set of values can translate into action under the right circumstances.

The story unfolded almost literally like classical Greek drama, right down to the two feuding cousins both named for the family patriarch. Arthur Telemachus Demoulas ("Artie T.") had been involved in the company in a hands-on way from boyhood and had continued to expand it steadily since becoming CEO in 2008. Arthur Stephen Demoulas ("Artie S.") had started out on the same work-your-way-up-through-the-ranks path, been forced off the board by Artie T.'s father in an acrimonious episode, then litigated his way back. Even before the events of 2014, the press liked to characterize these two as "Good Artie" and "Bad Artie," although there wasn't consensus on which was which.[13]

In 2014 Artie S.'s faction managed to gain control, firing Artie T. and some of his most loyal managers. The insurgent faction wanted Market Basket to act more like other supermarket chains, directing more of its profits to the shareholders and less toward things like employee bonuses and self-funded expansions. They were also frustrated by Artie T.'s insistence on making big decisions unilaterally, including the planned new store in Athol. He'd already spent $18 million of the company's cash reserves on that project before the board even knew it was happening, and some board members weren't happy, preferring to take on debt in order to expand the chain like everyone else.[14]

As battlelines were drawn in the early summer, there was a lot of speculation that the Artie S. faction wasn't actually interested in the grocery business at all but might be hoping just to sell the company to the highest bidder at the most opportune moment. Both Delhaize and Ahold, the European giants who already owned Hannaford and Stop & Shop respectively, were reportedly showing interest, along with U.S.-grown behemoths like Kroger.[15]

The grassroots backlash among Market Basket's workers, vendors, and customers still has business analysts scratching their heads. The press tended to draw comparisons with legendary labor organizing in the region, like the 1912 Bread and Roses strike in Lawrence, Massachusetts, but the participants in 2014 were often staunchly *anti*-union. "This company never needed, or ever will need, a union," one manager said when it was over. "We're far stronger than that."[16]

The mutineers made shrewd use of their intimate knowledge of the chain's day-to-day operations. The warehouse staff walked out first, knowing that this would instantly disrupt the complicated supply chains that brought groceries to the shelves. Replacement workers brought in to keep things moving took weeks to get things running again, and even after they did, inexperienced drivers faced nitpicking receivers at the stores who seized every opportunity to question and reject shipments that weren't packed or documented properly. Shelves emptied quickly, starting with perishable items and rippling out from there; customers noticed and wondered why.

All those brief moments of human encounter at the cash register turned out to mean something. They translated into customer sympathy and then outrage as the new leadership tried to clamp down on the protests by firing more managers and eliminating all of the shifts typically filled by Market Basket's thousands of part-time workers. Big mistake. Picket lines and rallies only grew. Politicians got involved. Sales dropped from $75 million a week to under $10 million.[17] At one point it seemed as though the stand-off might drive the company all the way into the ground.

It was the spontaneous mobilizing of customers that the new leaders seemed most unprepared for. The common wisdom was that shoppers were only interested in getting the best quality for the lowest price. But it turned out they weren't—or at least Market Basket's customers weren't. They literally seemed to see themselves fighting alongside workers for an embattled way of life where you knew the grocery store manager by name and cashiers could actually live on what they earned.

Customers bought a full-page ad in the Lowell *Sun* and launched the social media hashtag #YouCantFireCustomersWeQuit. They signed petitions, including one on the online platform MoveOn.org. MoveOn leans hard left politically, and while using its petition app doesn't equate to agreement with its politics, somehow the combination showed the scrambled realignments at the bleeding edges of corporate capitalism. The most memorable image from the summer was the fluttering cash register receipts from other supermarkets that customers taped to the windows of all-but-empty Market Basket stores, underscoring the point that there were other options for getting groceries and loyalists would continue to shop elsewhere until Artie T. Demoulas was restored as CEO.

By the end of the summer it was a national and even international story, a skewed David-and-Goliath saga in which Goliath was runaway corporate greed and David was a beleaguered billionaire. It was essentially a struggle over the unequal distribution of wealth fought by people who rejected any such language or the politics associated with it. They were defending capitalism's promises while pushing back against its effects.

A celebratory book about the mutiny cowritten by a journalist and a marketing professor states this very directly. "At Market Basket," they write, "associates are aware that they are not just selling groceries; they are raising consumers' standards of living through low prices. Other supermarkets advertise low prices too. What is unique at Market Basket is how strong and pervasive this sense of serving the community through the business model is. Executives remind associates frequently and explicitly. Their purpose at work is to make people's lives better, especially those who are in vulnerable or disadvantaged situations."[18]

This lovely, lofty sentiment is precisely where we need to start questioning the many feel-good qualities of the Market Basket saga. And I start with the question an anthropologist is always going to raise: which people are you talking about? The mutineers were fighting the good fight for a capitalism that works fairly for everyone—but define "everyone." Who's included, and who's left out?

Who's included, the people whose shared values were being defended, are the generations of immigrants who have come to the United States in search of a specific vision of a better life, defined as having plenty to eat, a solid roof over your head, and a decent job, or at least one that can support an education and a shot at prosperity for your kids. Basically it's the old American Dream of hard work and socioeconomic mobility, refined and entrenched in the late nineteenth and early twentieth centuries with the massive numbers of mostly European people who came to the United States in those years and those who have continued to migrate with the same hopes since then.

If there hadn't been a way to make food cheap and abundant, the American Dream wouldn't have been as feasible as it was for as long as it has been.[19] Lest you should question how much of an article of faith this is within the American civil religion, here are the words of the man who created the first true supermarket, Michael Cullen, speaking in the 1930s: "I would lead the public out of the high priced houses of bondage," he said, "into the low prices of the house of the promised land."[20] Market Basket's appeal comes out of a very historically specific pact between haves and have-nots, a newer version of the one that the medieval assize of bread brokered between hungry peasants and their liege lords.

In both cases, the bargain only works until food prices start to rise. And there are other instabilities too. Cheapness creates its own new problems, and the strategies that you have to use if you're trying to squeeze profit out of cheap food—scaling up, buying out competitors, undercutting prices—inherently favor the biggest players.

Like the small farmers of Shays's Rebellion and the New York City bakers who resisted the assize of bread laws, Market Basket's workers and customers were trying to shift that momentum without wanting to block it altogether. It was remarkable. It was magnificent. But it wasn't war. It didn't change the fact that larger supermarket chains—all of them avidly studying Market Basket's appeal for certain kinds of shoppers—were continuing to move into the region. It didn't stop the continued corporate concentration in the grocery business. (Having failed to acquire Market Basket and still determined to make inroads in the American Northeast, Belgian-based Delhaize went back to its own historical rival, the Dutch giant Ahold, and succeeded in arranging a 2015 mega-merger that doubled the reach of those European powerhouses in New England and far beyond.[21]) The 2014 mutineers made a stand around a particular moment—the decades between the 1950s and the 1990s—and tried to make it permanent. It was my own lifespan, the period when supermarkets were becoming normal and taken for granted.

It wasn't a coincidence that this was also when a lot of the people and places in Market Basket's core communities were becoming more suburban and white-collar. The lively, diverse Market Basket that I shopped at in Lowell's Acre neighborhood seemed to confirm that the American Dream could still work for everybody, no matter your race or national origins. But those weren't the people really driving the mutiny. It was people whose families had already made it to security—people descended from the kinds of white European immigrants who had once been able to parlay mom-and-pop corner grocery stores into regional and national supermarket chains—who were taping their cash register receipts to Market Basket's windows and taking out full-page ads in the papers. They were defending that very historically specific moment as universal and timeless, warranted by the twinned promises of America as the land of opportunity and capitalist modernity as a ticket to greater prosperity.

Those promises have become much more tenuous in recent decades, which is probably why they are more and more fiercely defended by those who define their own histories in terms of them. As wealth disparities grow and an ever-rising standard of living is farther out of reach for more and more people in the United States, not to mention elsewhere in the world, the industrial-era trajectory comes to seem like a one-time windfall rather than an endlessly unfolding cornucopia—a windfall, moreover, with devastating ecological consequences for all of life on the planet.[22] It's a lot to grapple with, and not everybody wants to do it. No wonder a lot of people fastened onto Market Basket as proof that the dream wasn't dead and framed the strike as "the last stand for the middle class."[23]

And that leads to the second big point about who's included and who's left out, which is that the cheap and abundant food in the United States and other industrialized places has *always* depended on even cheaper labor and land somewhere else. Our whole modern food system rests on that fact. Market Basket's providing bonuses and decent wages for cashiers and supposedly enabling a rising standard of living for customers in its own backyard doesn't translate into—and in fact actually subtracts from—better pay or working conditions in the fields or slaughterhouses or processing plants of California's Central Valley or the Midwest or Mexico or Canada or any of the other places that most of New England's food actually comes from.

The bulk of Market Basket's products comes through exactly the same long-distance, large-scale, low-wage, low-margin supply chains that all supermarkets rely on, the ones that made it possible for them to become super in the first place. There's a lot of invisible labor there, and most of the people doing it aren't getting a shot at any kind of American Dream even when they're actually in the United States.

So now that I've anthropologically undercut the happy ending, here it is: the 2014 Market Basket uprising was successful in forcing things back to the status quo. After six weeks of protests, interventions by the governors of both Massachusetts and New Hampshire, and a lot of rumors about possible sales to rival chains, the Artie S. faction sold its shares to Artie T. for $1.6 billion, most of it raised through venture capital.[24] The stores reopened faster than anyone expected. Reinstalled as CEO, Artie T. was lionized by his employees and supporters and many in the media, although he modestly refused the hero role and told reporters, "I'm happy just being a grocer."[25]

There were some predictions that the new debt load would hamper the company's ability to continue redirecting profits downward rather than upward. But a year later, the employee bonus program was still robust and sales overall had risen, in part because of the positive buzz from the previous summer. Market Basket opened in five new locations and took in about $5 billion in 2015, seeming to prove that you *can* value people over profits—as long as you're selective about which people you value.[26]

CHAPTER **6**

AFTER THE PLANTATION

ONE OF THE five new stores that Market Basket opened in 2015 was in Athol, Orange's neighbor and the largest of the nine North Quabbin towns. It anchored an equally new mall development wedged between Routes 2 and 2A on a piece of property that local businessmen and town leaders had been trying for some time to develop. The new store opened to great local fanfare in February and the honeymoon period wasn't anywhere close to over by the time of Quabbin Harvest's much more modest gala opening in May. It was one of the things that made me worry most about the co-op's chances of survival.

Market Basket's workers and customers had just made a resounding populist defense of the way things already were in the grocery business, or rather the way things had supposedly been not so long ago, before big corporations got so global and greedy, before everything was manufactured in China, in a time when people worked hard and got ahead and believed in America. The fact that that was a mythical time in a lot of ways didn't diminish its appeal in towns like Athol and Orange, with their majority-white, descended-from-immigrants, working-class-if-only-the-jobs-were-still-here ethos. And there was much to be said for defending decent jobs with decent pay and a spirited resistance—even if it was still only on behalf of one segment of the food supply chain—to the race-to-the-bottom logic pushing things toward ever-greater consolidation.

Market Basket coming to the North Quabbin at that particular moment made a powerful if selective case for hanging onto the food system we already had. Quabbin Harvest seemed to be trying to make a case for doing something different. But it still wasn't entirely clear what that was.

Some of the vagueness had to do with inventory. If the co-op's initial selection seemed to say, "We're a tiny Whole Foods," the gradually thinning shelves and long row of half-empty freezers in the center of the store suggested that a tiny Whole Foods was not really what the North Quabbin had wanted or needed. There were some local products but there seemed to be fewer of them all the time.

And the place still looked like a bank. When people asked me where the co-op was, I found myself saying, "It's the old Workers Credit Union," a description confirmed by the big, faded sign on the front of the building.

There was newer signage too, but it wasn't as helpful as it was clearly intended to be. A lot of the signs proclaimed the fact that everyone could shop at the store, which made sense. Most people had no clear idea what a food co-op was, and if they did, there was often an assumption that it was for members only, as had often been the case in the old days of bulk-buying groups. But the signs felt like they were protesting too much. Paradoxically, they had the effect of making Quabbin Harvest seem even less like a regular grocery store where you might just go to buy some food.

Regular grocery stores—and especially supermarkets—have worked very hard to make food shopping into a frictionless and passive process. You buy food so automatically that you don't even notice how you've been conditioned to know where things are in the store and where to find what you want on the shelves and how to pick the fastest checkout line. A store that seemed to be trying to undo that conditioning, asking shoppers to think about their own economic role in the whole process, is hard for most people to grasp, and the more signs you have explaining it, the more unsettling it becomes. Most people don't expect to be unsettled when they go to a grocery store. They expect to be coaxed and catered to.

The 2014 Market Basket mutiny made it even harder to make a dent in that comfortable, automatic shopping experience. The so-called strike echoed a lot of the ideas and strategies of co-operatives and collective action and unions while asserting that we don't really need those things in order to have good jobs and a flourishing local economy—oh, and low prices too. One of the recurring tropes during the 2014 strike was that Market Basket workers and customers felt a powerful sense of ownership of their supermarkets. As the manager of a New Hampshire store declared, "My life has been spent building this company. We own it."[1] That #WeAreMarketBasket sentiment came up over and over again, along with the idea that if people stand together they can accomplish anything.

On the surface, those seem like exactly the same ideas and ideals that have led people in the modern world to form co-operatives and other forms of shared decision-making and action in their work and economic lives, not to mention the countless ways of operating collectively that have always been found in small-scale communities—especially those that have been marginalized in some way—across time and around the globe. You can make a case that this is a basic human response to the challenge of needing to do something that no single person can do on their own. It's part of what makes us human.

But a lot of the modern versions of this response, like unions and co-ops, have arisen as a direct response and often resistance to corporate and industrial capitalism and its many unequal burdens and opportunities. The Market Basket strike was a ringing *defense* of that whole system, framed as resistance and solidarity, which made the strike even more complex and the fledgling food co-op's messaging even more confusing. Why go to all the trouble of trying to create an alternative to the supermarket system when you have a supermarket you can feel good about?

Quabbin Harvest hadn't begun to articulate an answer to that yet.

Even more challenging, Market Basket and nearly every other supermarket chain was turning in a big way toward precisely the kinds of products that the co-op's feasibility study had identified as its core niche: organic, healthy, natural.[2] There was always local, of course. Local—*real* local, from small producers close to home—was always going to be Quabbin Harvest's ace in the hole. But only if the store could stay open.

Shortly after my summer of deconstructed burgers, the co-op's first manager left. There were some personality issues with the staff and board; there always are. But fundamentally what happened was that everyone was still just realizing the magnitude of what they'd taken on. Yes, it was just one small store. But that made things harder, not easier. Small stores—all those legendary mom-and-pops that get a handhold and sometimes grow into something bigger—need total devotion, someone to pour their heart and soul into the business on a 24/7 basis. That's especially true if you're trying to sell food, with its excruciatingly thin margins and competition from giants. Quabbin Harvest, still in its startup phase but already out of working capital and with a manager burned out from trying to carry a greater share of the burden, was a mom-and-pop grocery store badly in need of a mom and a pop.

Or maybe more than one. When the manager's contract ended after that first year, the board's solution was to create a mostly volunteer management team that could share the load more widely and support the actual in-store management role, now scaled down to something called "Team Leader." It was clear that a six-day-a-week, brick-and-mortar store with employees and inventory and infrastructure couldn't run on all-volunteer labor like the old store in the Tapioca factory, not without volunteer coordination and training and supervision itself becoming a full-time job. But the business wasn't anywhere close to being able to pay for all the staff it needed, especially the key people whose jobs it was to worry about paying the bills and keeping the shelves stocked. That ton of bricks needed to be distributed a little—or a lot—more widely.

A lot of them landed on Karl Bittenbender. Karl was the pop that every mom-and-pop needs: boundlessly energetic, handy with everything from spreadsheets to leaky pipes, connected to people who could do the few things he *couldn't* turn his hand to, devoted to his community. Karl took on most of the financial piece and the responsibility for the building.

Julie Davis and Amy Borezo also agreed to join the management team. Both had young kids, and Amy also had her freelance bookbinding and graphic design work; neither of them wanted to take on the paying part of the job. But as founders of the co-op, neither wanted to see the venture fail so quickly either. Julie had continued to order the produce for the weekly shares, and it was relatively easy to fold that role into the day-to-day store operations and extend it to doing the ordering for the rest of the inventory. As chair of the board, Amy was already running the organizational side of things and handling the communications, something that also folded readily into the new management team structure. Now all they needed was a team leader for that not-quite-a-manager job.

They had a candidate close at hand: Nalini Goordial, one of the part-time staff. Like Julie and Amy, Nalini wasn't actually looking for a job. Newly moved to Orange, she'd been happy to discover the co-op on Facebook and responded to a call for volunteers during the runup to the opening. Like Karl, she could turn her hand to a lot of different things. After building a house in New Mexico, she'd gained a lot of construction know-how. A systems analyst for many years, she was also good with computers.

As she reached her fifties, Nalini wanted to be closer to her family in central Massachusetts. Her partner found an incredibly cheap fixer-upper in Orange and talked her into settling there. While he started to work on the house, Nalini helped paint and set up the cash register and inventory systems at the co-op. By the time of the soft launch in late 2014, she was on the payroll. And when the management team was formed a year later to try to share the burden of running the store, she was an obvious choice for the new scaled-down team leader position. She became the one employee on the management team, responsible for the day-to-day running of the store with support and input from Karl, Amy, and Julie.

Nalini also brought another set of experiences to Quabbin Harvest that helped connect the little store in Orange more directly with the immensity of the task of making real change in how people in the United States get their food. Born and raised in what was then still British Guiana—now Guyana—Nalini was the great-granddaughter of Indian migrants brought to the Caribbean as indentured laborers on British-owned sugar plantations in the late nineteenth century. That history gave her a much broader perspective on all that is present but invisible at Market Basket and other supermarkets: the kinds of places and people and processes that made—and make—the whole modern food system possible. She knew what kind of damage those histories could do, because she'd had to work to undo it in her own life. And she had a sense of what it might take to really step outside the taken-for-granted model and still make a food business that could survive.

It's worth a detour here to the plantation itself. The specific plantation where Nalini's father and grandfather worked had a charming name: La Bonne Intention. Guyana has a tiny strip of arable farmland along its Atlantic coastline on South America's Caribbean shoulder.[3] The Dutch, Spanish, French, and English fought and haggled over a set of small colonies along this coast for nearly two centuries until the boundaries settled into something like the present-day nation-states. La Bonne Intention, now the nationally owned Guyana Sugar Corporation, is just outside the capital of Georgetown, surrounded by other optimistic colonial names like Enterprise and Better Hope and Success and Bachelor's Adventure. During Nalini's childhood her family lived in the town of Mon Repos—"my rest."

Sugar plantations are not charming or restful places, even when they're named for good intentions. Sugar cane is one of the foundational crops of European colonialism, and it was twinned with slavery right from the beginning. The Portuguese created the first sugar plantations, worked by enslaved Africans, on their island possession of Madeira forty years before Christopher Columbus's first voyage to the Caribbean.

Columbus brought sugar with him on his second voyage, and the Spanish brought Africans to work on the plantations shortly afterward.[4] The extreme brutality of Caribbean slavery on the sugar plantations led to high mortality rates and frequent rebellions, which eventually helped push the British into abolishing slavery in their empire in 1834.

The story of La Bonne Intention shows how the distorted morality of colonial economies created opportunities for white colonizers while making it nearly impossible for others to prosper. A pair of British brothers named Booker snapped up plantations whose owners decided they were finished with the business as abolition loomed. That put the Bookers in line for the British government's compensation to slaveholders. In fact, the brothers cleverly bought *more* slaves in the four-year grace period before final abolition in 1838 and managed to get compensation for them too. They emerged from the transition with more capital and land than they'd had to begin with. (In case you have to ask, no, the formerly enslaved received no financial compensation.) The Booker family is still celebrated in the prestigious Man-Booker Prize for literary excellence; when John Berger won the prize in 1972, he donated half his winnings to the British Black Panthers and used the other half to fund a study of Caribbean migrant workers in Europe.[5]

And this is where the specific plantation where Nalini's family labored meets up with "the plantation" as a form, a concept, a mode in which some humans have encountered and interacted with their environments, with other humans, and with other species. You can make a case, in fact, that the plantation underpins our entire modern food system and therefore our entire modern world.

That case rests on the incestuously tight links between the plantation and the factory. Some of those are obvious. Plantations produce things that factories manufacture into commodities, like the cotton that got woven into cloth in the first integrated mills in both old and New England starting in the late eighteenth century. That field-to-factory route is very well-worn at this point. It's how wheat gets turned into flour, tomatoes into sauce, sugar and corn and palm oil into—well, nearly everything.

The more incestuous twist starts to appear when you look at how the early plantations and factories also served as markets for each other, helping to grow capitalist economies on a world scale right from the beginning. A lot of the cloth woven in northern factories went to customers in the newly industrializing towns and cities—that's the whole Market Basket model of raising (some) people's standards of living through access to cheap consumer goods. But a surprising amount also went right back to the source. Cotton woven in Europe and America was sold to clothe enslaved workers on the Caribbean sugar plantations and on the southern cotton plantations themselves. Materials came from wherever they were cheapest and went to wherever a market could be created, so, for example, it made economic sense to ship low-grade raw cotton from India to Britain to be woven into cloth and then shipped back to India to be sold to Indians who had formerly had their own thriving artisanal textile-making economy.[6] After Indian cotton was undercut by imports from the country that had colonized it, of course, people there had the option of becoming waged laborers growing export crops like cotton and tea and rice. With their wages they could now buy their cloth just like the working classes in the British and American factory towns did. To a lot of people, that looked like a win-win.

Those locations were mutually reinforcing in other ways too, as the anthropologist Sidney Mintz showed in 1985 in one of the classics of anthropological literature. *Sweetness and Power: The Place of Sugar in Modern History* traces how sugar circulated through the expanding global economy starting in the seventeenth century. By the time slavery was abolished in the British Empire, Europeans had developed a collective sweet tooth that made the sugar plantations highly profitable. Sugar, along with other tropically sourced stimulants like coffee, tea, and chocolate, went hand in glove with the burgeoning industrial economy in Europe, keeping workers alert and taking minds off bellies that weren't always adequately filled. It was a quick boost to energy and productivity, one hand literally washing the other, part and parcel of that vaunted "rising standard of living" for some people within global supply chains.

Mintz went further. The plantation and the factory weren't just economically linked, he said. The sugar plantation basically *was* a factory, or at least a prototype. It integrated multiple steps in growing and processing, which required—and created—a coordinated and highly controlled workforce. It also radically simplified the natural ecosystems from which it drew its raw materials. Look at a satellite image of Guyana today and you'll still see miles of rectangular fields transected by a kind of regular fishbone pattern, row upon standardized row of sugar cane.

Mintz wasn't thinking centrally about race, but you can't read *Sweetness and Power* without recognizing—as other more recent scholars have done much more directly—how the system depended on the division of humans into not only different classes but different races as well.[7] It was another aspect of standardizing and oversimplifying, shoehorning the extraordinary realities of human variation and difference into supposedly neat categories determined mostly by the singular factor of skin color.

More recently, anthropologists and others have been wondering about how the nonhuman species within these systems respond to being disciplined and fragmented in this way.[8] Some species seem to thrive. Sugar cane and corn and soy and many of the bugs and pathogens that feed on them go right along with our plans for those straight rows and simple ecosystems. Some are less collaborative; giant cane toads imported to control pests feeding on sugar cane had ideas of their own, colonizing Australia and other places in ways that get termed "invasive."

Humans themselves have responded in different ways to the demands of being a cog in a wheel. Sometimes people acquiesce, but they tend not to enjoy it very much. Over time there's been as much defiance as acceptance, all the way from strikes and machine-breaking and outright revolts to low-level worker snarkiness that manifests in things like "time theft," the posting of Dilbert cartoons, and cultures of heavy drinking and other forms of self-medication to dull the effects of doing work that feels dehumanizing. Worker dissatisfaction has been a problem to be solved for both the plantation and the factory right from the beginning, and it's been solved in some very consistent ways, from outright coercion and violence (slavery, union-busting, strike-breaking) to hiring other people who are struggling to subsist for one reason or another. It helps if you can engineer—or at least be ready to take advantage of—the conditions that lead to those struggles.

There can be no cheap food at Market Basket without that dynamic, no cars rolling along on rubber tires, no bolts of fabric or racks of shirts for people who no longer grow their own food or weave their own cloth. It's the reason Mahatma Gandhi's homespun *dhoti* and shawl were such powerful anticolonial symbols in a country where cheap British imports and exports had eviscerated existing smaller-scale forms of production.

One of the many Indian resources the British were exporting was workers to keep the Caribbean sugar plantations going after abolition. Nalini's family came from Uttar Pradesh, then as now the most populous, most rural, and poorest of India's states. British recruiters offered indenture contracts—five years of labor in exchange for five acres of land or a ticket home—that many struggling rural farmers jumped at. Nearly a quarter million came to British Guiana alone before the indenture system was ended in 1917.[9] Half the country's population is Indo-Guyanese today.

"They were basically treated as slaves," Nalini says. "But if you talk to most Indians, they felt like colonialism was this amazing thing for them. Like it did so much for them. But it's just how you're conditioned. And if you don't read, you don't realize that this colonialism was not a good thing!"

Nalini's father was determined that his children—including his daughters—*should* read, and also that they should find some way to get out of what was by then an impoverished and polarized postcolonial nation built on deep racial animosities between the descendants of the formerly enslaved and those of the formerly indentured.

"My father was a very strange man for his time," Nalini says. In his later life he took to saying, "God is not a woman, and you know how you know this? Look at the way the world is—God is not a woman!" He bought trousers for Nalini and her sister even though it wasn't socially acceptable for traditional Indian girls to wear pants, took them to get library cards, and insisted they should get more of an education than was open to them in Guyana.

Many Afro-Guyanese had moved into cities and towns after abolition. They constituted much of the political and professional classes by the time Guyana gained its independence in 1966. The Indo-Guyanese like Nalini's family were more numerous but also more rural, less well-educated, more insular, deeply attached to the traditional Indian culture that helped them subsist under the harsh indenture system.

The two groups were—and remain—associated with Guyana's two major political parties. But the British and then the American governments chose to back the Afro-Guyanese-led party after independence. In the Cold War era, the Indo-Guyanese party leader struck many Western politicians as too radical and likely to lead the country toward communism. The first Guyanese president installed himself for life; truly free elections weren't held until 1992.[10]

By then the Indo-Guyanese had fled the country in large numbers, moving elsewhere in the Caribbean or—if they could find a way—to North America. For the already poor and politically marginalized, conditions had become untenable. Nalini remembers her elementary school class being brought outside to wave national flags and cheer when the president's motorcade drove by, but she says, "Even then I knew there was something strange about it, because there was no food." One month her family had nothing to eat except the okra they'd managed to grow. Family members told stories of soldiers disrupting harvests and carrying all the food away. Nalini's parents decided to join the new diaspora, and in the early 1970s they managed to make the move to New York City with their youngest children. Nalini, at ten years old one of the eldest, was left with family in Guyana until her parents had established U.S. citizenship and were able to sponsor her own migration.

It took a few years. By then, Nalini's traditionally minded family had found her a husband. She was married at fourteen. At seventeen, already the mother of two small children but legally still her parents' dependent, she was able to leave Guyana—alone.

"It's the hardest thing I've ever done in my life," she says now. "But I kept telling myself this is for a better life for them, because I couldn't see them growing up in Guyana and having a chance for an education. And I believed that that was available here for them, that they would get that here."

Her parents and younger siblings were living in the massive housing development known LeFrak City in Queens, home to more than four- teen thousand people in twenty apartment towers, each seventeen stories high. "These buildings looked like you were in jail," Nalini says. "When you looked out all you saw was other buildings and the parking lot. It was crazy, because I came from very, very, very rural farm country, and it was just so scary to me. Eighteen, and I'm trying to figure out how to navigate the subway system in this big city and it's just crazy, because I've never really seen anything like that in my entire life. I mean, reading does not do that for you!"

The family members Nalini stayed with after her parents emigrated lived farther inland in Guyana. There were plantations there too—Nalini remembers the long rows of "coconut walks" and the canals that ran through the farms. But they were surrounded by tropical rain forest, and people were able to grow and catch more of their food than had been possible in the coastal towns. Plantation workers fished in the canals and grew big gardens. Nalini remembers her grandmother's garden, filled with beans, squash, taro, batata, and other plants. She learned to cook on an open fire in a home without running water or electricity, grinding spices by hand and making use of whatever ingredients were available. Recipes and cooking techniques handed down from Uttar Pradesh were readily adaptable and served to keep hunger at least somewhat at bay.

People in Nalini's new rural community referred to the food from their gardens as "provisions," a term handed down from the era of slavery when Caribbean plantation owners allocated small "provision plots" for enslaved workers to grow their own food. This was both a cost-saving measure and a hedge against the ever-present possibilities of both starvation and rebellion. But anthropologists and others have shown that self-provisioning also opened a space of independence—sometimes even small-scale entrepreneurialism—for the gardeners and farmers. The provision plots, Sidney Mintz wrote, were "an extraordinary by-product of New World slavery."[11]

Rugged tubers and root vegetables like taro and batata and yuca played a special role in this form of self-provisioning. Many of these foods are even more tangled up with colonialism than sugar cane. Cassava, for example, was probably first domesticated in the southern Amazon basin several thousand years ago by Indigenous people who may also have been cultivating peanuts and chili peppers.[12] It was carried to Africa and Asia by Spanish and Dutch traders and planters, then embraced in the Caribbean by the enslaved and indentured people brought from those parts of the world to work on the sugar plantations. These plants were harder to turn into commodities at first, but as foods familiar to people pushed to the margins by plantations or forced into the labor that produced the newly commodified crops, they were an essential part of the plantation model even when they weren't its central commercial product. Sugar only went in one direction, from the plantations to the markets. But the tubers and roots went every which way.

The names of these underground treasures map the routes that people and plants and cooking traditions took throughout European colonization and often long before. Taro comes from the Maori *te reo*, and the plant has countless other names in other languages, including kalo and gabi and "elephant ears," the ornamental monster that always loomed in a wicker stand next to my Canadian grandmother's dining room table. Yuca (no relation to yucca, the familiar ornamental garden plant) is an

Indigenous Caribbean name; it is also known as manioc and mandioca and cassava. Potato, batata, sweet potato, yam—the multiple forms and names for these foods sprout like their own abundant foliage.

What unites them is that they are all adaptable, high-carbohydrate foods. Especially in their older forms they tend to be tough and durable, able to grow almost anywhere, no matter how poor the soil or dry the weather. They can be stored and transformed, dried and ground into flour and starch, turned into belly-filling breads and long-lasting crackers. Unlike crops with a narrow window for harvesting, they're "indeterminate"—that is, they can be dug up when needed or left in the ground as insurance against lean times. Cassava is content to remain underground for a year or two or even longer.[13]

These plants tend to be indeterminate in other ways too. They've historically been able to stay under the radar, distributed, horizontal, suited to the small, the marginal, the ungovernable. The anthropologist and political scientist James Scott, who has studied ungovernability for much of his scholarly career, has written, "It is surely striking that virtually all classical states were based on grain. . . . History records no cassava states, no sago, yam, taro, plantain, breadfruit, or sweet potato states."[14] Scott and others see cereal grains, with their greater regularity and willingness to go along with monoculturing, as foundational to states and private property and plantation agriculture and patriarchy and what we call "civilization" itself.

The tubers and roots did play a role in creating and expanding those systems, however. Ships' crews and plantation laborers and sometimes even European planters stayed alive on foods like cassava. And the plants and knowledge of how to grow and cook them traveled back and forth and around both the Atlantic and the Pacific.[15] But the plants themselves also stayed off to the sides, often literally up in the hills.

In British Guiana, where the original inhabitants were driven to the upland interior with the coming of the plantations, Indigenous people grew—and still grow—the toughest, least accommodating types of cassava, known as bitter cassava. All cassava contains natural toxins, and all can be made safe for humans to eat by soaking, boiling, pounding, cooking, drying, and other techniques. But bitter cassava requires even more hard work and specialized knowledge to process.

For Indigenous people in what is now Guyana it also carries an even longer list of names and associations than those circulating in the colonial economy. Some farmers, mostly older now, nearly all women, know different varieties based on the characteristics of the tuber (straight or zigzag), who or where a particular plant came from, how old it was, what was exchanged for it ("paid for with a cutlass"), and so on. In a study done in Guyana in the 1990s, some farmers spoke of their cassava plants as *more yamî*, their "children," reflecting a sense of familial relationship to both the plants and the places where they grew.[16]

Those relationships were shaken by the coming of the plantation, but they have never been entirely severed. Enslaved Africans or indentured South Asians grew under-the-radar crops to keep their own bodies and souls together, but they never gained the more specialized ecological knowledge about bitter cassava from the upland regions of the Caribbean. For that they relied on the Native people: Nalini remembers her family buying spices and medicines derived from yuca from Indigenous vendors in British Guiana. As they have always done at the edges of the modern world, people operating at the threshold of subsistence could be resources as well as competitors for each other.

Eventually the plantation found a way to absorb the recalcitrant roots and tubers too. And that brings us back to Orange and the Minute Tapioca Company.

Tapioca is the starch that comes from cassava after you soak and grate and squeeze and dry it. You can leave the starch in powdered form, as flour. Or you can shape it into flakes or granules, the little "pearls" familiar to bubble-tea enthusiasts and generations of children who know them as fisheyes.

Cassava got onto Americans' radars around the turn of the twentieth century as a hardy crop that would grow in poor soils.[17] But it was the desserts that really captured the public's attention. Susan Stavers figured out how to make an exceptionally smooth tapioca pudding and the Minute Tapioca Company soon found an efficient way to precook it, making a convenience food out of a labor-intensive one and creating an easy route to sleek and impressive dishes that price- and image-conscious housewives were drawn to in the early twentieth century.

But mechanized processing and national advertising campaigns only got you so far. As John Whitman quickly discovered, successful mass-production needed a steady, standardized supply chain of raw or nearly raw materials.

It needed, in fact, the plantation.

There wasn't much of a world market for cassava or its derivatives at that point. But the plantation existed as both a model and a reality. Before long the businessmen who had taken over Whitman's struggling company sent out a scouting party to find a more robust—that is, a plantationized—source of supply for the factory in Orange.

The scouting party consisted of a single young man, twenty-four-year-old Eben Gridley. Gridley was a cousin of company president Frank Ewing, who took the young man under his wing after Gridley's father died suddenly in 1904. By 1905 Gridley was learning the ropes at the factory, "sweeping floors, unloading tapioca, and shoveling coal," he recalled many years later. The next year, he was on a ship to Singapore and Malaysia as a one-man taskforce charged with studying the small on-farm processing facilities where cassava was turned into tapioca flakes for export. "The very best," he concluded, "was none too good—certainly not what it should be for an American packaged food."[18]

Gridley turned his attention to the Indonesian island of Java, where Dutch colonists had developed cassava plantations as early as the seventeenth century.[19] He found fewer factories but was impressed by Dutch standards of cleanliness and quality. He pitched the idea of having planters export flour, not flakes, with the rest of the process being completed in Orange under more controlled conditions. Gridley's overture had the effect of helping to shift cassava growing and exporting patterns in Java, which became a major exporter of tapioca in the decades that followed.[20]

But Ewing and Gridley were thinking in other directions too. Why should the company be dependent on distant growers and processors? What would happen to Minute Tapioca if wars or economic shifts disrupted its flow of source materials? Wouldn't it make more sense to control every step of the supply chain?

This was the "vertical integration" model to which American corporations were beginning to turn as they scaled up and sought to dominate their industries. C.W. Post added his own box-making factory in the very early Postum years. His successors acquired Clarence Birdseye's General Seafoods Corporation to secure its flash-freezing technology. Henry Ford famously provisioned his Detroit-area factories with coal from Ford-owned Kentucky mines and wood from forestry operations in northern Michigan and rubber from a short-lived experiment with a plantation in a Brazilian town still called Fordlândia.

Minute Tapioca started down that road, only to discover it was something that only made economic sense for the biggest of the big companies, and sometimes not even for them. The tapioca business's short-lived plantation experiment launched in 1908 with the purchase of seven hundred acres of farmland in Bayamón, just inland from Puerto Rico's capital of San Juan. Puerto Rico was a lot closer to Massachusetts than Java, and thanks to the Spanish-American War it had recently become an American colonial possession, eliminating the risk of import taxes and tariff wars. Well on his way to an executive role in the company, young Gridley made the land acquisition and stayed long enough to oversee the construction of a factory building where cassava could be processed into flour.[21]

But it didn't take long for Minute Tapioca's leadership to realize that the numbers for this new venture simply didn't add up. To keep the company growing, they needed greater and greater amounts of tapioca, far more than could be cultivated and processed on a single plantation even when supplemented with some cassava from local farmers who were growing it on their own smaller plots of land.[22]

And size was the least of it. As any farmer will tell you, the most pressing, draining, day-by-day, season-after-season expense is for labor. It's one of the reasons that family labor has always been so essential for keeping farms going in market economies, especially small farms.

In a system that was already in 1908 based on mass-producing foods as cheaply and efficiently as possible, the labor of planting, tending, harvesting, and processing cassava into flour in Puerto Rico was simply too expensive for Minute Tapioca to turn a profit on the affordable convenience food it was selling at the other end of the supply chain. It wasn't that the Puerto Rican plantation workers were being paid a lot—it was that those in Java were being paid even less. The very cheapest labor could offset the additional costs of shipping the finished flour several thousand more miles. And that made all the difference.

"To be profitable," Minute Tapioca's plantation manager admitted in 1913, "tapioca must be gotten from yuca grown on cheap land."[23] And by "cheap land" he really meant "a place where labor is cheap." That's one absolutely essential piece of the plantation model.

Before long Minute Tapioca started growing other, more profitable crops in Bayamón. In 1919 they were cultivating about 150 acres for oranges, grapefruits, coconuts, and—yes—sugar cane.[24] It's not clear when they gave up on their experiment—probably sometime in the 1920s, perhaps when the company was acquired by Postum. But the plantation proved useful in other ways, including as a site for research and development. Eben Gridley spent most of a year in Puerto Rico with the company's chief engineer in 1911 and 1912, designing the precooking process that really launched Minute Tapioca as a true convenience food. With the cheap supply chain from Java secured and a new efficient design for steam-jacketed cookers and big rotary driers, the company could finally expand into the national market. At that scale, the profit on any individual package of Minute Tapioca was less than miniscule. But now they could make and sell enough to add up to a very solid return.

"When the business was taken over by General Foods," Gridley recalled many years later, "we were able to deliver a well-developed manufacturing process."[25] People who were schoolchildren in Orange in the 1940s and 1950s remember touring the factory with its big rumbling drums and belts and rollers, still churning tapioca through a highly efficient and sanitary system into little red and blue boxes that could be found in grocery stores all over the United States and beyond.

The high-value parts of that process—the research and development, the engineering, the advertising—stayed firmly in the hands of people in the higher-value locations, like Orange. But all of it rested on the plantation, running in the background like an unnoticed operating system.

The plantation is still in Orange. In 1913, the same year Minute Tapioca's leaders acknowledged they could only make cheap food profitably if the land and labor in back of it were even cheaper, the company donated two painted stage curtains as part of the renovation and expansion of the Orange Town Hall. In an era when every little American town had—or aspired to have—its own theater or opera house, painted curtains added either local color in the form of familiar nearby sights or a touch of the exotic and famous from farther away.

Orange's stage curtains offered both. Minute Tapioca's branding still invoked the patriotic Minute Man image in 1913, and the main curtain, seventeen feet high and twenty-six feet wide, featured the well-known statue of the Minute Man at the bridge in Concord, Massachusetts, installed to celebrate the national centennial in 1875.

The second one was more functional and also more complicated. It was an asbestos curtain intended to safeguard the beautiful auditorium, patterned after Boston's recently built Symphony Hall, by blocking draft

FIGURE 6. The now-hidden asbestos fire curtain in the Orange Town Hall depicting a tapioca field was one of two donated by the Minute Tapioca Company in 1913.
—Photographer unknown; image provided by Pennie Smith

and flames in the event of a fire. It hung from the ceiling and slotted snugly into a frame around the sides of the proscenium arch.

It's not clear how often this curtain was lowered and fully visible. Whenever it was, people in the hall would have seen a less familiar scene than the Minute Man statue: a field of low, rather straggly plants with a dirt road through the middle. There are palm trees in the background, and beyond that dense tropical forest. Next to the path there's a small, whitewashed wooden building on stilts, with a thatched roof and a single window, maybe a farm building, maybe someone's house.

The "someone" may be the lone human figure in this landscape, a dark-skinned man—Javanese? Puerto Rican?—wearing a white shirt and trousers and holding some kind of hoe or other implement. Within the faux-fabric border painted around this scene, gold letters read, "A Tapioca Field." It doesn't seem like a generic scene; there's a sense that this was painted from a photograph, or maybe a description, perhaps of Minute Tapioca's own yuca plantation or somewhere else that the company's executives visited in their search for a cheap and consistent source of supply that could make the whole tapioca venture profitable enough to succeed.

A few years ago, a group of people interested in local history wrote grants and raised funds to hire a company that specializes in restoring old painted stage curtains. That effort brought the Minute Man curtain back to something like its original vibrancy. But the fire curtain was a more intractable challenge. It would have to be wholly encapsulated to make it safe to work with, costing tens of thousands of dollars aside from the work of restoring the fabric and the image itself. Even just taking it down and storing it somewhere poses a health hazard.

So it remains where it's been for more than a hundred years: hanging high above the stage, its painted face against the interior brick wall. Its reverse side is dark brown canvas, making it even harder to see in the dim reaches of the backstage area.

In fact, it's a lot like the modern food system itself: big yet oddly invisible, firmly fixed in place, put there for good reason but now as much problem as solution, resistant to being changed even for the better, making a link with the most marginal people in the food system in the kind of place that has benefited most from all that cheap and abundant food but not in such a way that people on the two sides of the divide can directly know or encounter one another. The plantation is still in Orange in that more social and economic sense too. It's present but invisible in every grocery store, including the new co-op in the former bank right across the street from the town hall.

I call this chapter "After the Plantation." In truth, there is no such time. Our modern industrial food system still depends on the strange invisibilities inherent in the plantation model, the grotesque imbalances of power and wealth, the extreme simplifications of ecologies, the radical uprooting and transplanting and disciplining of both humans and nonhumans.

This food system—and our whole modern industrialized world—has given us many wonders, many conveniences and pleasures and seeming securities. But the way the plantation model has changed humans' relationships to earth and other species within the span of a few hundred years has also enabled us to change the very earth itself, the soil, the water, the air we breathe, the atmospheric systems we exist within. It's what has led some to dub this era the Anthropocene, a time when humans are the most powerful influence on those systems.

Some have recently suggested it would be more accurate to call this the Plantationocene.[26] It's not a word that rolls easily off the tongue, but it does a better job of naming the specific historical actors who set these processes in motion. It's not human beings as a species who have managed to destabilize and short-circuit so many planetary processes. It began with Europeans who developed plantation agriculture in their colonies in the fifteenth and sixteenth centuries and then built the model into the industrial factory starting in the eighteenth. It's all the people since then who have continued to merge and refine and expand those forms as a way to control and wring profit from nearly every "natural" thing and place on the planet, except for the few that have been set aside as parks and preserves to offer a kind of relief from this still-expanding, brutalizing logic of extraction and commodification. And you can make a case that even those places and the relaxation and sense of escape they enable are just another commodity, a mirror image of the industrialized ways of living that people are trying to escape.

I'm not trying to demonize all those humans, although there's plenty to question, criticize, and denounce. But we can't begin to see our modern food system clearly until we see its centuries-deep roots in this whole way of relating to the world that we depend on for our food. We need to understand that what most of us think of as agriculture itself has been shaped by the logic of the plantation and its sibling the factory, and not just on giant farms where monocropping and mechanization make the connection more glaringly obvious. The anthropologist Anna Tsing reminds us that the whole model of humans controlling plants and other species—the basic idea that most modern people have about farming—has become "so naturalized that many people believe that that is the meaning of the term agriculture; we forget that there are other ways to farm."[27]

Thus, there is no "after the plantation" for humans as a whole yet. But there are projects that set themselves *against* the plantation model and cultivate the mindset we now call "decolonized." One of them, the closest thing to a national food brand in the North Quabbin since Minute Tapioca moved away, is also in Orange, right across town from that invisible fire curtain in the Town Hall.

Dean's Beans Organic Coffee imports and roasts coffee in one of Orange's two small industrial parks, in an unassuming pair of buildings sided in red clapboard. The coffees have names ranging from the purely descriptive—Guatemalan French Roast, Timor Atsabe—to the whimsical—Aztec Two-Step, Ahab's Revenge—along with merchandise reflecting a retro-hippie sensibility ("Make Coffee Not War"). There's a pleasant kitchen and eating area for staff and always lots of activity going on against the backdrop of a hand-painted mural and an interesting playlist, suggesting a workplace that is both lively and chill.

Dean Cycon, the eponymous founder, started out as an Indigenous rights lawyer. He found himself working in coffee-growing communities around the world, meeting a lot of small farmers who felt trapped in the idea that their only option was to take whatever prices they could get from a system in which they had no real power. He recognized the root cause as a very simple one: people weren't making enough from farming to live on, let alone to invest in strengthening their own businesses and communities. He decided to make a move into the coffee business to see if it could be a more immediate vehicle for solving some of the problems he saw people struggling with.

Dean's starting point was to pay a fair price for beans plus a more-than-token share of the profits from the other end of the supply chain. He redirected those to community development projects that the farmers identified as their top priorities: new and cleaner wells; processing equipment so they could capture more of the market value of their beans; programs responding to the perpetual problems of poverty, life in conflict zones, and the growing challenges of climate change. Dean is always quick to point out that this isn't charitable or philanthropic—he calls it "simply a different form of payment for the coffee," one that tries to rectify some of the baked-in inequities and imbalances in the modern food system.[28] As he puts it, "This is a social justice organization that uses coffee as a vehicle for change. We're not doling out money because we have enough of it for ourselves and we want to give a little something back. Our fundamental business model is about the justice."

Of course, Dean isn't the only one thinking about coffee as a potential vehicle for justice. When it was founded in 1993, Dean's Beans was part of the burgeoning fair-trade movement that began with handicrafts in the 1960s and spread to other products similarly exported across gaping wealth divides. The fair-trade rate for coffee tends to be about double the commodity price, which means it's more expensive at the consumer end. It works because there are sufficient consumers who care about it enough (and are able) to pay more for coffee that doesn't exploit anyone or damage the places where it was grown.

All good—except that creating a new and popular premium brand inevitably captured the attention of bigger players who are following the standard "buy low, sell high" and "buy or be bought" playbooks. That included the older category-busters (Maxwell House, Folger's) but also the newer juggernauts of Big Specialty Coffee, companies like Starbucks, which absorbed a lot of its competitors on the road to becoming nearly ubiquitous.[29] Others, like Vermont-based Green Mountain Coffee, have managed to get big without entirely shedding their patina of craft and regional identity. All of them, big and bigger, are surfing a surging wave of global coffee supply, churned up by national development policies in places like Vietnam and Brazil where new and larger coffee plantations are being created all the time on newly deforested lands, further ramping up production and driving down the commodity prices while consolidating power in fewer hands.[30] You know the story by now.

Once the behemoths took note, it didn't take long for fair trade to be co-opted. It's Monk's Brew all over again—public confusion works to the advantage of whoever can shape the narrative. There are a lot of ways that the fair-trade promise gets watered down now. You're allowed to use the label on your brand even if you're sourcing only a small percentage of your beans that way. You can use parallel language and criteria and certifications that *imply* fair trade without actually following the formula set out by the original certifying organizations.[31] Starbucks has perfected this with its "ethical sourcing" terminology and partnership with a conservation organization that specializes in greening the images of huge multinational corporations.[32] Then there are the layers of intermediaries and banks and politicians and nongovernmental organizations and philanthropists whose agendas and hierarchies further complicate the seemingly straightforward business of paying small farmers a fair price for coffee grown in responsible ways.

To Dean Cycon, this is nothing more than turning social and environmental responsibility itself into another kind of commodity. He's been a persistent and vocal critic of greenwashing in the specialty coffee market; one of the T-shirts for sale at the beanery proclaims, "Fair/Unfair: There's No Middle Ground." In 2003 the company caused a minor national stir by taking out a full-page ad in a then-trendy coffee-shop magazine. The ad called out Newman's Own—a famously altruistic food company founded by a beloved liberal figure—for entering the specialty coffee market through a partnership with Green Mountain Coffee, which sourced only 12 percent of its beans under fair-trade conditions at that point. The ad asked Paul Newman, "How can you partner with a company whose meager percentage of Fair Trade smacks more of marketing than sincere commitment when farmers and their families are literally being starved off their land?"

The blowback was illuminating. Newman's Own and Green Mountain both insisted that bigger companies like theirs were able to do more good *because* they were big. Green Mountain pointed out that 12 percent of its $100 million sales amounted to a heck of a lot more than 100 percent of Dean's $1.5 million. It was a valid point, if you overlooked how many of the problems faced by small Indigenous coffee farmers were actually caused by the logic of bigness and commodification in the first place. Green Mountain also noted that it couldn't make any sudden moves toward greater equity for farmers without alarming its shareholders, which just reinforced Dean's point about what happens when you let purely financial calculations drive your decision-making.[33]

"The consumer really wants these things, they want justice and they're willing to pay for it," Dean says. "But the companies have figured out a way to make them pay for it without making a commitment." He recognizes what some have called the "limited pool of worry" among consumers, who are flooded with images and causes they want to care about.[34] "They may be well-intentioned," he says, "but they don't know enough to gauge what's B.S. and what's not. When they see what seems to be a guarantee of ethical sourcing, they say, 'Check, okay, coffee farmers are taken care of, I'm going to go worry about those Tibetans.'" One of Dean's Beans' roles, as he sees it, is to keep bringing attention back to the fundamental equation.

To some, that makes him old hat. He has heard disparaging comments: "'Yeah, Dean's Beans, you know they just keep doing the same old thing, year after year.' And I say that's exactly right! Because we're not chasing the newest thing, you know, we're digging a deep well here. And things haven't changed in the coffee fields enough to say, 'Okay, we're going to go work with Tibetans now.'"

Dean isn't above selling a little sizzle. In 2005 he took a brief leave of absence to be an extra on one of the *Pirates of the Caribbean* movies because he'd always fantasized about being a pirate.[35] He gained a bit of notoriety from that, to the point that some of the Peruvian coffee farmers he worked with got the mistaken impression they were selling their harvest directly to Johnny Depp.[36] Dean proudly calls himself a "Javatrekker" and relishes the opportunities for adventure that coffee-buying gives him. "I have been able to travel, meet interesting peoples, and experience different cultures," he wrote in a 2007 memoir, in which he also recounted a speech he made to farmers in Papua New Guinea: "Your job is to grow great coffee, make a strong organization, and keep your culture strong. My job is to introduce your culture and your coffee to America."[37] A cynical ear might hear echoes there of tourism and even colonialism, something that may be impossible to sidestep for a white man traveling entrenched routes carved out by colonization and the plantation economy.

One of Dean's great saving virtues is that he's perfectly aware of all of this and he has refused to let it stop him or even slow him down. He's also intensely pragmatic. He knows you have to start from where you are, and from where other people are. For him that means continually pushing resources back down to the level of small communities, whether that's in Orange or East Timor. Like his good friend Karl Bittenbender, who was instrumental in creating the business park where the beanery is located, Dean is all about keeping capital circulating close to home. And he knows you can't do that if you don't have any capital to circulate. Part of his pragmatism is about finding ways for a small business to be viable enough to be a force for good in whatever communities it interacts with.

It helps that there *is* money to be made selling coffee, unlike a lot of foods where the margin is so thin that the only possible way to find a profit is to chase the other options of either getting big or exploiting someone else's labor or land. There's enough breathing room in coffee to push against the mainstream.

And even so, Dean can only push so far. "Any time I talk about politics I get slammed left and right by our customer base," he says. But when he talks instead about values, people are more willing to listen, and to think. For him it's a good-enough starting point, a way to engage without having to know exactly where you might end up, to work in the direction of decolonizing and decommodifying without immediately having to resolve all the fraught legacies of the plantation, the factory, the market.

Far more than most socially conscious businesspeople, Dean recognizes how essentially simple this is. You actually only need one small, unequivocal word: no.

"Nobody's *requiring* you to maximize profit," he says. "Nobody's *requiring* you to use marketing as a tool for increased sales rather than honest transparency about what you do. It's just the business culture."

If there is no such time as "after the plantation," there is, for some people, a time after plantation *labor*. That time has been very different for different people, resting on transitions that are often incomplete and constrained. In the United States, descendants of the enslaved people who labored on American plantations are still struggling with the deep psychic, social, and economic wounds it inflicted. Many of those descendants left farming voluntarily or involuntarily because the struggles seemed impossible to resolve; some are finding their way back now, trying to reenter an agricultural economy that—like the grocery store—has been delineated by the scale and scope and methods of the plantation and the factory. How to farm in other ways, how to be in a different relationship to land, is a huge, open question for these new and returning farmers. Many of them are negotiating that question with great courage and clarity, often in dialogue with writers and scholars who have articulated the stakes and the histories in passionate and powerful ways.[38]

And some, like Nalini Goordial's family, found ways to move farther beyond the plantation and the fraught legacies of colonized places such as Guyana. Like many immigrant families, they put their faith in educational opportunities for the younger generation. Transplanted from rural Guyana, Nalini rode the New York City subway to community college where she studied computers—"That was my dad being practical too," she says—and caught the early 1980s transition from punch-cards into the more fully digital systems that would shortly become the backbone of a globalizing business world. After a year's residence in the United States she was able to sponsor her children as immigrants, mending that gaping hole in her life. With an associate degree in hand, she went to work in corporate America, moving with her extended family to central Massachusetts and taking a job with the Thom McAn shoe company, a beloved national retailer based in New England.

A lot changed in the next couple of decades. Her kids grew up; she and her husband parted ways; Thom McAn succumbed to the same competitive pressures as other older brands and disappeared as an independent retail presence. During its corporate dissolution Nalini met a technician from Colorado whose firm was helping to dismantle the company's gigantic systems. They struck up a long-distance relationship and eventually decided they'd both had enough of corporate life. That prompted the move west, then eventually back east to be closer to Nalini's family. And so to the co-op.

Nalini had moved a long way from the plantation, to and through the aspirational white-collar world that rests on that unseen operating system and then back out of it again. Moving away in a physical or socioeconomic sense is hard enough, often requiring immense reserves of ingenuity and determination. But truly moving away from the plantation requires finding a way to move outside of its emotional legacies too, its deep logic of disconnection and cheapness.

And its food. Given that the modern world is now almost entirely fed in ways conditioned by the plantation, escaping that logic requires developing a very different relationship to food.

There were many reasons that Nalini was a natural choice to take over the almost-a-manager position as Quabbin Harvest entered its second year in the storefront. She was clearly committed to the fledgling co-op, she lived nearby, she had a warm and welcoming presence, she knew how to deal with the computerized point-of-sale system that others had been struggling with.

Less obvious, but far more consequential, was her deep sense of why this all mattered—the thing most people involved with Quabbin Harvest hadn't quite found a way of communicating to the rest of the world yet, or perhaps even to ourselves. Nalini knew that moving beyond the plantation meant finding a way to mend the profoundly and often violently unbalanced relationship of people to food, to earth, to soil, to place, to work, to other species. And to each other.

"Each other" for most of the co-op's first members and supporters meant mostly other people who wanted to buy healthy local food and support local farmers. Like the Market Basket mutineers of the previous year, most of us drew our circles fairly close to home, and given who most of us were—white, middle-class, descended from European immigrants—"home" was a fairly circumscribed place.

Nalini's sense of "each other" was more capacious and much more challenging, more like Dean Cycon's vision of what it actually means to put people before profits and to look all the way across the long-distance food supply chains that have helped to build the world in which we now live. It wasn't something Nalini talked about much in the store, though she was always ready to have a conversation about colonialism if it happened to come up. It wasn't about embracing something that came before, because "before" was as much the problem as the solution. And anyway, "before" is no longer tenable. There are too many humans now, the great majority of us no longer able to provision ourselves.

That's the unresolvable paradox that the whole modern food system rests on. We have to change, not just to do something about the many moral and logistical and ecological problems in our plantation- and market-based model but because the changes we've already wrought through this altered relationship to the world now threaten everyone's ability to get food reliably, or at all. Yet change is next to impossible when so many people are so dependent on the system that's in place. We can't just shut it down for a few years or a few decades and create something different, even if we knew what we were trying to do.

What we're trying to fix took centuries to build in the first place. The English were trying to regulate the tensions between market prices and food quality and poor people's ability to pay as early as the thirteenth century. The Dutch were making sugar plantations in what became Nalini's home barely a hundred years after Christopher Columbus brought sugar cane to the Caribbean. The modernness of present-day grocery shopping, all that shiny newness, blinds us to how old and deeply rooted this actually is, and how foundational the changes will need to be if we truly want to eat—and live—in some other way.

CHAPTER 7

HINTERED LANDS

DEAN CYCON WAS happy to see the new food co-op in Orange. And he shared its founders' sense that it was smart to open sooner rather than waiting to raise more startup capital. "You really have to grab opportunity when it's brightest and most alluring to people, even if it means a rougher start," he believes.

Quabbin Harvest was definitely having a rough start. As it started its second year in the storefront location, its inventory was starting to be more closely aligned to what people actually wanted to buy, and the "Shop Co-op First" campaign had helped nudge some of us off our usual routes and into newer patterns of getting what we could at the little store before going elsewhere. But only a fraction of the six hundred members were actually shopping at the store. Even for those of us who were, the co-op was still a supplement to our regular trips to larger supermarkets. We were trying, and that seemed like it should be enough.

The board and management team knew it wasn't nearly enough. Karl Bittenbender was sounding the alarm at every month's board meeting: the store was losing far too much money to be able to sustain itself for long. There were bills that absolutely had to be paid—payroll, electricity—but paying them meant holding off on anything that could possibly be deferred. That included a lot of the invoices from food vendors, all the way from the big national distributor that brought a lot of the groceries to more regional suppliers like Squash Trucking.

Worst of all, it included North Quabbin farms and businesses like Dean's Beans, as well as Mount Grace Land Conservation Trust, the co-op's landlord. Mount Grace was fiscally and philosophically committed and willing to be forbearing about the rent—up to a point. No one was very happy about the situation, but no one wanted to see the store fold so soon after opening.

The lack of money drove everything, from desperate cost-cutting to agitated brainstorming about what kinds of new products and ideas might possibly turn things around. A lot of the suggestions were based on what seemed to work at other co-ops, without considering whether they would necessarily work in downtown Orange. And with the working capital already spent, there was no cash to make most of the changes even if there had been agreement about what to do. Nalini was continually being tugged between two contradictory messages: "Nalini, we don't have any money," and "Nalini, we need you to raise the sales—a lot."

Most board members were reluctant to go public about what was happening. And there was a certain wisdom in that. A doom-and-gloom message could undercut the tenuous gains the co-op had made, and people might be even less likely to come to the store if they thought it was already on the brink of closing.

As a shopper myself, I could feel how my own responses factored into this downward spiral. I'd decided that I would try to buy particular things at the co-op, and I was always peeved if those things were out of stock when I came in looking for them. It felt like a violation of some unwritten contract: I, the consumer, had decided to spend my money in the store, and the store should reward my virtuous behavior by providing what I wanted to buy. What could be simpler than that? Wasn't that what food co-ops were all about?

It both was and wasn't, but I didn't know enough to understand that yet. Food co-ops had indeed been created to provide foods their members wanted and needed. But that was before supermarkets created the expectation—and the reality—of being able to get absolutely *anything* you wanted whenever you wanted it. My feeling of being annoyed and unappreciated welled up in the gap between the frictionless experience of supermarket shopping and my bumpier, uneven interactions with the little co-op. I didn't have the patience or the interest to find out why there was no ground beef in the freezer on a particular day—I was just irked that I was going to have to change my plans for dinner. I'd been trying to make a commitment to the new store, but it seemed like the co-op was continually testing that commitment, and I already felt less and less guilty about just going elsewhere if I wanted to be sure of getting what was on my list.

The downward spiral was well underway by the summer of 2016. "Sales have tanked," the board minutes from August stated baldly. A new employee with experience running her own business took a hard look at the operations and concluded that the problem wasn't in how the store was being run. And she couldn't see any room to pare down expenses further. The management team had stepped in just in time to get things back on track after the failed experiment of turning everything over to a single manager. But by then the cash flow had dried to a trickle and there just wasn't enough money to stay ahead of the bills.

Quabbin Harvest was already hintered.

Another word for this would be "impoverished," which also conveys a sense of hintering as a process, something that doesn't simply happen but is shaped by whoever influences or controls what is done with a place over time—political and business leaders, landowners, corporate decision-makers, lenders, planners, voters, developers, both local and distant. But the idea of "hintering" conveys something more about the links between places and people, how they're tied together and what happens when the resources of a place are—or become—too meager to sustain what most people there conceive of as a good life. Sometimes the process of hintering uproots people, unsettling and dispersing them. Sometimes it keeps them locked in place, static in the same way the places themselves come to feel static, sticky, stuck.

The North Quabbin's hintering has happened gradually over nearly a century, with the creation of the Quabbin Reservoir in the 1930s and the slow seeping away of industrial capital, especially in the decades since the Second World War. The spatial and temporal metaphors we use to talk about this process reek of assumptions about the linear progressions everyone is supposed to be following: these places are "down" and they need to move "up," "behind" and struggling to get "ahead." This shorthand language doesn't leave room to tease out visions of what a good life might look like outside the linear drive toward a particular understanding of prosperity. It doesn't account for the other potential kinds of wealth—in skills, knowledge, connectedness—that exist in hintered communities whose impoverishment is measured in purely monetary terms, terms that can indicate the depth of the problems without ever naming them directly.

America's hintered landscape is an uneven mosaic, with strange archipelagos of poor among rich and rich among poor. What sociologist Saskia Sassen calls "the systemic edge" manifests itself in both rural and urban places and even within the suburban belts that formerly signaled arrival in the zone of prosperity.[1] As financial wealth and wealth in property become more concentrated in fewer hands, hintering is affecting the kinds of people and places that formerly didn't know what it meant to have to live outside of the affordances of the "developed" world.

You could feel that in the North Quabbin mill towns after the 2008 crash of the U.S. housing market. In eastern Massachusetts and the Connecticut River Valley, housing prices were starting to rise again by 2016. But in mill towns like Orange and Athol, the market was so glutted with foreclosures that the relatively cheap prices which had drawn a lot of us to the area were still stuck at rock-bottom. We were in a place that was poor and becoming steadily poorer, on the hintered edges of a wealthy state.

There are ways to keep a food business going in hintered places. If you're selling a product that has healthy enough profit margins, like Dean Cycon at Dean's Beans, you can push against the taken-for-granted assumptions of the business world and refuse to let profitability dictate the terms of what you're doing. Like Dean, Deb Habib and Ricky Baruch at Seeds of Solidarity were actively participating in a system whose foundational premise they rejected and whose legacies they were working to repair. By 2015 Ricky had been farming for twenty years, and he found himself wanting to spend less and less time in his truck, distanced from the actual cultivation he loved and from the land he and Deb had been rejuvenating. He'd made a decision to sell only to the most local venues, including Quabbin Harvest. His deliveries there were often accompanied by a handwritten yellow sticky note sharing his thoughts of the moment, which tended to circle around the question of what was coming as the world continued to become more overheated, more fractured. Customers at Seeds of Solidarity's small solar-powered farmstand on Chestnut Hill Road found many of these little notes on the walls too.

"No other creature would live as far away from their food source as we do," was one of Ricky's frequent observations, along with another: "The so-called first world lifestyle is killing the rest of the planet." Deb and Ricky found that maintaining some kind of balance and ability to function on the edge of catastrophe necessitated starting from gratitude and a sense of abundance rather than from a jittery alarm about everything that was demonstrably going wrong. "We must prepare in a loving way, not from fear," one of Ricky's farmstand notes insisted.[2]

Nalini had a similar way of refusing to be too ruled by the logic of food-as-commodity. Having come from a background of true privation, she had a very different sense from most of the co-op shoppers of what scarcity and abundance could mean.

"I don't talk about money because I think it's very constrictive," she says. "I strongly believe that the universe smells desperation. I always think I have enough to do whatever I want to do. And I always *do* have enough to do whatever I want to do. So I adopted that same thing here. It's like the universe is there, I'm here, money will be there!"

Since money was obviously *not* there at Quabbin Harvest, or at least not in sufficient amounts, Nalini's approach may sound a lot like magical thinking. But you can also see it as the exact opposite: it's a recognition that surviving within scarcity means not giving in to the kind of dread that will quickly eat you up if you let it.

It goes further: it recognizes how a sense of scarcity actually serves and drives the whole system that rests on plantations and commodities. That system responds to real needs and creates new ones in an endlessly self-reinforcing cycle. Europeans didn't need so much sugar before plantations made it widely available. It was an elite treat at first, spreading as it became more accessible to more people, many of them nonelites aiming to boost their social status through new modes of consumption.[3]

Sugar also boosted the effects of tea and coffee, which in turn boosted the energy of workers in the factories that mass-produced cloth and sewing machines and coffee grinders and water turbines and new desserts like instant tapioca pudding. Once that energy boost was felt to be a necessity, markets supplied ways for people to get it while helping them express a sense of individual or group identity at the same time. At the turn of the twentieth century, it made a statement whether you bought generic coffee beans from a bulk bin at an old-fashioned corner store or a red can of higher-quality, vacuum-packed Hills Brothers coffee at one of the new and more modern chain groceries. And from there it was a pretty straight line to pumpkin-spiced lattés and mocha cookie crumble Frappuccino, single-origin fair-traded yirgacheffe and twelve-packs of biodegradable K-cup pods produced using all-renewable energy certified by an organization dedicated to saving the rain forest. Saving the rain forest is felt by many consumers in the industrialized world as a new need, and the market can help you satisfy it without having to give up the coffee and sugar that keep you going through the day.

Refusing that cycle—refusing to need what our economic system needs us to need—is a principled stance, one that chooses to start from a sense of sufficiency rather than the fear of scarcity. And this isn't the distorted sufficiency of the mainstream food system, all those towers of cheap food resting on so many invisible Others, so much degraded Nature. It's rooted instead in internal resources of skill and commitment and care for people around you. Nalini knew how to do that, and she tried to bring it into what she was doing at Quabbin Harvest, in spite of the way the scarcity mentality had set in around her.

"I decided to focus on the things that were pleasurable to me and pleasurable to other people," she recalls. "And to me that made a lot of sense. I could make you feel really good when you walked into the store. I could do that."

She did it in part through food itself. She started making big batches of chai spices, using her family's recipe, and brewed up pots of hot chai that the co-op could sell alongside its coffee. You could get hot coffee almost anywhere, but nobody else in the North Quabbin sold real chai.

Nalini also found ways to make better use of foods that weren't being sold. One of the challenges in a small grocery store—especially one that prides itself on supporting farmers and selling healthy food—is to keep fruits and vegetables fresh and appealing. Grocers are always culling and discarding the tired-looking produce, something that comes under the grocery business term "shrink" (which sounds better than "waste"). Nalini rescued those foods and turned them into salsas and fruit cups and other little products that saved them from the compost pile and offered something different to shoppers.

There's an industry term for this too—"valued-added"—which means taking a food with a low profit margin, like a winter squash, and making it into something you can sell for a higher price by turning it into a soup or bagging it in precut chunks. But the value Nalini saw herself adding was equally a social and emotional one. It was an expression of care for the people who came into the store as well as for the food itself, especially the food that came from local farmers.

"I was working toward a certain energy in the store," she says. "I wanted to offer people something they hadn't had before, and I wanted to do it with love and just share that."

Again, this all sounds mystical and magical but there's a deep pragmatism to it, based in an acceptance of how profoundly you have to rely on other people when you don't have much in the way of material resources. It's one way of not needing as much, something Nalini had made a conscious decision to do when she left the corporate world. Her family has a maxim: "We should always at all times have both hands open, one to take and one to give." This isn't purely either self-interest or altruism—it's reciprocity, which is somewhere in between. It's closer to the kinds of "gift economies" that anthropologists have historically been very drawn to.[4] Studying more relationship-based economic systems, you come to understand that true mutuality isn't comfortable or easy. It knits you into webs of obligation that can limit your individual choices but also hold you up during hard times. And it's very, very different from the entirely transactional exchanges that happen in a supermarket.

"This is how the world works," Nalini says. "I'm going to love you by giving you this and then you're going to love me back by coming in and supporting the store."

It couldn't wholly offset the big operating deficit or the increasingly frantic efforts to find a solution to the cash-flow problems. But it did make a difference. I could feel it when I shopped in the store. Other things helped too. Julie Davis was now doing the ordering and making smart strategic decisions about what could and should be stocked with the co-op's very limited resources. Amy Borezo was crafting accessible and upbeat messages that reminded people of the reasons we might choose to step off our beaten paths and come to the store to shop. There was an electronic mailing list and regular radio spots on the local station. Karl Bittenbender was anchoring the complicated financial side of things, and while it was still depressing, it was a little more comprehensible than it had been. It felt like there was now something to build around and good reasons to hold on.

In the summer of 2016 I joined a working group convened by Mount Grace Land Conservation Trust, the co-op's landlord, to try to revive the Orange and Athol farmers markets. Over several years, both markets had hit that downward cycle of fewer vendors, little to buy, and a dwindling shopper base, a pattern seen elsewhere as the number of farmers markets reached a saturation point.[5] The remaining local farm vendors had asked for help to build things back up again.

Our group did most of the standard things that farmers markets do to attract customers: added a kids' area with games and toys, wrote grants to hire a market manager and pay musicians a little bit to perform, upgraded signage, got stories about local farmers into the newspapers. There were some impractical proposals: one participant gamely suggested taking the fight directly to Big Food by setting up in the Market Basket parking lot, not recognizing that even chain stores and restaurants leasing space at the so-called North Quabbin Commons had to sign agreements not to compete directly with Market Basket's offerings. But mostly the ideas were productive, like helping to revive the mostly inactive agricultural commissions in the two towns and getting votes of support passed at town meetings.

It didn't take long before it struck me that the farmers were grappling with a lot of the same questions as the people running the co-op: how to encourage more seasonal eating in the face of the supermarket's year-round abundance, how to mobilize a sense of mutuality and even (gasp!) obligation without preaching or moralizing, how to reach across the invisible divide between people who were on some kind of mission about local food and those who weren't. I invited some of the co-op leaders to join the discussions, and we did manage to do some cross-marketing, promoting Quabbin Harvest as a kind of year-round complement to the seasonal farmers markets.

But it always seemed hard to weave the co-op into the overall messaging. It was as if the store was a different kind of venture—more complicated, less truly local in some ways, selling food that was somewhere in between the decommodified, buy-directly-from-your-farmer offerings at the market and the conventional, got-there-in-a-big-truck goods at conventional grocery stores.

Some of Quabbin Harvest's produce came in a truck owned by a company whose founders had once sported T-shirts saying "Squash Capitalism." But that was almost more confusing. Like Squash Trucking, Quabbin Harvest was between the mainstream and the alternatives, making it hard to see and understand. The co-op sold bananas and lemons and other things that could never be local but that made it something closer to a full-service grocery store, which was what it needed to be if it was going to survive. The big sign on the front still said Workers Credit Union and the building still looked like a bank. There were also all those unpaid invoices from vendors, which certainly didn't boost the co-op's credibility with even the most supportive of farmers.

At the farmers market, it was relatively simple to create an atmosphere that felt festive and inviting. It helped that the experience of ambling along rows of vendor stalls, listening to live music on a sunny day, eating a fresh peach that you bought from the person who grew it, has become a kind of marketable commodity in itself, akin to picking your own fruit at an orchard or enjoying a craft beer in a brewery taproom. Other small businesses around the North Quabbin have also figured out how to mobilize atmosphere and experience to attract customers. An artisanal brewery in the Orange Innovation Center opened in 2015 with a rustic-chic tasting room whose bar was made of local materials by a woodworker friend of the founders and hand-lettered signs on the wall from the old Minute Tapioca Company, unearthed when the space was being renovated. Its beers' names often invoke local scenes, like "Accidental Wilderness," a phrase sometimes applied to the forested lands buffering the Quabbin Reservoir and protecting the purity of Boston's water supply.[6] A few miles away in the easternmost North Quabbin town, an orchard called Red Apple Farm has managed to keep going over four generations by producing, marketing, and exporting a particular brand of New England nostalgia (its tagline is "Your Family Farm"). It rests on fresh cider donuts and homemade fudge and pick-your-own options and—yes—a brewery and taproom, started when the apple crop was damaged by hail one year and the farmer and a brewer friend decided to make hard cider rather than letting the fruit rot on the ground. Red Apple's strategies would have been familiar to the enterprising nineteenth- and early twentieth-century farmers in the region who found new sources of income in a consolidating and competitive agricultural economy by offering farm-stay vacations to visitors in search of rural peace and tranquility, with a side of pickle relish.[7] These are the kinds of resources that hintered places often have in abundance, and the challenge is to connect them with people who can and will pay for them.

Over time, experiences themselves have become another new kind of product, a new commodity. It's not that farmers markets or artisanal breweries or farm tourism experiences are interchangeable—rather the opposite. Each has to find some unique mix of qualities that makes it stand out in a crowded market of local eating and drinking. But the ways in which each experience is unique have become standardized, in the same way that all tourist attractions and arts districts and waterfront parks have to be unique but within a highly consistent repertoire—the scenic vista, the striking architecture, the culinary discovery, the seren-dipitous encounter, even the unexpected misadventure. Taken together, they all signal authenticity and a sense of connection across space, time, culture, occupation. Shorn of that repertoire, travel is just moving from one place to another and going to the farmers market is simply buying food in a less convenient way.

"Outside the commodity" doesn't really exist yet in most of the mod-ern food economy, any more than "after the plantation" does. It's hard even to find the right language for talking about it. Most people aren't looking for political theory with their vegetables. So we default to feel-good phrases, selling the home-grown sizzle and marketing the earthi-ness, the friendliness, the post-and-beam-ness of it all.

Our working group managed to reactivate the local farmers markets, especially the one in Orange, by adding some of those signals of authen-ticity, and the organizers were justifiably proud of having accomplished at least part of what we set out to do. But the co-op was still an outlier, a piece of the puzzle that didn't quite fit, with problems that felt somehow more intractable, more real. The farmers markets and craft breweries were real too, but they had an appealing aura that could be pulled around them that softened the edges of the economic exchanges going on. The reality at Quabbin Harvest, always peering over the financial edge and in direct competition with the grocery giants, was both harsher and harder to see clearly.

It felt, in fact, like a lot of the problems in places like the North Quab-bin, where the gaps are obvious but the means of filling them are opaque, distant, slow, daunting. I'd gotten a very clear sense of this when I was teaching adult basic education before I went back to graduate school, in a program run by my friend Pat Larson. The program was in the basement of the low, flat building that had replaced the splendid clock tower in the center of Orange, and whoever plumbed it hadn't gotten the drains right, so water gushed out of everywhere whenever there was a heavy rain. There was nothing to do but evacuate and come back later with mops and buckets. Pat went after the damp like a Viking warrior, bleaching all the concrete floors to keep mold from getting any ideas about settling in. The first time it happened we had just started seedlings to be transplanted into the student plot in the community garden down by the river. In the free-writing that students did in blue composition notebooks at the end of the day, one woman wrote, "Today we finished cleaning up the back room and Pat bleached everything and killed all the little plants." It was a perfect reflection of how it felt to be trying to sustain life and health in an impoverished environment. Students' gains, when they happened, were nonlinear, messy, often sporadic, sometimes mundane, sometimes glacially and generationally slow, and almost always in tension with a world that continually demanded more—more credentials, more new skills, more mobility and adaptability—just to be able to make any kind of a grab at the edges of prosperity.

In many hintered places where the process of hintering is moving up along socioeconomic and racial hierarchies, it has been prompting the very opposite of the solidarity you might think would come from realizing you're now being screwed in ways that are similar to how a lot of other people have been getting screwed for a long time. Rather than feeling a sense of common cause, there's resentment and scapegoating, much of it across racialized lines. And sometimes there's also just a wholesale retreat from the immensity of the problems.

There were more and more inklings of this in Orange in 2016. The nomination of Donald Trump for president in July was a reminder of just how much resentment was there to be harnessed by someone willing to exploit it. In the "Make America Great Again" mantra you could hear the anger of people caught within those powerful and problematic metaphors, wanting to go back and at the same time desperate to move forward, people who hadn't expected to feel so left behind, nudged off the track, in places and positions that used to be more comfortable and had now been pushed aside, or that had never been all that comfortable but were at least not the most miserable, giving the aggrieved some sense of being a bit higher up in the pecking order.

Plenty of people were also just checking out and becoming numb. Like the national real-estate crash, the American opioid crisis hit particularly hard in hintered places. The county sheriff estimated that the great majority of people he saw coming into the county jail were addicted to opioids or heroin; with no detox facilities available, they were going through withdrawal alone in their cells.[8]

Out in the community, the reverberations of the opioid crisis were everywhere. The same day Trump secured the Republican nomination, the little farmstand at Seeds of Solidarity was robbed, its self-serve honor-system cashbox ripped from a secure spot bolted onto a shelf. The thief was a visiting brother of neighbors, a young man who had relapsed into an opiate addiction. Deb and Ricky were relieved to know who the culprit was so they didn't continue to suspect and wonder about others who came to the farm to volunteer or learn. "It sucks to start thinking and looking at people that way," they said.[9] But they were also troubled by the sense that there were more and more people who needed more help that wasn't available. The farm was working to build up health and strength in a place where things were continually falling apart at the same time.

The co-op's troubles felt like part and parcel of all this, although that only made it seem riskier to talk about the bigger picture too directly. It was hard enough to admit that the store was already failing—how much worse was it to invoke even larger, slowly unfolding emergencies like the increasingly unequal economy, the fracturing political sphere, the ever more volatile planetary climate? The summer of 2016 saw a historic drought—one of several within the same decade—across central New England. Farms like Seeds of Solidarity that used "regenerative" methods were finding they had some degree of protection from the wild swings of wet and dry, hot and cold, but it was still an anxious time.

One of Ricky's notes at the farmstand read, "When I was looking for my first farm twenty-five years ago the place to look for was river bottomland. Now river bottomland gets 100-year floods three years in a row! Things have changed and we must adapt. Farming up in the hills, cities, suburbs—making soil is the future."[10] But the future also felt chancy in so many ways. On the same bad day when the cashbox was robbed, Ricky was nearly struck by a falling tree in Seeds of Solidarity's own driveway. It seemed like just another sign of present problems and coming storms, and not a good one.

In August 2016 the co-op's leadership finally broke its silence and let the membership know how bad things were. The message was clear: the store would have to close by autumn if there wasn't an immediate and substantial influx of cash. Everyone needed to start buying as much as they possibly could in the store.

And people did. Shoppers who hadn't been there for a while were heartened by the changes Nalini and Julie had made—the prepared food offerings; the bountiful, beautiful produce in the cooler; the mix of staple items and local specialties; the tried-and-true weekly fruit and vegetable shares. People remembered their own enthusiasm of just a couple of years ago and the reasons they'd been so excited about the new venture. The increase in sales was just enough to stave off the worst and keep the store going for a little while longer.

But here's the thing about being hintered: just enough isn't actually enough. You're stuck holding on, telling yourself it could be worse, hoping worse things don't happen tomorrow.

Then they did. In early October, Orange was shaken by a vicious attack on an elderly couple in their own home, leaving the ninety-five-year-old husband dead and his seventy-seven-year-old wife badly injured. The assailants were in search of money and a vehicle so they could escape court-ordered drug treatment for heroin addiction and arrest for a prior car theft.

In a lot of hintered places this scenario is exhaustingly familiar. It's a measure of how insulated most majority-white communities are that this was so shattering to Orange. But shattering it was. People throughout the area felt it like a body blow. The victims were connected to and through family and social and organizational networks all around the North Quabbin. They were dear friends of the Bittenbenders; the wife had worked for many years with Pat Larson on youth and parenting programs. The irony of having spent much of her life working to nurture and support the lives of children only to be brutalized in her own home by two young people was not lost on those who knew her.

The news felt bruising for weeks. And then, the election. I wasn't actually able to vote; after all those years of living in the United States, I'd only recently made the decision to become a citizen, and in November 2016 I was still in limbo between passing the test and taking the oath. I'd been working up to it for a long time—it's a difficult step for many Canadians, for whom America is the Other, the thing we are not. And not only an Other but an often troubling one, especially whenever the national id asserts itself in response to some kind of threat, perceived or real, internal or external. For a long time I'd preferred to stay at arm's length from the nation-state itself, much as I loved the region and the state I had settled in. My blue vote wasn't going to change any electoral outcomes in liberal Massachusetts, and I could—and did—participate in campaigns and support candidates in other ways.

But somewhere in the middle of the 2016 presidential campaign I started to think it was time to make the big step. The no-longer-veiled animosity toward America's own Others, the demonizing of "bad hombres" from Mexico and Muslims from everywhere, the idea that the country should literally be walling out people trying to escape untenable lives, patriarchal prerogative reasserting itself in the grotesque caricature of pussy-grabbing and chants of "lock her up," all of it reinforced the sense of an established order desperately defending itself against a breakdown that had already been happening for decades or longer—one that needed to happen for so many reasons. As a woman, I was both furious and uneasy. As an immigrant who'd had the luxury of passing easily as American, I'd always been aware that the national animus was not toward immigrants per se but toward those who looked or sounded different from the white norm, especially if they were poor. With so many violent undercurrents roiling the surface, it felt like it was finally time to stop pretending that I could hold myself apart from the aspects of America that troubled me.

I spent Election Day afternoon planting next year's garlic. By the time I went to bed it was starting to look as though all that unleashed animosity might have carried the day. By the next morning it was clear it had. Like a lot of people, I stumbled through the day in a stupor, trying to be present for my distraught students, making anguished eye contact with other women on the commuter train and the city bus (one stranger spontaneously hugged me after we exchanged brief glances). It felt as though overnight the rupture that had been making itself felt throughout the long campaign had created—or maybe just officially recognized—two entirely different Americas.

The town-by-town map of blue Massachusetts showed a red belt that ran straight through the deindustrialized middle of the state, including Orange and Athol. It tracked the hintered places, the towns that were continuing to slide farther behind as others surged ahead. In the post-election phase of well-educated liberals trying to comprehend what had just happened, a group from a nearby (blue) town made an expedition to Kentucky in search of Trump voters and some kind of understanding. White New Englanders have been traveling to Appalachia on missions of cultural and economic uplift since the mid-nineteenth century, and the new project's focus on fact-finding and dialogue rather than assistance couldn't disguise the fact that this was a very well-worn path that led directly away from Massachusetts's very own Appalachia.[11] The emissaries to eastern Kentucky could easily have driven the few miles north to Orange, where white working-class resentment was not hard to find, and in many ways not all that hard to understand.

In the aftermath of the election I also felt I needed to do something more, but I looked closer to home. The co-op seemed like an obvious place to dig in and try to do some good in my own community, with a project that, for all its specific problems, was also connected to a lot of the larger, long-term challenges that troubled me most.

Pat and I had been talking about what might be done to improve communication between the co-op's members and its leadership. With the board's blessing we volunteered to convene what we called Co-op Conversation Circles, essentially focus groups to find out more about how people were shopping (or not) at the store.

We weren't surprised to hear a lot of comments about things not being in stock and the many reasons not to come to the center of Orange. But many of the conversations also circled uneasily around that recognition that good-quality food is inherently more expensive, especially at a small store. Even someone who cared about the store, someone who could and would pay more for coffee from Dean's Beans, wasn't going to sit still for a twenty-dollar pound of coffee. They would just buy it directly from the beanery or get it from one of the larger Connecticut River Valley food co-ops. There were price points that Julie couldn't go beyond, in the same way that farmers can't just simply charge a price that reflects what the food actually costs them to produce.

All of this intersected with the class politics of the North Quabbin and the country in general. With its higher-priced food and its members' generally liberal politics, Quabbin Harvest was a blue island in a red island in a blue state, and just about everybody knew it. Our conversations circled and sometimes tiptoed around that point, often ending in the phrase, "But we live in such a poor area," never really coming to grips with the financial or social underpinnings of what we were trying to do but at least getting a little more information flowing.

There was one piece of good news in the fall of 2016. Through an anonymous donor, the co-op received a two-year challenge grant that could help staunch the bleeding long enough to stabilize the business. The store would have to meet certain sales goals in the first year in order to unlock the second year's funding. It was a lifeline, extended just in time.

But overall, things still felt bleak. The woman injured in the home invasion earlier in the fall had been struggling to recover, but her injuries led to pneumonia and her death on the day after the election was one more hard loss. Her close friend Karl Bittenbender was carrying a lot of the weight of that ton of bricks at the co-op by that point. Nalini Goordial was holding the day-to-day operations together, but she found she could only do that if she didn't get drawn too deeply into the growing despondency at the store.

"I think the inner workings of the co-op was something I didn't want to see," she says now, "because I felt like I was going to lose something." What she was trying so hard to hold onto was her ability to feel and be generous with people who came into the store as well as the part-time staff who worked with her, keeping one hand open to give while also urgently needing to take with the other. The strain of it took a toll, physically and emotionally. "I was trying to stay positive in the store," she says, "up until I couldn't."

In December 2016 Nalini was diagnosed with breast cancer and left her job immediately to begin treatment. Because she'd been managing the store in a very collaborative way, a lot of things carried on relatively smoothly after the shock of this new loss. But the store badly needed someone to pay attention to the overall picture, to be part of the management team, to be responsible for keeping things running day in and day out. Karl was already carrying more than one person's share; Amy Borezo and Julie Davis were putting in a lot of volunteer hours but still weren't looking to take on an actual job. Ads went out quickly in the hope of finding someone to fill that all-important central role.

That's the moment when I decided to step across the line between just thinking and talking about the co-op and actually doing something more to help keep it going. I attended a board meeting in December to report on how the conversation circles had been going and learned that most of the directors would be stepping off the board in just a few months. The founding members were reaching their term limits and others had decided not to run for reelection, leaving only two returning board members for the coming year.

I also learned that there was no heat upstairs at the co-op. The energy-saving strategies put in place during the startup phase included taking the old inefficient oil furnace in the basement offline entirely and using space heaters instead. During the first winter the whole building had been frigid. Over the next few months, Karl and Bruce Scherer improvised a partial solution. They devised ducts to capture the excess heat from the basement compressor that ran the gigantic and equally inefficient old freezers, making the store itself much more habitable in the second winter. But the second floor, especially the large boardroom at the front of the building, was still glacial. Bruce and other volunteers made insulating inserts for the big plate-glass windows but board members still sat swaddled to the cheekbones in scarves and hoods at meetings.

Beyond the cold, I felt a pervasive inertia and misery at that first board meeting despite some efforts to look on the bright side and continue trying to find a way forward. The lifeline grant was good news, but it looked to me as though no one but Karl really understood the actual numbers. People eyed his photocopied financial reports like undetonated ordnance that might not explode if everyone just stayed very, very still.

I didn't know how to respond intelligently to a financial report either, and I wasn't quite sure what I could actually help with beyond the initial thinking and talking that hadn't felt like enough. But it also seemed as though there might not be anything to step into if I didn't do it now.

I expressed an interest in serving on the board and at the January board meeting I was appointed to fill a vacant seat. No one said, "Welcome to the board" or "Here's what we'd like you to do" or "Here's some information you should know." There was a sense that I was a warm and willing body and that was enough.

I was a lot less warm after another board meeting but still willing. I said I would run for a full term at the annual meeting that spring, having already heard from Pat Larson that she would do the same. I was willing, but I also knew I didn't want to do it alone, and I knew how much determination and practicality Pat would bring to the board.

And so I stepped across the line and into the grocery business. It made me nervous but with a familiar and anthropological kind of nervousness, the kind where you've done your preliminary research and have a lot of ideas in your head and you know it's more or less the right moment to stop hanging around on the sidelines and find your way into the picture, where things immediately become much more complicated, more interesting, and more real.

CHAPTER 8

THE C-WORD

AGRICULTURE ALWAYS BECOMES more mysterious, not less, whenever I try to write or teach about it. I started out like most nonfarmers, thinking of it primarily in terms of crops and seeds and animals and soil and weather. As it started to dawn on me that it was equally about commerce and land values and machines and banks, huge new connections opened up like crevices. I saw that you cannot begin to understand farming—especially in places like the older northeastern American states, where the ecological limits of commercialized agriculture made themselves felt sooner than in many other parts of the country—separately from industry and cities and fossil fuels and supermarkets and geopolitics and race and class and everything that those things connect to. Which is, basically, everything. It makes me glad I've had some training in a discipline that actually tries to think about everything all at once.

Over time I've found some bedrock. It's what I keep coming back to whenever I find myself pondering food systems problems, including the very real problems at the co-op. The basic insight I've gotten to is this: you have no hope of understanding what's going on in the modern food system unless you're willing to think critically about capitalism. It's actually very simple.

One of the things that makes it seem complicated is how resistant so many Americans are to taking a hard look at their own economic system. Many do, of course. And Americans are by no means the only ones in thrall to the idea that capitalism can enable endless economic growth and bring prosperity for all. But there's something that strikes me as particularly American about the way the topic gets evaded in both private and public.

I was thinking a lot about this in January 2017 because that's the month I finally became an American myself. Donald Trump and I were sworn in the same week, in my case in a big auditorium in Lowell. The master of ceremonies read out the long list of countries we had all come from and said that what united us was that we had all come to America because we wanted to make better lives for ourselves.

That wasn't true in my case, and that has always made me aware of how the American Dream narrative flattens the range of experiences that immigrants and refugees and sojourners bring to this country. No matter—we were all supposed to be living the dream now. And that meant, at bottom, not only a meritocratic and democratic but also a capitalist dream.

As I finally became an American, I kept reflecting on the moments that still made me feel alien. One of them is whenever someone from this famously optimistic, can-do nation whisks capitalism off the table in discussions about problems in the U.S. food system. I've heard it in countless meetings both in and out of academic life, in discussions that edge right up to the fact that capitalism itself creates so many of the problems we're trying to solve, and then dodge away again. It's often phrased to sound merely sensible—"Oh, we're not going to solve *that*, so let's aim for something more realistic" or "This is the system we have, we've got to work within it." But the underlying message feels stark and binary: "Don't go there." There's something in this American unwillingness to talk about the nature of capitalism that seems skittish, even phobic. If it's too risky even to air the questions, the possible answers must be unwelcome indeed.

When you do anthropological fieldwork there are always crystallizing moments when something big and important about your field site reveals itself to you. It's often just a casual remark or a fleeting expression, but it can break open room for insights you didn't have before. One of those happened for me during my dissertation fieldwork in Lowell, when I was sitting in a meeting in a very long-running exhibit planning process. For more than a year, the curators and historians and museum educators had been trying to figure out what to say about what had caused the capital flight that had gutted the city economically by the 1960s. The discussions were often circular, inconclusive, and hesitant, and one member of the team finally lost patience.

Why was it, he demanded, that everyone was so reluctant to talk directly about how capitalism had hurt the city? "If anybody even brings it up, it's like 'Who threw the dead cat on the table?'" he said. "If you're so afraid of this, why the hell are you in the exhibit business at all?"[1] The burst of laughter that followed this rant sounded relieved. It wasn't just that the emperor had no clothes—it was that everybody knew perfectly well that the emperor was also a real son of a bitch but nobody had felt quite brave enough to say it, because they also wanted him to like them. After all, he was, you know, the emperor.

I saw the same evasion in Ben Hewitt's book *The Town That Food Saved: How One Community Found Vitality in Local Food*. It's a good book, filled with thoughtful explorations of why food systems problems are so complex and recalcitrant. But Hewitt too stops just short of throwing the dead cat on the table. The title is catchy but misleading—Hewitt shows very clearly that the town in question, Hardwick, Vermont, hasn't really been "saved" by the local food movement, or at least not yet. In fact, there are a lot of sharply divergent opinions within the town about what that might even mean.

Hewitt is a skillful writer, and he traces the contours of those divisions clearly. In many ways they're the same ones that characterize the North Quabbin, between people who are on some kind of a mission with local food and those who aren't. As a good journalist, Hewitt seeks out opposing points of view to counter the media's enthusiasm about the "agrepreneurs" trying to rebuild a robust agricultural economy in Hardwick. At one point he finds himself listening to a diatribe from a couple named Steve and Suzanna about what's wrong with the new ventures. The couple are concerned that this is just replicating the same scaling-up and profit-seeking cycles that led to the problems Hardwick and Orange and countless other places struggle with in the twenty-first century.

"We don't need a bunch of white guys with money telling us how to adapt," Suzanna says. "People are always doing stupid things in the name of groovy ag movements."

Hewitt relays their ideas in detail, but only to show that he's doing his due diligence. He's even honest enough to note that Suzanna resents being included as a mouthpiece for ideas he's only including out of fairness. "Maybe you could just have those ideas yourself," she suggests.

But he doesn't. Instead, he makes the all-or-nothing argument I've heard so often when people don't really want to face up to what happens when you root your food system in the search for profit.

"Has [the U.S. economy] been corrupted by corporate interests?" he asks rhetorically. "Why, yes, it has. Is the only answer to that corruption the wholesale abandonment of this model, with all the societal havoc such transition would surely wreak? I don't believe it's quite that simple."[2]

Neither do Steve and Suzanna, of course. Neither do most—if any— critics of capitalism. Even if you think or hope that this economic system will eventually collapse under its own weight, I don't know anyone who believes that's going to happen tomorrow or anytime soon. Nor, given how dependent virtually all of us are on that system for the food that keeps us alive, should we wish for its sudden collapse. The problems we have now would pale in comparison with what would happen in that case.

But surely we have to be willing to face up to the ways that capitalism actually causes most of those big problems, not in the sense that it still has a few bugs in the system but in a truly fundamental way, how it can ultimately work directly against the goal of having a food system that's fair for everyone and doesn't despoil the planet in the process of getting food.

It seems to me that there's room within that perspective for those who believe markets can work for everyone if there's enough political will to come up with truly effective regulation. Equally, there's room for those who think we need to take the whole thing right down to its foundations and start from scratch. It's still early days, and there's an immense amount to do—too much to be spending time fighting with other people who at least see that a lot of big things need to change.[3]

But it also seems to me that at a bare minimum we need a common analysis of what we're trying to change. We need a shared understanding of how the tendencies inherent in capitalist markets have led us to the present moment of crazy overabundance and colossal concentrations of power. That analysis is what will give us some bedrock to stand on as we do the hard work of building something different, whether we're trying to take down the dominant system, build up something new while it's still in place, or move outside of it entirely.[4] And that means we need to resist the urge to whip the topic off the table just because it's too divisive or too daunting to solve all at once.

In the tiptoeing around that big question in the conversation circles my friend Pat and I convened shortly before we joined the co-op board, it was clear that Quabbin Harvest's members and most faithful shoppers didn't have that kind of shared analysis. Once I became the board chair in early 2017 it seemed important to find out where more people stood. As the academic year came to an end and some space opened up in my calendar, I embarked on a kind of anthropological listening tour to try to understand more fully just what I had gotten myself into.

I was suddenly the board chair because there was a gap around that key leadership role and no one else seemed to be stepping into it. The only two remaining board members were the secretary and Karl, the treasurer, and none of the other new recruits seemed eager to serve as chair. I wasn't exactly eager but I felt at least partly qualified. I'd done my obligatory coursework, over several years of reading and learning and thinking about how the modern food system worked. I had a big picture in my head, and I felt at least somewhat ready—and certainly motivated—to put some of that into practice.

That didn't mean I had any idea how to read a spreadsheet. The first thing that happened after I expressed a willingness to be the chair was that Karl invited me to sit down with him and Amy Borezo, the outgoing chair, to look over the budget for the coming year. I dutifully joined them in the upstairs office where the bookkeeping happened, and the three of us huddled in our coats around a space heater to look at a screen full of numbers. The bottom line showed a deficit of about a thousand dollars at the end of the year.

I was pleasantly surprised. I felt I should ask at least one probing question, so I said, "Are we really projecting that we'll only lose a thousand dollars in the coming year?"

Karl gave me an odd look. "Well, it's a *balanced* budget," he said.

If you know anything about finances you're smacking your forehead at this. If you're not smacking your forehead, you're probably like I was at that point, clueless about the processes of actually running a business, with a vague sense that the numbers on the screen must reflect reality in some way.

To be fair, Karl needed to say much more than he did. He needed to say, "Here's how you project your annual budget. You start out by seeing what a balanced budget would look like based on what you think your actual expenses are going to be, and that tells you how much money you need to bring in if you're going to break even." And then a vitally important point: "Your nicely balanced budget has absolutely nothing to do with whether you're actually going to be able to bring in that much money." And then an even more crucial piece of information: Quabbin Harvest was still a very, very long way from breaking even.

In hindsight, I know why Karl didn't say all of that. Partly it was because he was Karl, gentle and buoyant and shouldering a lot of the burden of knowing just how bad the situation was. I'd seen him trying to share that knowledge more widely at board meetings, and I'd seen people simply not wanting to hear it. If he'd shown me just how much money we were losing at that point, I might well have cut and run, and Karl probably knew it. It was better for the co-op to have me clueless and willing to learn than enlightened and gone.

So we agreed to present the budget to the board at the next meeting and we left the frigid office. The two-year challenge grant we'd gotten at the end of the previous year was buying us some time to get things in shape, although no one but Karl had any sense of how quickly we would be burning through that money even if we did get to the sales goal the grant required: $6,000 a week, on average, in the middle two quarters of 2017.

I latched onto that $6,000 figure because it felt like one concrete number we could build around. It was Point B, what we were trying to get to. I did find it disconcerting to realize how elusive Point A seemed to be. Amy had been reporting on our actual weekly sales at each month's board meeting, based on the cash register receipts, but those numbers didn't exactly match Karl's spreadsheets or the reports he generated from our bookkeeper's figures. I had a sense that there was some kind of translation between the cash register and the books that seemed complicated, but I'd resolved not to get sucked into that level of things. I was all about the big picture. So I just held tight to the $6,000-a-week goal as I embarked on my listening tour.

I talked with a lot of people that summer. I got some lessons from other board chairs (key takeaway: be prepared to go to a lot of meetings). I learned more about the co-op's relationship with its landlord, Mount Grace Land Conservation Trust. I had a long and illuminating talk with an early volunteer who had helped set up the co-op's financial structures— that mysterious cash register system and surprisingly complex chart of accounts. Dismayed, she had watched the initial plans for the store fracture as the first manager took over parts of the operation that others had once been involved in, gathering too many pieces of the business into one brain and one pair of hands that couldn't hold onto all of them alone. The volunteer had become somewhat bitter and disengaged from the co-op during that phase but was still shopping regularly at the store and still willing to talk. It told me something about the depth of support and expertise that existed in the membership, if we could reconnect to it.

One day I met with Karl and our loan officer from one of the cooperative funding organizations that lent the initial capital for the store. They made an annual visit to check on the health of their investment, and I had a sense of stepping into a cyclical conversation that these two had already had several times. Karl gave an overview of where we were financially and shared the progress we were making toward the $6,000-a-week goal. When he was done, the loan officer fixed him with a steely look.

"Do you think I'm ever going to drive into this town and look up at this building from the traffic light and see a sign that tells me this is a grocery store?" she asked. Karl smiled and gave a little shrug.

Note to self, I thought: *Get a sign on the front of the building.* How hard could that be? Karl's shrug should have warned me that like everything else at the co-op, there would be unexpected complications, but I added it to my mental to-do list and moved on.

The four-person management team structure was still in place, and besides Karl, I talked with the other members: Amy Borezo, who was beginning to step back from doing the communications and board side of things, and Julie Davis, who continued to order the weekly produce shares. And I started to talk regularly with the new not-quite-a-manager who had replaced Nalini as team leader.

The new team leader knew the North Quabbin area well and had experience in retail, including food retail, which seemed to make her a perfect fit for the job. And she had a strategy for marketing the store that seemed to make sense: don't even try to compete with the big stores that can always offer things at lower prices. Why reinforce the sense that the co-op was overpriced and out of touch with its market area? If people wanted things like canned tomatoes and butter and cheese, they could buy them somewhere else for much less. It was painful to keep having the same unwinnable conversation about prices. The co-op should stick with its strengths, the unique local foods and specialty products that the supermarkets didn't carry. It should also expand into prepared foods, increasingly the growth engine for all food retail.

Like the volunteers on the management team, I worried that the specialty-food part of this sounded too much like the first manager's approach, which had turned out to be such a mistake. I knew there were other shoppers like me who actually wanted to buy butter at the co-op and were willing and able to pay more for it. How many times could we alienate our most committed customers and then persuade them to come back again?

But there were also things to be said for playing to our strengths. After the near-bankruptcy of the previous year, the co-op's leaders invited a number of knowledgeable people to tour the store and make suggestions. Most of them agreed that emphasizing the unique and local was Quabbin Harvest's strongest approach. Several also suggested adding prepared foods to the product mix. Despite some reservations, the leadership—which now included me, in all my naïveté—gave the new strategy its blessing.

There wasn't an actual kitchen in the building where we could launch a prepared-foods division, but Bruce Scherer, ever resourceful, created one from scratch in an underutilized back corner of the store. Splash-guard material on the walls, some stainless-steel counters and tables that he and Rachel didn't need at their goat dairy, some shuffling around of one of the coolers and the existing hot beverage area, and voilà, Quabbin Harvest had a kitchen. The plan was to offer scooped ice cream and premade sandwiches and perhaps salads and other things.

We held a ribbon-cutting for the kitchen in early summer. It was the first time I'd represented the co-op in public and it felt novel and a little uncomfortable. As a scholar and a writer, I'm accustomed to using words to get as close to the contours of truth as I can. Even if "the contours of truth" is a nebulous notion, it's not an exaggeration to say that grop-ing toward it is an almost sacred imperative in my business. So I felt as though a big part of my new job as chair of the board was to convey the message that the co-op was in deep trouble, in a way that people could hear and understand.

But that's not the message you want to share at a ribbon-cutting on a beautiful summer day, with members of the Chamber of Commerce board there to cheer you on and volunteers serving up freshly made salads and a staff member dressed in a silly banana costume waving to people outside the store, encouraging them to come inside and have some fun and an ice cream cone. So I made the first of what I came to think of as my "upbeat-yet-urgent" (or sometimes "urgent-yet-upbeat") speeches, trying to say something about how challenging it was to keep a small food business going and why it was so important for people to support local stores. It felt crucial to say "this is hard," but also "this is important" and even "this can be fun." My own inclination was always to detour into "this is *why* it's hard," but I'd learned during my summer of deconstructing burgers that most people would only go so far down that road with you. You just needed to float the question and then let them get their ice cream.

In that summer of 2017 there were other things that made it feel as though we were making real progress, including inching toward that sales goal. One of them was Castle Rock.

You might have heard of Castle Rock. It's a fictional town in Maine that appears in some of Stephen King's horror writing. Its imagined history draws from the deep well of New England *noir*, the sense of something uncanny in this iconic landscape of white churches and brick factories, the other side of the celebratory national narrative of settlement and civilization. In 2017 a Hollywood production company was weaving the bits of Castle Rock's story into a television series and they needed an appropriately spooky town in the title role. They found Orange.

Orange's state of decline—its gap-toothed downtown, the big Victorian houses on the hill, the hulking New Home Sewing Machine Company buildings along the river—exemplified that feeling of something unknown working under the surface, something that might cause the ground to give way and swallow you up at any moment. Suddenly, hinteredness became marketable.

We negotiated payments that would offset the co-op's anticipated business losses on filming days and served up ice cream all day long when a casting call for extras brought thousands of hopefuls to town in the middle of July. It felt strange to be so busy, strange to have to wait through more than one cycle at either of the town's two traffic lights. People imagined Orange becoming a film tourism destination and Hollywood riches flowing freely into the area. Co-op members suggested ways for us to capture some of it. Could we convince the catering service to source local foods? What about asking for an outright donation to offset some of our operating deficit in the coming year? But there were no points of entry where those kinds of ideas could reasonably land. The production company's front people were friendly, accommodating, and communicative right up to the point when they weren't. We were going to have to be content with fame and hope at least a little bit of fortune might trickle down too.

Good days alternated with bad ones. One evening I was at a meeting of the farmers market support group in the big upstairs room when we noticed that the sky was nearly black and the wind was starting to blow sideways. John Moore, who was at the table, looked alarmed and suggested that we go downstairs right away. When a phlegmatic New England farmer gets worried, you should pay attention. We huddled in the back office, formerly the bank's main vault, until the storm blew through. When we came out we discovered that a big ash tree from the next yard had fallen over on my car. Bruce Scherer showed up the next day with his chainsaw and the little tractor he used for everything from moving fodder to digging trenches and got rid of the tree. It took him hours of hard labor, sawing and bundling and trimming and loading, yet another reminder of how good it is to have friends with skills and tools.

It was also good to have insurance. The damage to the car was reparable, if time-consuming. We didn't need to tap the co-op's insurance for the fallen tree, but we did need it later in the summer when the big bank of old freezers quit one night, leaving thousands of dollars of inventory melting and unsaleable by morning. The cause wasn't clear, and in listening to Karl and the repairman, I began to realize how complicated the installation of those freezers had been, and how much work had been done to try to minimize the enormous electrical load they drew. Was the malfunction somewhere in the energy-efficiency technology that had been added? Was that equipment just not working and playing well with the freezers' own thermostat system? No one was quite sure. But at least the insurance company covered our losses.

The first time. When the freezers quit again later in the summer, the company dug in its heels. Their logic wasn't air-tight, and we debated continuing to fight it out. But there was limited energy for fighting; it seemed smarter just to absorb the hit and carry on.

One of the reasons we were able to refill the freezers even without the insurance money was that our cash flow improved tremendously as the summer went on, almost entirely due to the launch of a new state initiative. The Healthy Incentives Program (HIP) provided an additional benefit for people receiving federal food assistance: full reimbursement for the purchase of fresh fruits and vegetables from local farmers, up to a monthly cap based on household size.

This seemingly simple idea emerged from many years of planning and discussion among Massachusetts social service and public health agencies and advocates for the state's farming sector. A single-county pilot version had run a few years earlier and Quabbin Harvest had been quick to pursue the idea of becoming a HIP vendor when the program launched statewide. True, we weren't a farm, but we were an outlet for farmers' products—it was a core part of our mission. And so was making good food more affordable for everyone. HIP felt like a big part of an answer to the question of how to make money selling good food without pricing it beyond the reach of many people in our area.

The weekly produce shares that had been a mainstay at the co-op from the beginning were easily adapted to the new program. Amy Borezo negotiated the contract with the state so people could sign up and pay for shares using their SNAP (Supplemental Nutrition Assistance Program, formerly called food stamps) benefits. Pat Larson mobilized her network of contacts in the North Quabbin area's social services to get the word out. Applications flooded in, and by summer Quabbin Harvest was the top HIP enroller in the state, with more than a hundred households getting fully subsidized fresh fruits and vegetables through the store. On Tuesdays, when the produce was delivered and volunteers showed up to weigh and pack it, the co-op was crowded and lively, overflowing with beautiful fresh food. And the payments from the state helped get us a lot closer to our $6,000-a-week goal. It all felt good.

It *was* good. But there's much more to say about HIP, which is far more radical than it appears at first. To understand why, you have to take a tour of the strange marriage of convenience that undergirds the great majority of American food aid.

You may assume that the goal of food assistance in the United States is to get food to people who need it. You would be wrong. That's *one* goal, certainly. But it's not the only one. Arguably, it's not even the main one. Bear with me while I connect a lot of dots to explain why.

Most Americans are aware by now that an immense amount of food ends up being thrown out, left to spoil, or never harvested.[5] People tend to be appalled by this, and rightly so. But most of us don't really understand why there's so much food to waste in the first place. The truth is that the United States produces far, far more food than is actually needed to feed everyone. We can waste lots of food because we have so much of it, because we produce it so very efficiently. And it's not just the United States. Every region of the world where industrialized food production has taken hold—which is to say, every region of the world— already produces more calories than are needed to keep everyone alive.[6]

How nourishing those calories are is another question. But in some ways it doesn't matter. As a species, on a global level, we're clearly capable of growing all the food we need—even for the projected 9 or 10 billion people who are often held up as the rationale for why we need to figure out how to produce even more. The next time you hear someone say, "But we have to double food production to feed all the people that will be in the world by 2050," tell them it's simply not true. Not only do we already have enough food, we actually have too much food. And the problem is not just that a lot of it gets wasted, although that's bad enough. Overabundance also creates an economic dilemma for farmers, in ways that can be hard for nonfarmers to understand.[7]

When there's an oversupply of something, prices go down. That's market logic. The sensible thing to do, when prices are low, is to produce less or switch to producing something else. That's how markets are supposed to balance out supply and demand.

But farmers can't just switch to something else or scale back when prices fall. When your money is tied up in land and livestock and equipment, you have to keep producing—and producing whatever specific things you're set up for—in order to keep the cash flowing at all. If it's a lean harvest, prices will be high but you may not have enough to meet demand. If it's a bumper year, prices drop and the cost of the labor for harvesting might be more than you can make back from selling your crop. That's market logic too.

That's part of the insoluble koan of trying to mesh a market economy with a food-producing system. It's what drives farmers to try to get big. If you have to grow food to make any money at all, you might as well grow as much of it as you can and roll the dice that the markets and the weather will be on your side that year. It's also what drives farmers out of business, and sometimes to suicide, when they get so far in debt that there's no hope of ever making enough money selling food to get out of it again. That's been the history of American agriculture for the past two centuries, especially the last hundred or so years when industrialization supercharged the whole cycle of growth, efficiency, consolidation, and overproduction. Increasingly, it's the story of agriculture all around the world.

There have been brief moments of balance along the way. New technologies like tractors and silos helped small farmers stay competitive in the early twentieth century. But then the cycle kicked in again and farmers had to buy bigger tractors, taller silos, more cows, more acreage to stay in the game.[8] Before supermarket chains got big enough to dictate terms, they sometimes played nice—agreeing to buy up agricultural surpluses during a bonanza year, for example, and passing the food along to customers at bargain prices. In the Great Depression years of the 1930s, there were periodic sales on whatever was overabundant—peaches one year, grapefruits the next—and for a minute or so everyone got something out of the deal.[9] Policymakers and administrators in the federal government's New Deal agencies had been tying themselves in knots trying to figure out how to solve the problem of agricultural surpluses, and here the supermarkets seemed to have done it for them. The market could work for everyone!

Except it really didn't. By the postwar decades the supermarket chains had managed to withstand a slew of midcentury antitrust challenges and were getting bigger and bigger, to the point that only the largest of farmer cooperatives could still do business with them at all. And by then it was entirely on the supermarkets' terms.[10] So individual farmers and farmers' organizations continued to expand and consolidate too, if they could figure out a way to do it. And they kept producing more and more and more, and making less and less profit. By now, farmers get a very small percentage of the "food dollar" and are producing food at a loss much of the time, often unable to make back their costs no matter what the market may be doing.[11]

It's not only farmers who are overproducing—giant agribusinesses do it as well. But because the giants have managed to get such a stranglehold on the food sector as a whole, they're able to capture the lion's share of those excruciatingly thin slices of profit from selling any specific food. Remember the joke: when you lose money on every sale, you have to make it up in volume. That's what the big food brands and supermarkets do. It's why they're so big, and why they keep getting bigger all the time.

So American farmers overproduce because they're more or less permanently stuck in the red, and agribusinesses overproduce because it's the only way they can actually make money selling food. And government has always been the referee.

Occasionally—mostly during the Depression years, when the whole system really came unglued—government agencies have tackled the destructive effects of market logic head-on. There have sometimes been political efforts to ensure farmers could reach "parity"—prices that are in line with the cost of production. But those efforts have always been contentious and over time they've given way to the "get big or get out" approach famously espoused by Secretary of Agriculture Earl Butz in the 1970s. Overall, politicians and regulators in the United States have followed the national pattern of not wanting to talk too openly—or at all—about market-as-problem. So we've ended up with a convoluted system of subsidies that consumers vaguely realize are skewing things in hard-to-understand ways. We have larger and larger farms that still can't survive without subsidies and a colossal amount of food that piles up and goes to waste in ways that are strangely invisible to most of us.

Thank goodness there are also so many people who can't afford to buy food on their own. This is the marriage of convenience that nobody wants to talk about—"the particular genius of emergency food," in the words of one scholar who has spent decades unraveling the enigma.[12] Surplus food and hungry people are two problems that appear to solve each other, and pairing them has helped to deflect attention from both root causes and actual solutions.

Whenever Americans are forced to see overabundance and need in the same frame—Depression-era "breadlines knee-deep in wheat" or farmers dumping milk and "depopulating" their herds in the early months of the COVID-19 pandemic—they're shocked and mystified all over again. There's a deep feeling that it simply isn't right for this to be happening in the land of plenty.

But there's never really been a robust national conversation about all that surplus food, outside of a few policy and advocacy circles. Over time, and more and more quietly, the people charged with helping farmers stay in business and those who are trying to make sure everyone has enough to eat have redirected some of the surplus toward food aid, some of it at home, some abroad. That's why the great majority of the U.S. Department of Agriculture's budget isn't spent on agriculture but on food assistance—three-quarters of its $200 billion budget in 2022.[13]

Of course, this does help agriculture. It soaks up some—by no means all—of that troublesome surplus. It creates secondary markets for what the market itself can't absorb. People who operate in the domestic wing of that secondary market—the national food banking system and all the pantries and schools and other places that it funnels food to—often talk about trying to "end hunger." But hunger in America is a kind of bizarre solution in itself, or at least an indirect justification for all that extra food. It protects Americans from having to look at the way their food system combines and perpetuates some of the most troublesome features of industrial capitalism while acting as though they're trying to solve both its excesses and its disparities.[14]

Back to Massachusetts and the Healthy Incentives Program. The radical innovation at HIP was to dissolve the marriage of convenience between industrial food and food assistance. Instead, the aid went toward direct purchases from the Massachusetts farmers who were trying to stay afloat economically in a region where the topography, soils, and climate had always placed sharp limits on just how big a farm could get and how competitive it could be in national or global markets.

This wasn't a new idea in Massachusetts. People in the state's policy realm—and especially a man named Gus Schumacher, a Boston-area-farmer-turned-economist-turned-Washington-official—had been more or less connecting the dots for decades among nutrition, poverty, and the farming sector. Starting in the 1980s, Massachusetts provided incentives to people receiving federal food aid so they could shop more affordably at farmers markets, a then-new model that the USDA eventually adopted on a national level. HIP was just a further extension of that.[15]

I say "more or less connecting the dots" because this approach still isn't any kind of serious challenge to either the market logic that originally set the whole cycle in motion or the wealth gap that makes food aid necessary in the first place. You could see it as just another workaround, another way to try to help both those who can't afford good food and farmers who can't make enough money selling it. In some ways, it's the same refusal to talk about market-as-problem, the same insistence that if you just make the right interventions—if you inject public or charitable funds at strategic spots in the supply chains—you might be able to get the equation to balance.

But the *scale* of this intervention was very different. And that's what made HIP more radical, in the sense of coming closer to root causes. By linking low-wealth eaters more directly with the economic well-being of local farmers, it opened the door to a whole new conversation.

That conversation was breathless right from the beginning. Quabbin Harvest wasn't the only HIP venue bowled over by the immediate surge in demand. Around the state, and especially in more densely populated urban and suburban areas, farmers markets were suddenly seeing long lines of new customers buying up every fruit and vegetable in sight. Vendors were running out of stock and struggling with the clunky technology for processing payments from people's electronic benefits cards. And a lot of things were being revealed in a big hurry.[16]

First, the meteoric rise of HIP showed very clearly that poor people were ready and eager to buy good food. It was a powerful corrective to the assumption that they needed to be educated about nutrition first so they would make the right choices. You'll hear this idea all around the nutrition and "food access" fields; Pat and I heard it in some of the conversation circles at the co-op in the year before HIP launched. The implication is that if people aren't eating well, it's because they don't really know what's good for them. The follow-on implication is that those who *do* know (oh, look! it's us, the middle-class, well-educated, white progressives—mostly women—who are so much to the fore in local food projects) are in a position to enlighten others through recipes and cooking lessons and tips for shopping on a budget. That assumption has run through American food assistance projects ever since the dawn of nutrition science, home economics, and similar food reform efforts.[17]

Then, as now, the targets of middle-class reform had their own ideas. The tsunami of new HIP customers proved that people knew perfectly well that it was good to eat fresh fruits and vegetables. They just needed help to be able to afford it. This was Gus Schumacher's foundational epiphany when he was working at his family's stand at a farmers market in Boston. He saw a young mother avidly gathering up fruit from a box of pears that had spilled onto the ground. When the woman explained that as a food stamp recipient she couldn't afford to buy fresh produce, the lightbulb went on for Schumacher. It motivated his long crusade to counter the ways that the interests of food-assistance recipients had become directly pitted, over time, against those of small- and midscale farmers.[18] Schumacher was an economist at heart, and he never lost faith in market-as-solution. But he also didn't shy away from the problems inherent in food-as-commodity, and he thought government had a responsibility to offset them.

A related revelation in the first year of HIP was that distinctions along lines of class and race within the "good food" world went disturbingly deep. There were lots of stories about tensions at the bigger farmers markets, including complaints that the newcomers didn't understand proper market etiquette. They would muscle each other out of the way and handle and squeeze the produce to assess its freshness. Some tried to haggle to get the prices down—unheard of!

The irony, of course, is that many of the new HIP customers were immigrants from places where outdoor food markets and robust face-to-face bargaining are still the norm. All the familiar conventions of the American local food sector—the neat rows of pop-up tents, the leisurely conversations with a farmer or artisan—were shaped by the invisible dominance of the supermarket that the farmers markets had emerged as an alternative to. It was one thing to talk about widening the market for local foods or including "culturally appropriate" fruits and vegetables in those beautifully curated displays. It was quite another for committed and mostly white American locavores and farmers to encounter the less sedate realities of outdoor food marketing in much of the rest of the world.

Some of the complaints came from farmers cut out of the new windfall. Kate Stillman, a livestock farmer from central Massachusetts, was particularly vocal in her criticisms, arguing that the program had cherry-picked one sector of the local food economy and that this was part of a wider demonization of meat and fat. "It's really changed the entire dynamic of the farmers market system," she said, noting that her own sales were down by 75 percent at one of the largest Boston markets where she had sold for years.[19]

A sympathetic podcast host picked up the demonization angle. "How is it okay that we're allowing folks to get twelve-dollar bags of mesclun mix and twenty-dollar tomatoes and saying that that's nutritious but that a steak isn't, when dollar per dollar there's just no comparison in nutrient density value, pound for pound?" she demanded. It was a strange echo of one of the questions that defendants of the mainstream industrial system had been asking for years—that is, whether high-priced boutique foods were a realistic way to nourish people adequately on a large scale.

It's a reasonable question. But it was jarring to hear it from within the local food sector itself, especially when it was prompted by the fact that poorer customers were suddenly able to access those higher-priced items. The word choice—"we're" allowing "them" to get these expensive foods—was particularly revealing. "We" were the hard-working taxpayers, "they" were the people spending our money, and that gave us the right to have an opinion about what they were buying. We were happy that they weren't using it on Twinkies, that long-running target of conservative critiques. But neither did it make sense that they were able to buy expensive mesclun mix, especially if it hurt hard-working farmers raising healthy pasture-based meats. As with the Market Basket uprising three years earlier, there was a powerful defense of a particular and particularly white farming and marketing tradition. Others were welcome to join in and invited to raise their standard of living or seek out their unfamiliar foods as long as they followed the established American-Dream progression. But HIP helped them jump the queue right into the more expensive locavore markets, and not everyone was pleased by that.

At Quabbin Harvest we *were* pleased, and not just for the sudden boost to our cash flow. It felt good to have at least a partial answer to people who saw our store as too expensive. And it was exhilarating to be able to place larger and larger produce orders every week, and to see all that good food going out the door on Tuesdays and Wednesdays.

By late summer, though, the number of HIP shares was already starting to overbalance our hyperlocal supply chains. Julie was finding that she wasn't able to get enough corn from John Moore or enough greens from Seeds of Solidarity to fill all the shares every week, and she had to turn to Squash for more. That wasn't a big problem—she'd been working with Squash on ordering for the weekly share program almost from the beginning. But the surge in demand from HIP meant that "as local as possible" couldn't always be as local as we wanted. And that was the other big revelation from the first heady year of HIP.

With food assistance programs yoked to the industrial surplus of the mainstream food system, there was a kind of equilibrium. The tremendous need was shameful in the richest country on earth. But there was also tremendous overabundance. It was like a barbell with two huge but evenly matched weights. HIP took the weight off the farmer side and replaced it with something like a ball-bearing. It exposed the current limits of Massachusetts's local food capacity, sharpening that question of whether local food could really feed everyone. The answer, clearly, was "no." Or at least "not yet." It showed how much work was still to be done to build a more functional regional food economy. And it laid bare some of the societal fault lines that were likely to complicate that work as it went on.

The new HIP income helped us inch our way toward the $6,000-a-week sales goal. But the abundance of fresh produce streaming into the store every week couldn't mask the fact that the inventory on the shelves was both changing and thinning out. Following the new stocking philosophy, there were more processed and packaged foods from nonlocal companies and fewer everyday staples and truly local products. In truth, there was starting to be less of everything again, a disquieting reminder of how things had looked at the end of the store's first year. We had a custom-made rack for honey and maple syrup from a local distributor and a dedicated shelf for bags of coffee from Dean's Beans, but both frequently sat empty as we waited for enough cash to pay the previous bills and restock. It wasn't a good sign.

And there were other problems. Staff morale seemed low. There were cliques and divisions, a lot of back-channeling and text storms. One staff member was fired, another resigned. Fingers were pointed. Again, personalities and styles inevitably came into it, but so did the fact that the authority structure for the store was anything but clear. Did the management team include the paid team leader? Or did it actually comprise the three super-volunteers—Amy, Karl, and Julie—who supported and consulted with (but maybe also supervised) the team leader? Where did the board of directors come into it? It didn't take a lot of experience for me to see that this was a classic co-op problem: you wanted everyone to feel a sense of ownership and empowerment, but if you decentralized authority too much you ran the risk of the whole thing falling apart.

As tensions around the management structure started to be really palpable, I went back to the bylaws and discovered that we were supposed to have a personnel committee to stay on top of staffing issues. Quickly we reconvened one and found ourselves meeting more often than any of us had quite expected to. It became an extension of my ongoing listening tour as staff and volunteers shared their own analyses and ideas about what should be done—ideas that still went in every possible direction with no kind of center or consensus.

I remember coming out of one meeting and finding Karl changing a fluorescent tube in the upstairs hallway. "Everybody in this place lives in their own separate version of reality!" I said.

Karl gave me his little philosophical smile. "Welcome to the party," he said.

The sense of being at an impasse, not really able to move forward *or* back, infected everything. Once again there were desperate, long-shot proposals, people retreating into themselves, further cuts to expenses that had already been pared down. On slow days we started scheduling only a single staff member per shift, which made the store feel desolate and unwelcoming. If that single staff member called out, as increasingly happened, we sometimes had to close altogether.

To me, that was the death-knell of any business. If people couldn't count on you being open when they came to spend money, why on earth would they keep coming back? The board floated whatever ideas we could think of. What if we trained a few more super-volunteers who could run the cash register? Wasn't that what co-ops had always done?

But it turned out that labor law had moved on since the old "hey, kids, let's have a grocery store" days. In 2017 we risked running afoul of workers compensation laws if we had volunteers doing jobs that we would otherwise be paying people to do. Volunteer cashiers were a nonstarter.

Merchandising was the next frontier. As Thanksgiving approached in November, stock in the store had dwindled dangerously low, and staff hadn't had the heart or time or initiative to try to make the place look even moderately festive. Sales should have been rising as the holidays got closer, but they were headed in the other direction. Amy Borezo and I formed a merchandising committee with the team leader to try to turn that around. There were more meetings, more circular conversations, more dead-ends where we ran up against the fact that we simply didn't have any money to work with.

We did manage to get some seasonal decorations up on the outside of the building. Pat Larson wrangled a crew of volunteers; a neighboring family came with all their kids and helped; Julie Davis, whose supermarket experience had included running an in-store florist, made evergreen swags and filled the big wooden tubs outside the store entrance with fresh pine boughs. We participated in the Chamber of Commerce's annual late-night holiday shopping spree one Saturday, with volunteers staying until midnight and Christmas carolers dropping by. Nalini came to visit too, looking happier and healthier after a couple of rounds of chemotherapy. Like the decorating party and the Tuesday share-packing shifts, it was a moment when the imagined reality felt real, when you could see that the store not only reflected a community of people but was helping to create one. The feeling that we were making things up as we went along made me nervous. But at least we were still moving.

Around us, Orange was being transformed and retransformed. Filming for the television series had started at the end of the summer, and for each successive visit the set-dressers were recreating a different decade so the show could flash back and forth through Castle Rock's tortured history. Barber poles and a faint "ghost sign" for Schlitz beer evoked the 1960s, a video store the 1980s, strangely reminiscent of the actual succession of downtown businesses over the decades.

In Castle Rock, most of the stores were closed. Awnings were taken down and replaced with dusty, mold-streaked ones. The building next to the co-op, which had recently gotten a new coat of paint, was repainted to look dingy and decrepit. A cheerful mural on the side of the outfitter store in the center of Orange was covered over to look like a boarded-up hardware store; ironically, it was next door to what had actually been a hardware store until the 1990s. For the television version of the 1990s, there was a sushi restaurant, which caused a mild stir among those who weren't in the know. "Did you see there's a sushi place opening up in Orange? And it's going to be open until 11 on Fridays and Saturdays?"

One of the New Home Sewing Machine Company buildings on the river, still known to many residents as the needle factory, became the Castle Rock Police Station. The actual police were deeply involved in the logistics for filming days. There were detailed maps and schedules and well-organized rerouting of traffic around the shooting locations. It was like being occupied by a benign military force, with drones overhead and street signs removed and a small army of people walking around, carrying equipment, standing in huddles, endlessly waiting and then suddenly snapping into action. There were some sightings of movie stars. Night filming lit up the dark, vertiginous streets behind the town hall. During filming for a scene where the woods were on fire, Julie Davis looked out her front window and saw a flaming animatronic deer bounding down the street.

Quabbin Harvest was cast as Hemphill's Market ("Grocery–Bakery–Deli–Butcher"). The faded red awnings that replaced our own on filming days were as grubby as all the others, but the store was intended to seem fully functional, or as functional as anything can be in a town possessed by evil. For the 1960s, the set-dressers applied retro-looking window signs that spoke volumes about what present-day designers thought small-scale grocery retail had been like back in the day when it had actually been possible. "Heirloom tomatoes $5 per pound," one sign read. "Organic zucchini $1 each." Never mind that the terms "heirloom" and "organic" didn't start appearing in grocery stores until decades later. In 2017 they evoked a simpler time and a simpler food system, and that was close enough for TV.

But there was concern about the price points. A jovial artisan spent a whole afternoon in the store adjusting the signs to something closer to what the set-designers imagined to be reality. He was happy to have me watch him at work and to chat about his company, which specialized in making places look dilapidated on film. I wondered what it cost to repaint even a single building to look shabby and then restore it again when filming was over, but it felt awkward to ask too directly. When the adjustments were made and the window signs reinstalled—now saying four dollars a pound for heirloom tomatoes instead of five—it did occur to me that this tidbit of faux historical detail might well have cost most of what we were trying to bring in every week in sales. It was a lesson in perspective: there was a lot more money to be made pretending to sell groceries than in actually doing it.

I can trace a straight line from that day in 2017 to a day almost exactly seventy years earlier when the Minute Tapioca Company was celebrating its fiftieth anniversary. The actual anniversary had happened during World War II, when the Orange plant was churning out dehydrated potatoes and K-rations as part of the war effort. Imports of tapioca flour were cut off after Japan occupied Java, and it wasn't until 1947 that executives negotiated a new source of supply from cassava plantations then being carved out of the rainforests in Brazil. In September 1947 the war was

FIGURE 7. A set-designer amends produce prices on a sign for "Hemphill's Market" during filming for the Hulu series *Castle Rock* in Orange, September 2017.

—Photograph by the author

won, the soldiers back home, the plant gearing up to make its signature product again. Everyone was ready for a party.

It was, the local newspaper said, "the grandest clambake in the history of the company."[20] Like many corporations, Minute Tapioca owned a piece of land that it used for employee recreation, an eighty-six-acre pleasure-ground east of the center of town along the river, known locally as "the Ranch." For the fiftieth anniversary, the company rented a huge tent and gathered several hundred current and former employees, including Eben Gridley, the past president who made the first scouting trip for an industrial-scale source of tapioca as a young man back in 1911.

The guest of honor was the chair of General Foods' board, Clarence Francis. Francis was a true captain of industry, a fierce Cold Warrior at the forefront of the twinned battles to keep U.S. food production growing and to deal with the problems that continual growth was causing. It wasn't just that he was the head of one of the largest food companies in the world or that he'd been tapped during the New Deal and the war to lend his expertise to the economic recovery and mobilization for military victory. His entire career had tracked the ascendancy of industrial foods and American agribusiness. At the turn of the twentieth century, as an Amherst College student hoping for a summer job with Standard Oil, he had accidentally walked into the New York offices of the Corn Products Refining Company and found himself getting into the food business instead.[21]

The line between food and oil was already being blurred. American geneticists moved the first hybrid corn seeds onto the market just in time for World War I, part of a surge in food production that temporarily replaced the shattered agricultural economies in much of Europe. Francis's first employer was in the thick of things, developing new starches, sweeteners, and other products that in turn helped stimulate the growth of other sectors like processed foods, pharmaceuticals, meat production, and mass-market publishing (corn products are an important binder in papermaking). They're still doing it: a hundred years after Clarence Francis entered their New York office by mistake, the Corn Products Refining Company opened the world's largest tapioca processing facility in Thailand.[22] In 2012 the company changed its name to Ingredion, reflecting the fact that what it really makes is components for making other things, in exactly the same way that New England's metal-working companies made tools and machines that people used to manufacture other things. On some level, it's all just widgets, and a full-scale industrial economy doesn't run without a lot of them.

With the recent turn toward biofuels, everything comes full circle. Petroleum turbocharged the whole cycle of growth, bigness, overproduction. Farmers could—and often felt they had to—grow more and more of the higher-yielding new crop varieties. Petroleum-based fertilizers made it possible to keep doing it on soils stripped of their natural fertility. Bigger tractors and harvesters helped. When overabundance drove prices down below the farmers' costs of production, the government provided subsidies to keep the agricultural sector going—but only for the major commodity crops, mostly the grains. The cold chain, the highway system, and long-distance trucking all played roles.

At this point we're pouring about thirteen calories of energy, most of it from fossil fuels, into each and every calorie of food energy that comes out of our food system, including the ones that die in landfills or get turned into industrial ingredients that don't provide much in the way of actual nourishment.[23] It's nonsensical. The whole point of growing food is to fuel ourselves, but we've created a food system that actually serves as a sink for our own uncontrolled growth while pumping out greenhouse gases that are destabilizing the ecosystems that food production depends on. And now we're putting the surplus calories back into our cars and trucks and tractors in the form of biofuels that are touted as a partial answer to the climate-altering emissions from burning the fossil fuels that jacked this whole system to the level it's now at. This is capitalism literally eating itself alive, refusing to admit it has a problem, and desperately looking for ways to keep the cycle going.[24]

You probably already know some or all of this. Clarence Francis knew most of it too, although he wasn't around to see the current state of things. He died in 1985 at age ninety-seven, a day after he got to shake Ronald Reagan's hand in a White House newly rededicated to letting the market have its own way. But even in a world where only the blindest or most deluded can still deny the connections between the burning of fossil fuels and the destabilized planetary climate, Francis would probably tell you—as many people still do—that keeping the cycle going is our only option. He accepted that there were problems inherent in industrial capitalism, and he spent his career figuring out how to keep those problems from slowing down the American engines of commerce.

In 1924 he went to work for Postum, then well along to road to becoming a multisector agribusiness. When the company ran short of its usual raw materials during World War I and its partner corporations were pulled into the war effort, its CEO complained that the government was "practically trying to put us out of business." But Postum's wartime experiments with cheaper grains and grinding its own flour turned out to be quite profitable. And they led to new spinoffs. By the time Francis joined them, the CEO noted that "we found ourselves in the chicken-feeding business, food for cattle, oils, everything you can think of."[25] It was a big step toward what has been called the "feed-meat complex," the pairing of cheap (subsidized) corn and other grains with the livestock industry.[26] Like hungry people, it turned out, animals' bodies could serve as a sink, transforming surplus crops into higher-value products, some of which had the added benefit of signifying prosperity and status for many eaters. Affordable meat was one of the things that made supermarkets so integral to the dream—and reality—of socioeconomic mobility in twentieth-century America.

Postum's acquisition spree in the 1920s made plenty of room for an ambitious young executive who understood that his job was to keep the cycle of growth churning. By the time Postum changed its name to General Foods, Francis was its vice president of sales. He was there when the company bought Minute Tapioca in 1926, and I get the sense, reading his speech from the fiftieth-anniversary party in 1947, that he had a particular fondness for the company, and for the town of Orange.

"You cannot come to a group such as this without being refreshed," he told the crowd assembled under the big tent at the Ranch. "I believe that people in communities such as this think a lot more sensibly and a lot straighter than the people in the big metropolitan areas where they are subject to high pressure and different pulls."

Some of those pulls were toward the socialistic idea that government ought to play a very active role in refereeing and rectifying the imbalances within the nation's economy, including its ever more industrialized and corporatized food sector. Francis had no time for that. He served as a consultant to Franklin Roosevelt's National Recovery Administration in the early days of the New Deal, but he shared his CEO's certainty that government's true role was to do what it could to support the business leaders who really knew how to manage an industrial economy. The geopolitics of the Second World War, with its renewed opportunities for America to export both surplus foods and political ideas, was more aligned with Francis's brand of capitalism. He'd seen the nascent agribusiness sector figuring out how to generate profits from ever-cheaper, ever-more-abundant food crops after the First World War, and he was confident that should be the way of the future.

As for the surplus food problem, that could be solved with purposeful cultivation of more new export markets. Francis and others like Nelson Rockefeller, whose family foundation and fortune were already underwriting some of those global export ventures, found solid niches for themselves within the Truman and Eisenhower administrations. In the 1950s Francis was asked to chair the new Interagency Committee on Agricultural Surplus Disposal, a baldly revealing title for a group whose functions were soon folded into the more benign-sounding Office of Food for Peace. That office remains the federal government's main conduit for food assistance programs that export some of the persistent oversupply of food.[27]

Never mind that farmers at home were struggling with below-cost prices and those abroad were starting to cry foul with accusations that low-priced American imports were undercutting their own farm economies. Francis and his fellow titans of industry knew you couldn't make omelets without breaking eggs. Markets were inherently volatile and uneven; you just had to stay the course and behave rationally instead of running to the government for help whenever there was a problem.

In 1947 Francis was on the stump circuit with the message that people needed to calm the heck down about inflation and continued postwar shortages. Everything would even out in time, he promised. Food prices might indeed be rising, but he assured the National Restaurant Association in a speech earlier that year that "the law of supply and demand is waiting at the head of the stairs to push them back."[28]

His speech in Orange ran along the same lines. "These depressions and these recessions are man-made and there are a good many people in this world who believe because they are man-made that they can be stopped," he said. To Francis, that was interfering unnecessarily in the natural workings of the market. His advice? "If we will just be courageous, I think we can avoid depressions. Do not get panicky when you see things starting down a bit. I think it is purely idealistic to think that you will never have decline, to think that everything will always go up. And when it does come, if we can keep our sense of balance we can defeat it. In the main I think we are going to get along."

It was a message that resonated in Orange. Earlier in the year, the local paper printed a jubilant editorial about the end of the interventionist policies of the 1930s. "Working under the handicap of government controls for so long, managements will welcome an opportunity to produce under conditions which resemble more the freedom about which there has been so much said and so little done for a long time," the writer crowed. "With New Deal influences lifted at Washington it should be full speed ahead without some government agent sneaking in to throw sand in the carburetor. Orange is fortunate in having industries which have consideration for their employees and who try to promote a friendly working spirit. There are no union affiliations and no continual strikes."[29]

In other words, if people just let the market do what it did naturally, all would be well. It's an argument that carries a lot of weight in the United States in the era of neoliberal economics that Ronald Reagan's presidency ushered in.[30] And it remains ascendant elsewhere too, of course. It's the same hope that Nalini Goordial saw in her youth among Indo-Guyanese people clinging to the deceptive promises of colonialism or that Dean Cycon encounters all around the coffee lands where Indigenous growers desperately try to attach themselves to the promised benefits of global markets.

But there's something particularly American about the almost religious quality of this belief in capitalism. It touches some peculiarly sensitive bundle of nerves here, prompting the oh-we're-not-going-to-change-that-so-let's-not-even-talk-about-it response that always makes me feel like an alien again. You can feel how determined people are to keep believing in a system that has repeatedly let them down. If I were a psychologist rather than an anthropologist, I might say there's something fundamentally abusive about the relationship between Americans and their economic system, something that makes it feel impossible to leave or to change and that insists on seeing the bad times as aberrations and the good ones as the happy normal state that we just have to get back to. Again, this isn't unique to America, but it seems woven into the national mythos here in a way that gives it its powerful and persistent charge. And it's not unrelated to all that cheap meat in the supermarket cases and the way that towns and cities continue to chase the next economic development trend to fill the empty spaces left by the departure of earlier ones.

It must have felt immensely reassuring to have one of the high priests of American capitalism come to Orange and give this industrial trajectory his personal blessing. "You cannot be wondering about this country," Clarence Francis told the audience under the big white tent in 1947. "Have faith in the future, faith in the country, and I think it is going to come out all right."

This is the vision that a lot of people have in their minds when they yearn to make America great again, the one that motivated the Market Basket mutineers of 2014 to defend the idea that you could put people before profits yet still turn a handsome profit while keeping prices low, the reason so many people in towns like Orange voted for Donald Trump

in 2016. In 1947 Orange was a place where you could believe wholeheart-
edly that all of this could be sustained. You just had to not look too hard
at all the evidence to the contrary, like the Great Depression that the
country had just come through or the New Home Sewing Machine buildings that had defined the town for four decades but now stood empty.
People in Orange were gambling that General Foods would prove more
faithful, and Clarence Francis's speech must have felt like a renewal of
that vow.

The renewed vows were sealed after the picnic when the company's
executives got onto a Boston-bound train together to meet a ship that
had just arrived with the first postwar shipment of tapioca flour from
Brazil. More than a million pounds of it came back on the train to Orange,
enough to get the plant back up and running at full capacity.

In 2017 it was much harder to keep believing the promises that corporations made to communities. In neighboring Athol, the town's major
tool-making firm continued to be an industry leader but only because
it had moved much of its manufacturing to China. In 2015 Orange lost
the last—and oldest—of its industrial plants, one that had specialized in
making things like water turbines that let other companies make other
things. There was no longer a local paper in Orange, a sign of the media
consolidation that paralleled what was happening in so many other sectors. But the nearby paper that had taken over the North Quabbin beat
editorialized in much the same bitter tone that the old Orange one had
used when General Foods did, in fact, eventually abandon the town.

"Promised a deepening of [a] relationship . . . that stretched back 175
years, Orange today finds such pledges hold no water," the paper said
bluntly. The new owners, based in Wisconsin but controlled by a global
private equity firm, had said all the right things when they came to town.
But it took only five years for those promises to prove hollow. The paper
hoped that Orange could find its way forward, "hopefully with help from
business owners who keep their commitments."[31]

By 2017 the property was sold to a company based in India, which soon
resumed operations on a much smaller scale, paying quite well but not
creating any permanent jobs. This was just-in-time supply-chain capitalism, a world where almost anything—even industrial abandonment
itself—could be turned into a product for the voracious, capricious,
ever-expanding market. In 2017 Orange was Castle Rock, a place where

nobody had any idea what an heirloom tomato should cost but where there were a lot people who couldn't afford one without help from a government program and where a lot of other people were excited to be turned into a simulacrum, a stage set, because it was a way to remember—or maybe just to imagine, even briefly—what prosperity felt like.

It was preposterous to imagine that an actual small-scale grocery store could possibly succeed in such a time and place. But to those of us involved with the co-op it seemed equally unimaginable not to have some kind of alternative to the relentless and ever shorter cycle of booms and busts, courtship and breakup, extraction and abandonment. As I looked toward my second year as a participant-observer in the grocery business, I was beginning to have a sense that keeping this venture alive was going to require walking some kind of fine line between denial and determination.

"Anyone who takes even a cursory look at our books knows we're going down," Karl Bittenbender said at one board meeting toward the end of the year. "We're the only ones who refuse to know it."

How can you refuse to know something while simultaneously trying to do something about it? That was the paradox we needed to exist within as we started into our fourth year in the old bank.

CHAPTER 9

MARGINS

THE SUDDEN SUCCESS of the Healthy Incentives Program helped Quabbin Harvest reach its sales goal and unlock the second half of the grant that had rescued the store the previous year. It was enough to keep us going as we started into 2018.

But it also masked the fact that regular cash-register sales were continuing to fall. I came into the back office one morning to find the team leader staring bleakly at a computer screen showing the previous week's numbers: barely above $3,000. We knew there was always a post-holiday slump and things would probably pick up again as we got into the spring, but the number was still shocking. It was one thing for the grant to be stabilizing things as we worked toward higher sales. It was another to realize it might be nothing more than a form of life-support.

I was still holding onto the hope that I could draw some clear boundaries around my role as the board chair, staying on the big-picture level and not letting this volunteer position encroach too far on the time and concentration I needed for my actual job at the other end of the state. The new semester was just starting and I was back in the thick of things. I was aware of the irony of trying to keep my involvement in the food system from interfering too much with teaching a class called "Practicing in Food Systems." But I was still compartmentalizing as much as I could, trying to pick and choose from among the ton of bricks that had to land somewhere if the store was going to keep going at all. It felt like that should be enough.

And this, my friends, is what marked me as a very typical white, middle-class person who had never actually had to survive outside the parts of the world that are set up to respond to my needs and wants. Even in my more impecunious younger days, things never came down to life-or-death, make-or-break choices. It's a very cushioned kind of existence, a nice way to live.

As I started to get further into my second year of participant-observation involvement at the co-op, that comfortable cushion got pulled away. Part of it was coming face to face with the implacable realities of business. And the business world in general is inexorable enough; operating a small business that loses money year after year is much, much harder.

This became clearer after Karl brokered a meeting with a colleague who offered to help the board come to a better understanding of the financial mess we were in. Karl was a doer and a cheerleader, not a teacher—or rather, he was the kind of teacher who hands you something to read and lets you go off on your own to puzzle your way to enlightenment. That approach can be generous and life-changing. But it wasn't working with a board and staff caught between our own lack of financial expertise and the anxiety of hearing over and over again how much trouble we were in.

Karl's friend Seth had a different style. Seth was the kind of person who can break things down into comprehensible smaller pieces and help you build up some kind of understanding from there. He'd been involved in food co-ops since the days of the early hippie-anarchist efforts in the Connecticut River Valley, the ones where Squash Trucking had gotten its start. Even then, he'd been the quiet voice of experience and reason insisting that you had to pay attention to what the numbers were telling you. A friend from one of the long-ago valley co-ops once commented to him, "You always manage to find these little parcels of reality and apply them somehow," no small feat amid the swirl of emotions and philosophies and personalities that tend to surround food co-ops.

Seth came to a board meeting at the end of January and asked us some seemingly simple questions that helped me start to think about our problems in a different way. How much money did we actually need to bring in every week in order to break even? That figure was still somewhat elusive, but Karl estimated that $8,500 a week would do it. Seth took the gap between that figure and what we were making now and asked us how many more shoppers would need to add twenty dollars a week to their purchases to make up the difference.

The math was simple. So was the conclusion. We were still a *very* long way from generating the sales we needed.

It should have been deflating, but somehow it wasn't. For one thing, it felt much more concrete than the $6,000-a-week lump sales goal of the previous year. We had X customers spending an average of Y dollars each week. Seth's calculations showed us that we needed this to increase by Z amount. It was possible to visualize what that meant and to imagine talking with other people about it. These numbers had a kind of action plan built into them. Instead of sitting dumbly receiving the bad financial news, everyone on the board suddenly started generating ideas for messaging, imagery, strategy, timing. We could launch a member challenge campaign, with a phone bank and signage and handouts in the store. We could make this the centerpiece of the annual meeting, coming up in a couple of months. We could list the different ways a person could add twenty dollars a week to their shopping. We keyed off the older "Shop Co-op First" campaign and brainstormed specific tips for *how* to shop co-op first: for example, be flexible and adapt your shopping based on what you found at the co-op, rather than sticking rigidly to your list and heading to the supermarket in a snit if you didn't find everything.

We didn't actually say "snit." But when I eventually wrote all of this up into a set of campaign materials, the message was fairly blunt. "Supporting small businesses," one of our handouts stated, "often means resisting the convenience of large corporate chain stores." It touched on the pain points that Karl had been telling us we couldn't keep avoiding forever, but it didn't press too hard, walking that fine line between preaching and persuading.

Seth's breakdown of the numbers also made it clear that while we were doing all of this our unpaid and deferred bills were going to continue piling up at a perilous rate. And this is where it actually helped that so many of us on the board were from the nonprofit and educational and arts worlds. It seemed perfectly obvious that we were going to need to do some old-fashioned fundraising. So we started to plan for that too.

In some ways this was the easy part, at least for me. The hard part started when the team leader resigned early in the year to take another job and the store was suddenly without anyone to manage the day-to-day operations.

My first call was to Julie Davis to see if she would take over ordering inventory and stocking the store in the short term while the personnel committee figured out what to do about staffing. It was a huge relief when she said yes.

Staffing fell to me because there didn't seem to be anyone else to do it. After an astonishing amount of texting, I managed to get a month's worth of shifts scheduled with our part-time workers, most of whom were also juggling other part-time jobs. I started waking up every night worrying about what would happen if someone couldn't make it to cover their shift on a day that I had to be at work in Boston—not that I really knew enough about opening, closing, and running the store to be able to fill in for them if I had to.

Fortunately I didn't have to, because from the very first week it felt as though the not-quite-a-manager role was fitting around Julie Davis like the proverbial glove. Nalini said to me later, "Julie was always meant to be the person running this store." The moment just hadn't been right for her to do it.

As soon as she took over the ordering again, there was a sense of things shifting in the right direction. She started strategically rebalancing the stock, bringing back the staple foods that a lot of members were looking for along with the local items that were always going to give us whatever slim competitive advantage we might have. Some farmers and other vendors were permanently soured on the co-op by this point, or at least leery about committing too much product without knowing when or if they might get paid. But others were willing to keep going farther out on a limb with us, despite the mounting bills. From the dismal low in January, sales started to rebound as soon as Julie was back on board.

I remember the day I found Julie in the grocery aisle of the store and said, "God, I wish you wanted this job," and she said she thought she could actually take it on now. I don't think I literally fell to my knees and wept with gratitude, but that's how it feels in my memory.

I don't mean to overdramatize this. But it was a crucial moment in my relationship to the co-op, a turning point that's central to what I'm trying to say about making fundamental change in the food system, and I want to try to make it clear what it was that shifted for me and why I think it matters.

It wasn't that everything started to be fine because we finally had the right person managing the store. In fact, a lot of things kept getting worse.

Not long after Julie joined the staff, the Healthy Incentives Program (HIP) was canceled without warning, eliminating a now-vital chunk of the co-op's cash flow. Enrollments had been continuing to rise as word spread about the program. There were farmers around the state already planting in anticipation of continued growth in HIP sales in the coming season, and farmers market managers making plans for the kind of explosive growth some markets had experienced in 2017. Behind the scenes, though, administrators had been scrambling to deal with the fact that the amount allocated for the first three years of incentives had been used up in the dramatic success of the first few months. The funding infrastructure at the state level hadn't been solidified yet, and there was simply no more money to keep the program going. HIP seemed to be a victim of its own success.

Julie called me with the news while I was on the commuter train on the way home after a long day at work. It was the first time I realized she and I had the same basic response to calamity: regroup fast, come up with a Plan B, carry on. There wasn't really a good Plan B in this case but we talked over some options: contact our state reps in the morning, find a way to add this to our fundraising pitch in the longer term.

It wasn't until 2 a.m. when I woke up abruptly with my heart banging against my chest wall that I realized how hard another big brick had just landed on me. Or rather, on us—I was truly becoming a part of "us" now, for better and worse.

Even with the upturn in sales, our unpaid bills were engulfing everything. And they just kept on coming. The big inefficient freezers used nearly $2,000 worth of electricity every month and the electric company was starting to send demand notices, then shutoff warnings. I started to get phone calls at home from some of our local vendors who had somehow gotten my number. This felt annoying at first, then depressing as I realized that they too were financially stressed and needed to call in whatever payments they could get their hands on by whatever means possible.

That didn't mean we could pay them, though. One of our new board members, a young woman recently returned to the area after college, had gamely agreed to take on the treasurer role as Karl started to step away from it. But she had no clear sense of what she was walking into, and she was already starting to have a deer-in-the-headlights look as the bills kept coming and there was simply no money to cover them. I asked MaryEllen Kennedy, a longtime volunteer who had also recently joined the board, if she would be part of the finance team to give the new treasurer some moral support. MaryEllen didn't have a background in finance either—like Nalini, she'd worked in the tech sector—but she was staunchly devoted to the co-op and wanted to help. There was enough awfulness to go around, and I figured we needed as many people as we could find who were willing to shoulder a part of it.

As the spring went on, the awfulness was amplified by the trial of the two young people who had committed the double murder in Orange eighteen months earlier. It was big news in a small area and the local papers covered it in excruciating detail. Every article rehashed the whole miserable saga and added fresh particulars that meant families and friends had to relive things over and over again. Karl attended the trial every day, feeling duty-bound to be there. He came back to Orange in the afternoons looking gray and drawn, his usual sparkle utterly extinguished.

In late spring, while I was in Canada visiting my family, I got another urgent call from Julie. The electric company had given us a shutoff deadline of that day at 12:30, and she hadn't been able to reach anybody on the finance team or the board to figure out what to do, not that there was any money to do anything with anyway. I knew we couldn't let them cut the power, so I started making phone calls. I reached the utility company number Julie had been given and told them I would make a payment with my credit card. I could work out the details with the co-op later. They took the number, then called back a few minutes later to say that the payment wouldn't be fully processed for another day, so it wasn't enough to stop the shutoff. We argued about this for a bit. Julie tried arguing from her end. The lightbulb finally went on when the voice on the other end of the line said I could pay in bitcoin if I could get myself to an ATM that handled it. By that point Julie's instincts had kicked in too and she'd done some quick sleuthing. It was a scam, and we'd come very close to falling for it. I canceled my credit card and reflected that this is what desperation did to your brain. When the next crisis is always just one phone call or demand notice away, you don't have the luxury of careful reflection.

In a lot of ways the shift that was underway in my relationship to the co-op that year was all about moving farther away from convenience and choice toward real mutualism, the lifeblood of co-operative and communitarian projects of all kinds. I'm not sure what I expected that to feel like, but it was much harder and a lot less fun than I'd imagined.

The four young mothers who formed the core organizing group for the North Quabbin Community Co-operative in 2009 hadn't needed to start a co-op to access good food, including from local producers. They could drive around to area farmstands or go to the farmers market in season; they could go a little farther afield and shop at one of the valley co-ops or Whole Foods. By the 2010s, even Walmart and Market Basket had some organic produce, if you didn't mind that it came from thousands of miles away. Quabbin Harvest's founders, like people at many white-led food co-ops, were motivated more by ideas than necessity.

But at bottom the ideas were essentially the same ones that have spurred countless less-well-resourced people to pursue projects of mutual aid and food-sharing and community-centered economic development— people in immigrant enclaves collecting funds for medical or funeral costs, consortia of Black-owned businesses publishing directories to keep more capital circulating within their own communities, Indigenous groups building cultural resilience strategies around traditional foods, miners and industrial workers pooling their resources to buy better-quality provisions than they could get at the company store.[1] Those ideas are about consolidating resources within your own community and giving people a stake in deciding how to get and share the things they want and need. At bottom it's about taking more power over the conditions of your own life, often including how and what you eat.

Here's the thing about taking on more power. When you actually have it, and if you're using it for the right reasons, it just feels like responsibility. That's a truism but nevertheless true. Most things about modern middle-class life don't equip you to deal very well with this level of responsibility for the bare necessities of life, with actual obligatory mutualism and social encumberedness. Except in family life, and sometimes not even then, modern middle-class humans have been able to live in a way that provides—or at least gives the illusion of providing—an enormous amount of autonomy and choice. Stepping away from that is what feels so hard for many of us to do.

As I started into that unlearning process in a more serious way in 2018, some of my family and friends started to remark that maybe I had taken on more than I could really handle. Maybe I should step back. My actual job was demanding enough. Did I really need all this additional stress?

But I knew the bricks I'd picked up would just fall on someone else, and how could I do that to Julie, to Karl, to MaryEllen, to Pat? Even with a lot of people working together in a more or less concerted way, things were still so gappy and fragile. It wasn't that I thought the co-op would fall apart if I wasn't involved. But it seemed very possible that it would fall apart faster if any of us pulled away when we were teetering on the edge.

And I was entangled in this web of mutuality not only with the people at the co-op itself. There were also our local vendors, businesses like Squash. Astonishingly, given how small and fragile we felt, we had become Squash's largest organic customer, an actually significant node in that still-patchy landscape of regional food supply. Eric Stocker, Squash's CEO, was one of the people who sometimes called me at home to see when we might possibly be able to pay some of our back bills, and it was hard to keep putting him off when I knew there were people calling *him* to demand payment in turn.

I asked Eric later how much our cash flow woes had hurt Squash, and he was philosophical but frank. "It's like if somebody punches me in the eye. It's not going to kill me," he said, "but it's still going to hurt me." And it hurt me in turn every week that we weren't able to send Squash a check. Pain, it turned out, was integral to mutuality—who knew?

We were deeply embroiled with Mount Grace Land Conservation Trust too, in complicated ways. Mount Grace and the co-op had signed a ten-year lease when the land trust bought the old bank in 2014. The assumption was that we would pay rent at a steadily increasing rate as the store became more financially viable and would be in a position to buy the building outright at the end of the lease term. By 2018 it was clear just how overly optimistic those projections had been.

Some people at the land trust were still deeply committed to the co-op's mission and saw the store as an important complement to the farmland preservation work Mount Grace was doing. Others were convinced we were a drag on the organization and that they should cut their losses as soon as they could, even if it meant a greater likelihood that the co-op would go under. Still others worried that if we went bankrupt they would be stuck with a hard-to-rent commercial building halfway between a bank and a grocery store in a mostly empty downtown. The land trust was going through a leadership transition of its own and things felt very unsettled.

As we tiptoed around the big questions with Mount Grace I started to realize how hard it was to convey the brutally unforgiving economics of the grocery sector to people who had never tried to operate inside of it. To our detractors we just looked like a little business that didn't seem to be able to generate enough money to cover our bills. People gravitated to the obvious explanations: we must be selling the wrong things, we were in a market area that just couldn't support our kind of store, we were trying to operate with too much debt or not enough capital, we didn't know what we were doing, maybe all of the above.

None of those things was completely untrue. But looking to the store itself for the root causes of our problems missed the whole vast sea of cheapness and bigness we were trying to swim in. It missed the point that it's nearly impossible to make money selling groceries except at the largest of scales or the most niche of ways. It overlooked the stark calculus of price and margin: of every dollar's worth of groceries you sell, you get to keep, on average, about thirty cents, and those accumulated 30 percent bits are all you have to work with when it comes time to pay your bills—payroll, rent, utilities, advertising, loans. If you let those bills eat up all of the margin, you have nothing left to buy more inventory. So if you're operating below profitability, you can't possibly pay all your bills if you want to keep operating at all.

It's even harder if you're selling things that are inherently not cheap—meat and eggs from pasture-raised animals on small farms, high-quality ice cream, real maple syrup, organic vegetables from small- or midscale growers. But even with regular groceries from industrial food supply chains, anyone buying at a tiny scale, as Quabbin Harvest was, can't get the price breaks that larger stores—and especially whole chains of stores—can command from their suppliers. When well-meaning people with no sense of the economics of the grocery business tried to help us figure out what was wrong with the store, Julie often pointed out that she could go to Hannaford or Market Basket, buy a lot of the items we carried on our shelves, mark them up 30 percent, and they would *still* be cheaper than our current prices. In fact, some small and community-owned grocery stores have been driven to doing exactly that, sourcing from big-box stores and industrial surplus outlets in order to stay stocked at all. But we were trying to do something different, something that could survive outside the logic of bigness and cheapness.

With supermarkets continuing to bring their huge economies of scale to bear on foods that had once been available only in what used to be called health-food stores, it was harder and harder for the alternatives to stay competitive. People who saw Quabbin Harvest as hapless or unrealistic probably didn't know that by 2018, even many of the much larger, well-established, and well-run food co-ops in the Connecticut River Valley were operating below profitability, wrestling with ever-increasing market pressures from Whole Foods at the high end of the grocery sector and Walmart at the low end.[2] And don't forget the logic of cheapness: you can't simply raise prices, even in a more prosperous market area. Most people, whether they admit it or not, and whether they need to or not, are looking for the lowest prices they can get on their food. When Amazon bought Whole Foods in 2017, you frequently heard the comment that maybe this would bring down the prices at a chain that even many of its faithful shoppers referred to as Whole Paycheck.[3]

It was other people's incomprehension about the fundamentals of selling food that finally helped me understand the line I had crossed myself. This wasn't just about supporting an alternative: it was about taking on more of the actual day-to-day responsibilities for keeping the alternative alive. And there was a very big difference between the two. The fact that this was "alternative" was central to why it was so hard. Quabbin Harvest was trying to do and be something that the whole mainstream food economy not only didn't support but actively worked against. We were trying to swim against that riptide of bigness and cheapness while somehow making enough money to stay afloat.

That's what was so revelatory for a white, middle-class person like me who had never truly had to struggle against the mainstream world. I'd been out of sync with it in many ways since childhood, standing back and observing and pondering its many strangenesses, resisting most of capitalism's obvious avenues and markers of success, content to stay on its artsy and academic fringes. But fundamentally I believed that the system would work for me if I played by its rules. And I assumed that even at its most maddening and obtuse, it wasn't actually out to get me. Until I became a participant-observer in a grocery store, I had no idea what it felt like to exist within a vast, entrenched structure that's been set up in a way that's directly antithetical to your own ability to thrive.

It was not welcome knowledge at first. It felt inexorable and unfair, and it impinged on my taken-for-granted autonomy in all sorts of ways. It was often depressing, occasionally terrifying. But it also started to make some new connections clearer.

For one thing, it made me realize that the way we were managing at the co-op, just staving off whatever bills we could, trying to keep the store stocked and the lights on, was simply how things were on the margins. In fact, it was how most farmers coped all the time with the insoluble puzzle of making money in the modern food economy. I remember listening to a spring 2018 radio news story about a farmer who had to plow under his entire crop of romaine lettuce because of an *E. coli* scare. His own lettuce was actually fine. But nobody was buying romaine after some farms near Arizona's Yuma Valley had been contaminated by water in irrigation canals contaminated by manure from a gigantic cattle feedlot upstream.[4]

The interviewer was aghast. How, he wanted to know, could you come to terms with having to destroy whole fields of beautiful food, simply because consumers were too nervous to trust that it was all right?

"We just put one foot in front of the other and keep thinking two weeks at a time," the farmer responded. "Same as we've been doing for the past sixty years."

When I heard that, my thought was, Well, all right then. What we're doing is light-duty compared to that. If farmers can hold on decade after decade in the face of structural impossibility, surely we can find a way to keep doing it too. It was humbling and spine-stiffening.

You'll hear a lot of this kind of stoicism from farmers, especially the mainstream American kind: white, male, land-owning. Some of the stoicism may be a way to keep from questioning the can't-possibly-succeed logic of the modern food economy too deeply, because that could lead to questioning a lot of other things that white American farmers, and white Americans generally, have also benefited from and want to continue believing in.

Accepting the fact that the co-op was actually poor, having other people from the comfortable middle classes misunderstand or patronize or disparage us because we didn't seem able to get our act together, knowing we were consigned to the economic edges and there weren't any easy or obvious ways to move from there toward the center even if we wanted to, all of that pointed me toward another set of connections which expanded my sense of what it was that we *were* actually trying to do.

Margins are chancy places. It can be too easy to wax romantic about them, as anthropologists and others have sometimes been accused of doing. It's hard work to exist there, hard and often painful. But in finding ways to do that work, there are also things to be learned about human existence that a more buffered life is never going to show you. The writer and critic bell hooks understood that fact when she described marginality as "more than a site of deprivation." Rather, it is "a site one stays in, clings to even, because it nourishes one's capacity to resist. It offers the possibility of radical perspectives from which to see and create, to imagine alternatives, new worlds."[5] In a lot of ways my time as an anthropologist in a grocery store has been about understanding and accepting what it means to exist within conditions where it's essentially impossible to prosper in conventional terms, rather than simply trying to get beyond that state as quickly and lastingly as possible.

And the "lasting" part of this is important. The whole American Dream of socioeconomic mobility, the culturally induced trance that is middle-class life, the world built around certain kinds of assumptions and norms that have everything to do with race and class and capitalism, the vision that was so forcefully defended in the 2014 Market Basket strike and the 2016 U.S. presidential election—all of that is an artifact of a very specific moment in human history, birthed on plantations, built in factories, floated on fossil fuels, defended by massive investments in military might.

And that moment is coming to an end. As it does, the lines of struggle between those trying to hold on and those who recognize that we have to let go are being drawn more and more clearly. For those of us who have been floating along in the dream world, coming to terms with what it truly means to be on the "letting go" side is going to mean entering into a fuller sense of what a radically different kind of subsistence and coexistence looks and feels like.

That realization didn't put our little food co-op in Orange into direct solidarity or relationship with the kinds of people and projects and modes of survival and resistance that have been on the margins of the modern world ever since it first started to take shape. But it put us structurally into a place where we had to learn just how hard it was to do something that that world didn't enable and approve. It was a necessary humbling, a further undoing of what I and people like me have so easily taken for granted—not just having enough or being able to choose but not having to struggle or sacrifice or learn anything in order to get our food or the other necessities of life. It's just always been there for us on a platter, whether the platter is a plastic tray from the supermarket or a rustic plank at the farmers market.

Quabbin Harvest and projects like it represent some kind of in-between, something glimpsed and not yet fully defined. And we were working to define it—and create it, very much against the odds—at a time when the realities of life on the margins, the awareness or actual experience of the catastrophes always lurking within modernity, along-side worlds that have already ended and been remade multiple times over, are starting to become real for people who haven't experienced them before, or who thought those struggles were over once their families had made it safely into middle-class prosperity. The catastrophes are looming for all of us at this point, with each new extreme weather event and each new step in the polarization of political spheres, and no amount of either dogged denial or ethical consumption is going to change that.

One kind of response is to retreat into a bunker or homestead or space-ship. Another, the more generous and generative kind, is to work toward remaking our shared infrastructures and our daily practices of living so that they directly challenge the assumptions that have eased some kinds of lives to this point. We can do that by refusing the appeal of solutions that seem new but don't actually change or challenge anything—another new technology promising to fix the problems of the old, another workaround that ignores root causes, another alternative that is simply a different choice within the same pageantry of consumption. Instead, we can figure out how to get our hands on more embedded and ordinary and necessary things like grocery stores.[6]

And we need to know how to do that both within and in opposition to the logic of a system that is in no way hospitable to or compatible with actual alternatives, without simply being worn down by the challenge. We need to know what's on the other side of struggle, what to do when the world is not only ending but has already ended. That's what we were finally starting to figure out at Quabbin Harvest in 2018, and despite the continued setbacks, there were signs that we were actually getting some-where with it at last.

The member challenge campaign that we launched in the spring, along with the change in the inventory mix, had an immediate effect on sales.

We called members on the phone, sent letters and emails, put up posters and signs. It was a lot of work to coordinate all the pieces of the campaign but well worth it. Nearly a hundred members pledged to spend an additional twenty dollars a week in the store; many of them thanked us for reminding them that it was important to support the co-op.

Supporters of the Healthy Incentives Program had also been hard at work since the program's sudden cancellation, making the case to state legislators that the overwhelming demand of the first year showed clearly this was the right idea at (almost) the right time. With farmers already committed for the new planting season, it was unfair to pull the plug. Elected officials and others were looking for ways to build additional funding into the state's pending budget, and as the summer got closer, people at the agency in charge of enrollments began signing recipients up again.

There were bumps. Recipients weren't happy about having to do more paperwork for something that had already seemed—let's be honest—too good to be true. When HIP relaunched later in the spring, enrollments were lower around the state, the level of skepticism higher. State officials also decided to hold the number of HIP vendors steady while the funding was solidified, and farmers who hoped to share in the new revenue stream felt boxed out and disgruntled.

But despite these growing pains, HIP was back. And the vigorous advocacy on its behalf was strengthening connections and communications among groups around the state. It was a larger version of what we were relearning at the co-op: networks need a lot of maintenance and attention, but when they articulate a shared purpose clearly and well, they can magnify the power of any individual actor exponentially. It also showed that political will could be built around an actual alternative without having to resolve all the paradoxes within food-as-commodity. In fact, those paradoxes even created the kind of wiggle room we'd been learning to operate within at Quabbin Harvest. Politicians across the political spectrum found reasons to support the program, some as a means for economic development in the farming sector, others out of concern for public health. Pretty much everyone shared the deep feeling that it was just plain wrong for so many people not to be able to put good food on the table.

Admittedly the political spectrum in Massachusetts is not as wide as in many other places, but politics can be plenty contentious here too. The broad support for HIP showed that if policymakers could find ways to cut through the Gordian knot that tied food production and prices so tightly to the harsh logic of the market, the benefits could ripple across sectors and issues. Shining a spotlight on those benefits, as advocates for HIP were doing very energetically, made other efforts, other futures, seem more possible too.[7] If being in business with Dean's Beans put us into a kind of indirect solidarity with others struggling to hold on at the margins, being a HIP vendor knit us directly into changes within the mainstream structure itself, giving our own struggle to hold on a new significance within broader efforts at change.

There was one other big course correction at the co-op in 2018 when Julie Davis invited Nalini Goordial to launch a prepared-foods division. The proposal was open-ended: Nalini could decide how many days a week she wanted to work and what she wanted to cook. Julie knew Nalini was an inventive cook who genuinely loved feeding people and couldn't stand to see food go to waste. There had never been enough time for her to do more when she was managing the store, but just as it now felt like the right time for Julie to take over that job, maybe it was time for Nalini to start cooking there.

At first Nalini wasn't sure she wanted to take it on. The stresses of her earlier experiences at the co-op were still fresh in her memory. But she also had ideas about how to meld her own approach to food and cooking with the still-emerging vision of Quabbin Harvest as a different kind of resource for people. And her idea of how to prepare foods—and more importantly, *why* to do it—was very different from what was happening at all of the supermarket delis and cafés and hot bars trying to capture some of the money that Americans were spending on food they hadn't cooked themselves.

Over lunch with Deb Habib one day Nalini laid out her reservations about getting involved with the store again. As usual, Deb immediately grasped the possibilities and reinforced them in Nalini's own thinking. "She told me, 'Ultimately you're going to do what you're going to do,'" Nalini said later, "'but what an amazing thing to do for your community. This is so wonderful, your food is great, and you're going to love doing this.'" Why not propose a trial period, Deb suggested, so Nalini didn't feel locked into anything too quickly? "But she knew I was going to get sucked into it," Nalini added. "That woman knows more than she says!"

Julie was fine with Nalini's conditions, including starting with a trial period. And Nalini could make her own rules for the kitchen.

One of the rules was "no sandwiches." You could get sandwiches almost anywhere. Nalini wanted to start with the kind of cooking she'd learned to do as a girl, rooted in traditional Indian understandings of taste and spices and balance.

But she wanted to go beyond that too. She'd learned a lot about southwestern cooking while living in New Mexico. She loved to experiment with flavors, especially in combination with ingredients that you might not have thought to throw together—broccoli apple slaw, celery salad with figs and walnuts and feta cheese. Julie was quickly reviving the co-op's produce case as a central feature of the store, training staff how to refresh it every day so it always looked bright and appealing. Nalini's good food was the flip side of that. Kale that hadn't sold out the week before and was now a little tired could be turned into a colorful salad with a bracing vinaigrette. Potatoes that had sprouted slightly made wonderful potato-leek soup. And almost anything could go into one of the Indian dishes Nalini had at her fingertips—masalas and dals and chutneys and things that came under the catch-all colonial term of "curry."

Nalini came in to work the first week with her *masala dabba*, the circular, stainless-steel box with a set of smaller circles nested inside it that holds the basic repertoire of Indian spices—turmeric, cumin, coriander, cayenne, fenugreek, black mustard seed. I watched her as she started to lay things out, looking for ways to make the barebones, hundred-square-foot area at the back of the store into a more usable kitchen. There was no stove, just a toaster oven and the single-burner induction unit that staff used for making chai in the mornings. A narrow strip of countertop along one wall and a small stainless-steel-topped table were the only workspaces. An incompletely thought through exchange of equipment from members' home kitchens a few months earlier had left a stock of odds and ends at the co-op, random pots and whisks and baking sheets. It was like renting a cabin by a lake and making do with whatever you found in the cupboards and drawers.

Nalini's early years in a place with no electricity or running water and her later experience of off-the-grid life in New Mexico turned out to be just the right preparation for cooking in the co-op's improvised kitchen. The larger challenges were in turning out food at a commercial scale—tablespoons have to become cups and cups gallons—and figuring out how to market the remarkable mix of dishes that quickly started to appear next to the produce in the cooler: samosa wraps, smoky chilis, Thai butternut squash soup, Singapore rice noodles. Indian and Indo-Caribbean foods were the bedrock, and things like lentil and sweet potato masala quickly became customer favorites. But there was also enchilada casserole, burrito bowls and wraps with bright green homemade chimichurri, roasted corn on the cob as we got into sweet corn season. Nalini braised bok choy from local farmers and made panzanella or bread pudding with chai if there was leftover bread from the artisan bakery. She made quick pickles from anything that came to hand and turned the summer abundance of hot peppers into jerk marinade or sambal oelek ("Hot! hot! hot!" the handwritten note on the label warned). Her colorful handmade spring rolls with peanut dipping sauce gained an instant following. One faithful fan said of the sauce, "I would happily bathe in this stuff."

How to communicate all this to a wider public that still didn't really know that the old bank in the center of Orange was now a grocery store, let alone that it was now offering this hard-to-capture assortment of fabulous and healthful food? For the first couple of months Nalini experimented with labeling some of her compilations "Ayurvedic bowls" to signal that she had put them together to balance energies and elements in nourishing ways. But that felt unbalanced in itself, not quite in keeping with the audience we were trying to reach. There were people around the North Quabbin area who knew about Ayurvedic principles of health and balance, but it was clear that broader awareness would take some sustained effort, including in figuring out how to label things. The label for one early Ayurvedic bowl read, "Chana masala, brown rice tempered with nigella, cumin and mustard seeds, raita, shrikand." As the weeks went on, this got simplified: "Chickpea masala, spiced brown rice, raita, sweet yogurt dessert."

Nalini and I made a couple of little videos for our Facebook page where she explained some of what she was doing, but somehow the approach didn't feel quite right either. On the continuum from preaching to persuading, it leaned toward preachy, and we didn't want to do that. Nor did we want to invoke terms like "ethnic food" or "authenticity," with their subtle or not so subtle othering of anything outside the Americanized mainstream. For one thing, Nalini could and did cook those mainstream things too. There were days when she made comfort food like mac and cheese or corn chowder with bacon. Her chocolate pudding was killer. More important, however, was that even though nothing could be more authentic than eating jerk yam and black beans made by someone who learned at her Indo-Guyanese grandmother's knee, authenticity wasn't the point.

The point was that the food was incredibly good and Nalini loved cooking it for us as much as we loved eating it. She also loved the way it enabled the co-op to put something out into the world that then made the world want to give something back to the co-op. What came back to us was in the form of money, but the money alone also wasn't the point. The point was the exchange, the reciprocity. At last we were able to have both hands open, one to give and one to receive.

Generosity, in fact, was the point—generosity as principle, generosity as strategy for moving toward something that was after the plantation, outside the commodity and the corporation, while still existing within the world that their cheapness and bigness had made ubiquitous and unavoidable. Generosity was the right response to the insoluble puzzle that was the modern food system.

FIGURE 8. Nalini Goordial returned to the co-op in 2018 to open a prepared foods division. —Photo: Oliver Scott Photography

It was Julie who suggested the obvious name for the new prepared foods division. We should just call it "Nalini's Kitchen." Nalini resisted the idea at first, but she also saw what we all did: that it *was* Nalini's kitchen, and it was Nalini's understanding of food and nourishment—in the very broadest senses—animating it. As a tagline, we came up with "Food cooked with love with flavors from around the world." It would have sounded facile and maybe appropriative applied to someone's boutique sauce business. But it felt absolutely accurate for Nalini's food and our scrappy, struggling little store. That new sense of generosity and adaptability was what was on the other side of struggle, counterbalancing the still-awful weekly panic over finances. Even if we couldn't pay all our bills, we could eat like the proverbial kings and laugh in the kitchen and nourish each other in ways that hadn't felt possible before Julie and Nalini came back.

I designed a logo for Nalini's Kitchen, and we had a new sign made for the sandwich board outside the store. We started to buy a few more pieces of equipment so it wasn't quite so much like camping out, although I came in one day to discover a big batch of homemade biscuits and asked how in the world Nalini had managed that, only to be shown a clunky old turkey roaster that she'd repurposed as a bake-oven. Suddenly, out of almost nothing, there was abundance. And it wasn't the absurd, distorting overabundance of the supermarket but something fitted precisely to our own scale, our own resources. When you did that, those resources started to look like something after all, instead of perpetually coming up short.

In the fall of that year we held a fundraising auction and invited members to contribute items to be auctioned off. There was a sense of generosity and richness there too—all those craftspeople and artists and naturalists and farmers, all of the DIY skills and know-how embedded in the North Quabbin region. People brought potluck food; the artisan brewer in the old Minute Tapioca factory donated growlers of beer; Julie and a board member who ran a dance studio spent most of a day decorating. There were fierce bidding wars over unexpected items and sudden caesuras when everyone in the room recognized that a particular bidder really wanted something that they couldn't afford to spend a lot of money on. Seamlessly, wordlessly, everyone else just stepped back and let the right person take the winning bid. At the end of the evening we were several thousand dollars to the good, and perhaps even more significantly, we had reminded ourselves of the multiple kinds of wealth that did surround the co-op in spite of our undeniable financial poverty.

Seeds of Solidarity sends out its annual newsletter in the fall, and our copy arrived in the mail shortly after the auction, with one of Ricky's scribbled sticky notes attached. Ricky was effusive about the auction: "No matter what, the coop creates community!!" he wrote. "Will the numbers ever add up? Who knows but the coop is so important and will be more so as this system continues to collapse with bigger economic disaster than 2008 down the road. Keep up the great work!!! Let us weather through all of this."

The numbers, meanwhile, were still a long way from adding up. We were paying only the most urgent and immediate bills and hanging onto as much money as we could to buy new stock for the store, trying to stay clear of the dangerous downward spiral of not having enough to sell so that sales dropped even further and we were even less able to keep things on the shelves. But as Karl Bittenbender kept pointing out, there were dangers in letting bills pile up too, especially to vendors who supplied us with staple products that we knew people wanted to buy.

One of those was the large national distributor that had managed to gain a near-monopoly on the natural-foods business over the past couple of decades by buying up most of its competitors and aligning itself with the biggest natural-foods supermarket chains, including Whole Foods. If we wanted to carry certain products—organic canned and processed goods, crackers and snacks, bulk beans and grains—they were really the only option left, or at least the only one we could remotely afford to do business with.[8]

And clearly we couldn't even afford them, because month after month had been going by when we weren't paying their invoices. We kept doing it because they weren't demanding payment, and it created a tiny bit of wiggle room in the financial corner we were boxed into. But as the unpaid bills continued to accumulate, Karl was increasingly sounding the alarm.

So it wasn't a complete surprise when the demand finally arrived, in the form of an abrupt request for a phone meeting with the regional accounts supervisor, our friendly sales rep's boss and obviously the bad cop to her good one.

We gathered upstairs in the big meeting room above the store—Karl, the young board member who'd replaced him as treasurer, Julie, Mary-Ellen Kennedy, and me. The upstairs was at least comfortable by that point, because Mount Grace's board had gotten tired of meeting there on frigid winter days and had paid to have an air-source heat exchanger installed. At the same time, the co-op had borrowed money from the Garlic and Arts Festival's philanthropic wing to install a similar unit in the store, making the building overall much more habitable.

When I think of that meeting, though, I remember it as cold—all of us clustered together at one corner of the big board table, focused on someone's cell phone, listening to a tinny, implacable voice coming out of the speaker telling us that unless we could come up with the whole amount we owed, now well into five-figure territory, the company would not be delivering any more groceries to us, starting immediately. Essentially we were holding onto their money, the woman pointed out. They sent us the products we ordered and we hadn't paid for them. It wasn't fair to ask them to keep financing our store. Was it?

It was hard to dispute. And the demand was made more inexorable by the timing: the company itself had been in a potentially shaky position since Amazon acquired its own biggest customer, Whole Foods, the previous year. No one was quite sure yet what Amazon's entry into the grocery sector would mean, but it was clear that there was some kind of shake-out coming. The big were going to have to continue to get even bigger, especially now that one of the giants of the internet economy had invaded one of the few more lucrative pockets in a business with such famously slim profit margins.

The company we owed money to had already responded by acquiring yet another corporation, a bargain supermarket chain with its own national distribution network. They didn't want the stores—over the next couple of years those were quickly off-loaded. The goal was to bulk up the distribution side of things, to try to compete with Amazon's outsized clout there.

"There's Amazon, there's Kroger, and there's Walmart on the selling side," an investment consultant said of the deal. "You do not want to be on that side. If you're on the distribution side and you're good at it you're going to be in a much better position."[9]

We had to wonder if this sudden calling-in of our debt was part of the company's own cleaning house, bracing for a new era of even fiercer competition for those wafer-thin slices of profit. This was the world of Big Food, the corporate agribusinesses that Clarence Francis and General Foods had been so instrumental in creating, where whole companies like Minute Tapioca or supermarket chains with thousands of stores could be sold and traded and sometimes dissolved overnight like so many tattered baseball cards. Our tiny store didn't even register on that scale, except as an annoying speck in someone's Past 90 Days column.

It was strange to feel a kind of empathy for the corporate enforcer, a sense of how inescapable all of this was if we wanted to be involved in the business of selling groceries at all. This multi-billion-dollar company was no more secure within the impossible riddle of the modern food system than we were—they were just a lot bigger. In some ways, that actually made them more vulnerable because they had a lot more to lose. And that meant they couldn't afford to be nice. It made a dismal, discouraging kind of good sense.

We went back and forth about the all-or-nothing demand for a while. We pointed out that if we went out of business, our lenders were first in line for the scant assets we had left and the distributor and our other creditors would end up with nothing. Wasn't it better to work with us than to shut us down?

The supervisor replied that the time for trying to work together was over. It seemed like an impasse, and I felt like a sulky teenager who knows she's in the wrong but is still seething about the greater injustices of the world. What was there to say to this distant authority figure who wasn't willing to concede even an inch?

It was Karl who found the right thing. Calmly, quietly, sounding at first as though he might be just a kindly old guy heading off on a tangent, he started to describe the vision of what Quabbin Harvest was intended to be. He told the supervisor something about Orange, about the empty downtown storefronts and the numbers of people in the area who couldn't afford to buy healthy food. He mentioned the Healthy Incentives Program and the fact that our little store had been the top enroller in the state in the program's hugely successful first year. He talked about the volunteers who helped keep the store running and the local farmers we were trying to support with our buying. And then he stopped and waited.

There was a long silence from the speakerphone, and then an audible sigh. When the supervisor spoke again, her voice was different.

"It certainly is a problem," she said. "It's just not right that so many people can't get good food. You're doing a wonderful thing in trying to help." And then we went on to chat for a while before coming to an agreement that everyone could live with.

Karl hadn't been playing the poverty card or making a calculated bid for sympathy. He was just drawing attention to something that it seemed even Big Food, if you could just get it to pause in its own headlong scramble for survival, had to acknowledge: there was something profoundly and fundamentally wrong with the business we were all a part of. The change in the supervisor's voice, from adamant to tired, almost regretful, seemed like a tacit admission that it didn't always feel good to be on the side of the status quo.

I left the meeting relieved and elated. Yes, there would now be a tight limit on how much Julie could order each week. We were going to have to pay on delivery along with a weekly payment of several hundred dollars applied to the older invoices. But we weren't going bankrupt—not this month anyway. And we would still be able to keep at least some of those core grocery items on the shelves. Plus we'd managed to find some common humanity, if not quite common ground, with someone who had clearly started the meeting determined not to give us anything at all. It felt like a victory for the small and quixotic.

Karl was more subdued, and I should have paid more attention to that. He knew what I was overlooking in my relief at having dodged another disaster in the short term: that this new arrangement, while it would allow us to keep stocking things on a minimal level, was also going to throttle our cash flow down to almost nothing. The twin dangers of tight cash and overdue bills were starting to converge, and he could see more clearly than the rest of us where that was headed.

CHAPTER 10

SIGNS

AFTER FOUR YEARS, the big faded "Workers Credit Union" sign was still the most noticeable thing on the front of our building. And I had come to realize why Karl had sidestepped our friendly funder's questions about it a couple of years earlier. Everyone agreed we needed a better sign. But it was surprisingly hard to decide what it should say.

The co-op's original signage—"Your community market—Everyone can shop—Anyone can join"—seemed to confuse many people rather than enlighten them. After a lot of discussion the board agreed that it was better not to lead off with the fact that we were a co-operatively owned business. But then what *should* we lead with?[1]

You'd think this would be simple. And maybe it would have been simple in the make-believe days of Castle Rock, when Hemphill's Market and other small stores just like it dotted the landscape of every town and city in America, selling some of this and some of that, some foods coming from nearby and some from the industrial supply streams that had been gathering momentum since the late nineteenth century. Customers wouldn't have expected to be able to buy absolutely everything at one store because there weren't yet stores where you *could* buy absolutely everything. Many things would come and go with the seasons. There would be bushels of sweet corn from the farm up the road in late summer and fresh turkeys from another farm for Thanksgiving. Regular customers would know that the fresh bread came from the bakery by midday on Thursdays and some things might be running low by Saturday because the delivery truck didn't come again until Monday.

It's still possible for small grocery stores like that to survive in certain places, mostly densely populated urban neighborhoods where there are enough people to support them. They're often run—as has long been the case—by immigrant families. And their specialty items aren't usually from nearby farms but rather from global circuits of supply that can provide familiar products for people living in diaspora.

Supermarkets have pushed their way into that niche as they have with so many others. A stroll down the so-called ethnic or international aisle of any supermarket is a strange tour of imagined, opportunistic, and hijacked product lines—not, in fact, unlike the simulacrum that was Hemphill's Market. Corporate versions of ethnic cuisine, like taco kits from Old El Paso (part of General Mills), sit side by side with items from big distributors that have grown alongside immigrant populations themselves, like Goya with its ever-expanding universe of beans and grains fine-tuned to immigration patterns from Latin America and elsewhere. Occasionally an item will make the leap from niche to mainstream, buoyed by culinary trends in sought-after consumer demographics. Think sriracha, its now-iconic status as a kind of hipster ketchup boosting sales of everything from the well-known Huy Fong "rooster sauce" brand created by a Vietnamese refugee in California to versions by Big Food (Frank's Red Hot, owned by McCormick, now makes sriracha in handy half-gallon containers).[2]

I digress. But maybe not. In the fantastically fragmented, overlapping, shifting flows of foods, images, and desires that make up the modern food system, small, diversified grocery stores like the one we were trying to bring back in downtown Orange are all but unintelligible in most places, familiar and strange at the same time, literally hard for people to see and understand. What could we convey in three or four words on a sign glimpsed by a driver waiting for the traffic light in the center of town to change?

The supermarket's long shadow looms over the phrase "grocery store" now, implying a larger selection than we could possibly offer. "Local food" was our stock in trade, but that phrase carried its own overtones, suggesting the whole food-with-a-social-mission approach that was compelling for some people and alienating for others. Besides, we sold more than just local food—there were lemons and bananas and other things that people had told us they expected and wanted if they were going to shop at the store at all. We got those things through Squash, a distributor that was, like Quabbin Harvest, both local and not local, pointing up the slipperiness of the term itself. Probably best to stay away from "local" on the big sign.

"Market" was more promising. It suggested "farmers market" but in a more general way, minus the pop-up tents. It could lean in a boutique direction, but it also invoked a long history of small-scale vending by people close to the source. Market encompassed a lot of what food-selling had been before supermarkets made it super. Stripping back down to that old term felt right.

And to get the main idea across to that person driving past who was only going to have three seconds to take in our message, we thought "food" should be somewhere on the sign too. After a lot of discussion and scribbling on sheets of newsprint on the boardroom wall one evening, we arrived at a consensus about what should go on the big sign: "Quabbin Harvest Food Market," with the logo at both ends to sneak "food co-op" in there for anyone who happened to notice or care.

Of course, there was no money to pay to have the sign fabricated anytime soon. But at least we finally knew what we wanted it to say.

At the start of 2019 we were starting to wrestle with another kind of legibility, this time in a language most of us didn't speak: the language of numbers, or more specifically financial reporting. The state of Massachusetts had thrown us another lifeline in the form of a new revolving loan fund designed to help food businesses like ours. But to apply for it, we needed to be able to explain more clearly to outsiders just how things stood for us financially. And that meant we needed to face the fact that we couldn't explain it very clearly to ourselves.

Before we moved to the North Quabbin, my husband and I worked as janitors for a colonial-era Boston church heated by a furnace that was a veritable museum of central heating technologies. No one seemed quite sure which parts of the giant contraption were still functional, and it wasn't a stretch to imagine that the whole system might be ignited by some fur-clad cave-dweller in a dark chamber at the very center, striking a spark with flint and tinder.

Periodically something malfunctioned and we would have to negotiate with various repair people, none of whom fully understood how their own piece fit into the whole. Early on, I had my own fantasy that I would be able to solve the puzzle. I find heating systems interesting, and it seemed as though it should be possible to understand how this one worked. But the thing defeated me long before we left the job. As long as someone was able to get it going again, that was enough for me.

Opening the lid on Quabbin Harvest's financial reporting felt exactly like that, except that we were dealing with just a few years instead of a couple of centuries. But there *were* centuries in the co-op's finances—those centuries of food being made cheap and small-scale food-selling being made all but impossible and people continuing to try to do it anyway for a whole raft of reasons under circumstances that were usually far less than ideal.

It was all there in the books, in the optimistically overbuilt chart of accounts and point-of-sale system, which had led to countless in-the-moment guesses by staff and volunteers about which item might belong in which category, with no more sense of the whole than the pipefitters and electricians had when they were looking at the behemoth in the church basement. It was there in the way those two crucial systems didn't quite mesh, reflecting the uneasy division of labor between the volunteers who set up the accounting side and the staff running the store day to day.

And there was much more inside that gap. There was the desire to know, to master, to really understand what was going on inside the inner workings of the food system that keeps us alive, right up against the wish just to turn it all over to someone else and have the food magically appear on the shelves whenever we wanted it. There was the vital idealism of wanting to be part of making something different and the terrible naïveté of thinking you could make it work when so many others had failed. Those moments of key people stepping away, dropping their share of the ton of bricks, all left holes in the numbers and in our collective knowledge about the numbers.

There was gender stuff tucked away in there somewhere too, in the way everyone had so gladly turned all the financial work over to Karl, the former banker and the sole male in the small core group trying to keep day-to-day operations running in the store. Karl had made a layer of Google Sheets to translate between the point-of-sale system and the accounting software, and that layer was a classic black box—data went in one side and came out the other and no one but Karl had the slightest idea what happened in between.

Not all the problems were with the books themselves. There were a lot of things that simply didn't make sense to try to do at all at our small size, like breaking down which parts of the weekly produce delivery from

Squash ended up in the HIP shares, which ones were sold directly in the store, and which ones went to the kitchen for Nalini to use. A larger business would have been able to order by the case for each of those; at our size it would have meant literally tracking individual apples and heads of lettuce—theoretically possible but logistically irrational. That meant we couldn't know exactly what we were paying for the things we sold in three important areas of the business, which meant we couldn't figure out what our profit margins were in those areas.

That was one of the first questions the consultants from the new Massachusetts Food Trust Program asked us when we sat down for our first meeting with them: can you tell us what your margins are? The rest of us were relieved when Karl said he could get those figures—he just needed a bit of time to pull some information and do some math. But he also explained why we weren't going to be able to get beyond a reasonable approximation for some of our sales categories.

The consultants seemed willing to accept that, and it was one of my first inklings that the language of numbers might not be as cut and dried as I'd always thought. Granted, we weren't exactly sitting across the table from Big Finance: these folks were in business to support small enterprises like ours, and they were actively trying to help us survive. But they also needed to build a loan portfolio that wasn't going to lose the state's investment.

What was surprising in that first conversation and the many others that followed was how readily they folded all kinds of information into their calculations—the level of reliability they saw in Karl's figures, the signs of potential growth in the member shopping data we'd been tracking after our challenge campaign the previous year, the fact that unlike many small struggling businesses we were current with our loan payments and payroll taxes, the implications of what Julie was telling them about stocking decisions and price points in our economically straitened area. It all seemed like a process of translation, or maybe a translation of translations across totally different alphabets and ways of thinking, always working in the direction of something reasonably realistic that could be expressed in a spreadsheet while also holding open room for hope.

It was surprising in the same way that the conversation about our unpaid invoices at the big regional distributor had been. There was the same tacit acknowledgment that the whole system was fundamentally torqued, that at bottom there was simply something wrong with lashing food provisioning so tightly to profit-making, that some kind of basic humanity demanded we find more rational ways to feed ourselves and each other. It was as though deep inside the co-op's financial records we'd stumbled on something like the caveman at the core of the church furnace, in this case the pen-scratches of a harried medieval scribe keeping track of the price of wheat and the price of bread and trying to make it all balance out so no one starved or revolted. It was flawed and archaic and deeply limiting and over the centuries it had generated vast coping and accounting and mitigating mechanisms that almost no one understood. (There's a grim joke in the dairy business that only three people really know how the federal price for milk is set, and two of them are dead.[3]) But it was the spark that still set a lot of other things going. If we were going to have anything to do with the modern food system as it actually exists, we couldn't just ignore the language of numbers and the logic of markets. We needed to be able to translate ourselves into its language in a way that was both truthful and just-good-enough.

As we worked with the consultants over the spring of 2019, it started to feel as though the demands of the co-op were overrunning my life at the very busiest time of year in my real job. The new treasurer was struggling with the emotional burden of being the one faced with angry creditors and implacable demand notices, and she stepped aside gratefully when MaryEllen Kennedy agreed to take on the role. And Karl had been saying for a while that we needed something like a management team again, to support Julie in her day-to-day running of the store and to enable communication across the surprisingly complex areas of the little business.

"No single person can run this store by themselves," he kept insisting. I knew enough by now to recognize that was true. So MaryEllen, Julie, and I started meeting first thing in the morning every Tuesday, when Julie had to be there early to take delivery of the milk. Monday was my longest teaching day in Boston, and it was hard to get out of the house early the next morning, especially when I needed time and concentration to get ready for another long day on Wednesday. But Julie was doing the early Tuesday milk run week in and week out and MaryEllen had gamely taken on the toughest volunteer job in the place. And the role that was growing around the pile of bricks I'd taken on—communications coordinator, systems untangler, chief fundraiser—felt like it needed to be at the management team table. So I waded a little farther in.

I remember being at a professional conference in April frantically emailing spreadsheets back and forth with one of the consultants who was finalizing our loan application, feeling as though the two sides of my life were in a tug of war. But our loan application was approved, which let us stave off some of the most pressing bills and fill some of the ever-widening gaps on the shelves. And there was more: the Massachusetts Food Trust also approved us for two grants to help us with problems they'd noted in our operations. One was for additional consulting help to get our books and financial reporting systems in better order. The other was for marketing—including enough that we could finally fabricate that sign for the front of the building. These felt, literally, like hopeful signs.

Our 2019 annual meeting marked the tenth anniversary of the first produce share distribution under the pop-up tent in the parking lot of the old Minute Tapioca factory, and we used the occasion to reflect on what we'd done in those ten years and to celebrate—to marvel at, really—the fact that we were still in business. We made an illustrated timeline and buttons for everyone: you could choose one that said either "I was here at the beginning" or "I'm ready for the next ten years." We picked names out of a basket to choose people who volunteered to tell their piece of the co-op's story, and the five names that came up spanned the entire trajectory perfectly from germ of an idea through setting up operations to shared adversity to recent arrivals finding a sense of community at the store. At the end of the evening there was a strengthened sense of shared purpose and commitment and a somewhat clearer understanding of where we were financially.

Good things continued to alternate with bad. In May we were a stop on a North American tour by a Canadian who had written a book called *Grocery Story: The Promise of Food Co-Ops in the Age of Grocery Giants*. Jon Steinman was a food media professional who was visiting more than a hundred co-ops across the continent, making the case that more people who wanted to see real change in the food system should roll up their sleeves and get actively involved in the grocery business itself rather than simply "voting with their dollars" or putting too much faith in the much slower tools of public policy.

"The evolution of the market can outpace the political process seeking to reform it," he warned. "Co-ops allow for change to emerge from *within* the system and at the evolutionary pace of the system itself."[4] It was an argument that helped me understand my own involvement in the grocery business as a form of participant-observation, a necessary learning process that could only take place by engaging firsthand.

Jon's book also included a list of the main reasons new food co-ops fail, and it turned out that we ticked nearly all of those boxes: start in a small space after an abbreviated development process with an insufficient startup budget and too heavy a reliance on member labor. But Jon also noted that smallness and leanness could be advantages. He quoted the manager of one recent small startup in Indiana who used the same term we often applied to Quabbin Harvest: "scrappy."[5] Scrappiness meant flexibility, adaptability, collective grit, an awareness of what it felt like to survive on the margins and a willingness to try to hold on there no matter what it took.

Grocery Story was part of a wave of recent books that peel the shiny surface layer off the grocery business to show how deeply strange our current way of getting food really is.[6] It's as though a lot of us have been starting to stir out of the convenience-induced trance that the supermarket has been lulling us into over the past five or six decades, and we're starting to wonder how in the world we let this happen.

It's partly that the structural cracks continue to become a little more visible all the time. In the month before Jon's visit, more than thirty thousand New England supermarket workers went on strike at Stop & Shop, one of several U.S. chains now owned by the European colossus Ahold Delhaize. When Julie Davis worked at Stop & Shop during her high school and college years, the company was known for offering good pay and good benefits—automatic raises, premium pay for working on holidays, health insurance for full-time workers, paid vacations even for part-timers. Ahold inherited the union when it bought the chain in 1995.

But by 2019, as the Market Basket uprising of five years earlier had shown, cut-throat competition in the supermarket sector meant that everyone was trying to whittle down their labor costs. Ahold Delhaize had already made inroads into both pay and benefits; when it reneged on some promised concessions during union contract negotiations and simultaneously announced an increase in its shareholder dividend, workers walked out.

As with the Market Basket strike, public opinion was heavily against management. Most shoppers honored the picket line. So did the Teamsters union, which choked off supplies for the chain's 240 stores. Many Jewish and Christian religious leaders urged their congregations to shop elsewhere for their Easter and Passover foods and flowers. As the United States geared up for a presidential primary season, most of the Democratic candidates visited and tweeted out pictures of themselves with workers (Elizabeth Warren brought doughnuts).[7]

After eleven days, the company settled. But it was clear that this was likely to be a recurring fight as long as the supermarket wars continued to rage.[8] And as long as they did, the existing system didn't offer customers any kind of real alternative if they wanted to make things fairer or better. True, people could always shop elsewhere during a strike or a boycott, as they'd done so visibly with Market Basket five years earlier. But "elsewhere" wasn't really very far away, when the same few giant corporations owned most of the supermarkets and even the regional heroes like Market Basket only managed to hold the line by competing successfully on bigness and cheapness.

Jon Steinman's book and tour shone a light on what was already being done to build something new inside the shell of the old. If our tenth-anniversary timeline helped give us a shared sense of our own trajectory, being a stop on the *Grocery Story* tour knitted us into a much wider landscape of intent and determination. We were scrappy and still struggling, but we were very far from alone.

In late May the freezers quit again. The weather had been cool and we hadn't yet opened up the basement ventilation system that Karl and Bruce Scherer had rigged to dump the excess heat from the big compressors in the warmer months. On Memorial Day weekend the temperature suddenly spiked into the nineties and the whole giant unit overheated and shut down. By the time Julie got there on the holiday Monday morning everything had started to soften.

It was depressing to spend the first glorious early summer day standing inside at the cash register ringing up soggy semi-frozen food to document our insurance claim. My husband and I went to Walmart and bought more trash and recycling bins for the containers. A board member who ran a compost company came and took away the food itself. The worst part was dumping Nalini's good food. We sometimes froze things from the kitchen when they were nearing their "sell by" date and after a year we had quite a little stock of soups, chilis, and other things on hand. With every plastic lid I pulled off there was a ghost of whatever wonderful smell had permeated the store on the day that dish was cooked. It felt awful to throw so much away, tragic to undo so many of our efforts to be frugal and use things wisely and well. The oversized, outdated freezers were like a constant reminder that we were still trapped inside a system we couldn't control.

But that didn't mean we couldn't talk about it. When Julie restocked the freezer, she decided to fill only the four bays we actually needed. We couldn't take other ones offline—the thing came as a unit—but she covered the five extra doors with black chalkboard wallpaper and a staff member who was also an artist lettered and illustrated our intention to right-size the freezers at some future moment. "We are re-imagining the store," the chalked letters said. It was a reminder that the co-op was always a work of imagination as much as a reality.

FIGURE 9. After multiple malfunctions, the store's unwieldy bank of freezers became a canvas for a reimagined and more energy-efficient store. —Photograph by the author

The marketing grant pushed us to sharpen that still-coming-into-focus quality in how we ourselves were understanding the business and how we were communicating it to the rest of the world. On the recommendation of the Food Trust, we engaged another consultant from Boston to help us write a marketing plan.

We had some trepidation about that, born out of many years of experience watching people from Boston or the Connecticut River Valley try to get acquainted with the North Quabbin. And the first visit was not auspicious: the consultant arrived at the store with a troubled look on her face.

"I knew these little downtowns were having a tough time, but I didn't expect the center of Orange to look *quite* so bad," she said—and then wondered why we burst out laughing. We'd forgotten to tell her that the Castle Rock production company was back in town for a new season of filming, hard at work making everything look as sinister and decrepit as possible.

Explaining it was complicated. After all, the difference between Orange as Castle Rock and Orange as Orange was a matter of degree, not of kind. On its very best day, the downtown still had that mostly empty feeling, a sense of time having stopped and energy moved elsewhere. There was a reason the film company had chosen Orange, and it had everything to do with the town's long history of abandonments and its search for some kind of renewed prosperity in the present-day economy.

The consultant asked a lot of useful questions and helped us take stock of our scattered communications and marketing strategies—legacies, like our financial reporting systems, of the many different hands involved over our short lifespan. By the end of the summer we had a marketing plan that focused on the things we were already doing well and the unique items that couldn't be comparison-shopped, with an emphasis on our commitment to local farmers and to making good food as affordable as possible for as many people as possible. We tried to present ourselves as a reflection of the area: unpretentious, outdoorsy, independent.

The financial reporting cleanup was a tougher nut to crack. I didn't have a lot of time to devote to it until the academic year was over, but then I jumped in with both feet, determined to untangle things before school started again. We hired another consultant and tacked a finance meeting on to our regular Tuesday morning management team meetings. But it soon became clear that this was going to be a multiyear task which a platoon of consultants wasn't going to be able to do for us. The knowledge we needed—including knowledge about what we didn't yet know—was scattered across a whole network of people, some still present, some no longer available. It was the classic problem of the elephant that everyone is grasping only a piece of—the tail, the trunk, an ear—and extrapolating a whole animal that is nothing like the whole.

Two things helped.

First, those Tuesday meetings, initially so draining and distracting, came to seem less like an imposition as the academic year went on. I'd been trying to keep my work and avocational lives more or less separate, but the separation felt increasingly artificial all the time. I'd started teaching a new introductory-level course about food systems that year and found my experiences with the co-op were helping me figure out how to help undergraduates grasp the elephant as a whole and see it for the wondrous and stupefying creature it was. I was surprised at how much new authority I felt about this—surprised too at the credibility it gave me in the eyes of my students who were increasingly demanding that their learning have some applicability in the nonacademic world.

Sometimes that undergraduate zeal gets ahead of itself. There are times when you need to just sit and think deeply about things outside the rush of daily living, and that's what academic learning can help you do. But especially for a generation that has grown up with the awareness that the entire planetary system is in crisis and it's on them to do something about it, impatience with purely theoretical knowledge is also completely reasonable. It's the same urgency that motivated me to get involved with Quabbin Harvest in the first place, and it felt good to be able to merge the two sides of my life in a way that hadn't seemed possible before. From being a side project, a slightly guilty intrusion, the co-op now felt more like part of my real work, or maybe my real education, something I could share in turn with other people who were trying to learn about the systems they were trying to change.

The other thing that helped was that Tuesday was share day, when the fresh produce was delivered to the store. After some determined efforts in the state legislature by supporters of the program, HIP was now running again. For several years we'd also been distributing food through a local seasonal program for seniors. And because it was summer, most of the food in the shares was coming from closer to home. So as we sat around the big round table at the front of the store on Tuesday mornings wrestling with incompatible account categories and opaque software systems, we were buoyed by the steady parade of farmers coming in with boxes and hand-trucks brimming with beautiful fresh fruits and vegetables. The sheer amount of good food moving through the little store was dazzling and uplifting.

It all coalesced on one glorious late August day. We had signed up to staff the children's activity table at the Orange Farmers Market, turning tired vegetables from the compost bucket and the dollar rack into fantastical monsters held together with toothpicks. We took lunch from Nalini's Kitchen to our neighbors in the town offices across the street from the store. And we marshaled a volunteer crew to help cook a locally sourced dinner for the food pantry's weekly community meal. It was another of those moments when we realized how much we could do with what was at hand, how rich our collective resources actually were even though we were still so strapped for cash.

The cash crunch got worse as we started into the fall. A couple more vendors told us they couldn't keep delivering to us if we couldn't make inroads on our unpaid invoices, so we set up more payment plans and hoped for the best. One desperate creditor emailed us at 2:30 a.m., just a little earlier than I tended to wake up for my own obsessive fretting about the co-op's finances.

There came a Tuesday morning when we had to ask ourselves if we'd hit the wall for the final time. The stock on the shelves had been getting dangerously sparse, no matter how creatively the staff tried to spread things out to fill the gaps or camouflage it with seasonal decorations.

Perhaps fortunately, we didn't really have time to deal with the financial emergency because we'd committed ourselves to selling chai at the North Quabbin Garlic and Arts Festival that weekend. The festival is central to many good things happening around the region, and the co-op had had a presence there since its earliest days. It was an annual intersection of a lot of overlapping networks—food and farming and art and craft and music and various ways of living lightly and skillfully and responsibly on the earth—all centered around the community of farmers and artisans along the hilly roads on the western edge of Orange who had always been central to the co-op's own community.

There are ways in which the Garlic and Arts Festival is just like any hippie-inspired back-to-the-land gathering and ways in which it is unique. It's been unusually successful over twenty-five years in finding ways to maintain the vision and energy that fueled it in the first place. I remember waking up for my financial fret on the night before the festival, caught somewhere between the logistics of getting enough ice and coolers and the larger worry about our soon-to-be-negative bank balance, and saying to myself, "You know, it's Garlic and Arts weekend. I'm just going to tap into that and sell chai and be outside and let the bigger picture go for a couple of days."

When I woke up properly several hours later there was a new idea floating around in my head: could we ask members and supporters to split the cost of buying new inventory with us in exchange for a share of the product? People could underwrite the foods they really wanted to see on the shelves, and we could also draw up a list of things we knew were most important to keep in stock—coffee, honey, bagels, meat—and see if anyone wanted to adopt one of those. It was in keeping with the basic idea of a co-op as a way to pool resources. And it might be a way to eke things out a little longer while we got out from under the weight of those payment plans and had a chance to do more fundraising.

As we set up the chai operation and got things underway, I talked this over with others at the Quabbin Harvest tent. It turned out that Julie had come up with virtually the same notion as well as a catchy name for it: Share a Shelf. Two or three other people had been thinking along the same lines. It was as though that good Garlic and Arts energy had gotten through to all of us and helped us see a way where there had been no way just a few days before.

It was a flawless New England fall weekend, sunny and crisp. The festival was mobbed. There wasn't a lot of time to make plans but by Sunday afternoon we'd mocked up a pitch and enlisted a first round of donor commitments. We also sold a lot of chai and listened to a lot of great music from the main stage. The final act was a local blues band who played the last of the crowd off the field and then stayed around for one more number so the vendors and volunteers and organizers could come out and dance too. That end-of-the-festival moment seemed particularly sweet that year. We'd all been on our feet for two solid days but it was enlivening to be out on a freshly mown hayfield with friends and neighbors who knew that sometimes you just need to stop fretting and dance.

As we got the new Share a Shelf program underway, I put together a hand-drawn flip chart detailing how we'd gotten into the hole we were in and how we'd managed to claw our way back from the depths of it before. It showed that we'd made substantial inroads into the pile of back bills but at a cost of not being able to restock the store. It was a rationale for why we needed Share a Shelf, and it helped motivate some donors to contribute some or all of the cost of goods for foods they wanted or things we knew it was important to have on hand.

It felt good to set it all out so clearly, even though there wasn't anything like a happy ending yet. It also felt good to be making some headway with understanding the deeper layers of our financial reporting systems. The consultant's work had wrapped up at the end of the summer and Karl had made good on his intention of extricating himself from the co-op's finances by then too. But MaryEllen Kennedy and I continued to chop away at things, learning as we went and occasionally making new messes as we tried to clean up older ones. (Share a Shelf itself turned out to be something of an accounting nightmare, with money coming in that was somewhere between a donation and a sale and a member preorder and cost of goods, which couldn't really be captured in the chart of accounts.) We turned out to work well together, MaryEllen digging in single-mindedly just at the point where I got frustrated with the minutiae and wanted to jump back to bigger-picture thinking. It felt like the start of a joke: An anthropologist and a systems analyst walk into a grocery store. . . .

In early November there was another convergence of good things. We held a second fundraising auction, and the next day we were part of a larger celebration in Orange. A community group had spearheaded the restoration of the historic Minute Man stage curtain in the Town Hall auditorium and they held an unveiling on the same day that we dedicated a new grant-funded mural by a local artist on the side of our building. The mural was vertical, with intertwining corn and bean stalks and vines rising from ground level to the top of one of the brick chimneys, interspersed with birds and other animal species against a backdrop of rounded hills and the river that has always been the east-west spine of the region.

And—miracle of miracles—the new signage on the front of the store had been installed the previous week. I arrived one day to find a lift truck parked outside and the bright teal panels of the big Quabbin Harvest Food Market sign finally starting to cover up the faded Workers Credit Union wording. It had taken nearly five years, a lot of debate, and some financial help from the state, but the outside of the store was at last telling the rest of the world who and what we were.

It was an accomplishment as well to have come to some kind of terms with the language of numbers. From thinking of them as something unyielding, like implacable gods requiring interpretation by adepts in secretive shrines, I'd come to recognize that numbers, like words, could in fact be a way to tell a story about what had happened or what was happening right now or what you wanted to happen in the future. Just like words, numbers demand a certain facility and a certain clarity of thought—otherwise you end up with muddled prose and impenetrable accounts. A lot of people at the co-op—most of us non-native speakers in the language of numbers—had been telling disparate pieces of the story in our own ways, usually while short of time and overwhelmed by the scope of what we'd taken on. It made for a very tangled narrative that we were now finally starting to sort out.

In at least one case—mine—there'd also been a tendency to conflate what I didn't understand about numbers with what I didn't like about capitalism. I'd felt as though using numbers to tell the story at all meant we were somehow giving in to the imperatives of pure profit-seeking. It sounds simplistic, phrased like that, but I think that idea is in the back of a lot of people's minds when they try to come up with ways to fix what's wrong with our food system. It's probably one of the reasons that so many of the proffered solutions—the ones that aren't actively chasing profit itself—stay outside the marketplace and don't really engage with the economic realities of the system as it actually exists. After three years as a participant-observer in the grocery business, I was finally coming to see that there might be a way to position yourself in between the two, between accepting the market as it was and refusing to deal with it at all, a way to use its language to say and do something radically different. And if more eaters could gain some real fluency in even a few phrases from that language—some of the basics, like profit margins and cost of goods and economies of scale—it might be more possible to reach a shared understanding of why the current system is so intractable and what kinds of commitments and changes are needed if we're going to make something different.

Jon Steinman's argument about this—that there are advantages to inserting yourself into the actual propulsive force of the market—reminded me of the Zen parable about the man who falls into a raging river at the lip of a high waterfall. Horrified onlookers, assuming the worst, are astonished to see him swimming calmly away at the bottom of the falls. When he comes ashore, they ask him how he survived. He tells them he simply accommodated himself to the tumultuous water rather than trying to fight it. The co-op was like that. We were all being buffeted, continually tossed and upended, always just one breath away from drowning. But we'd found a way to keep on moving with the current—right up to the day when we finally couldn't anymore.

CHAPTER 11

FUTURES

W HEN THE END came, one Tuesday morning in February 2020, it felt strangely sudden. Julie, MaryEllen, and I sat at the little table in the upstairs office looking at the sales from the previous week and the list of bills that had to be paid. The numbers made it plain: there was no more room to maneuver. Even with the new revenue coming in from the Share a Shelf program, our trickle of cash flow had finally stopped.

My immediate thought was, Wouldn't you know that we would go bankrupt two months after finally getting a sign onto the building to let the world know we were there?

My second thought was, I will personally pay to have that sign taken down again so it doesn't haunt me and the town forevermore with yet another broken promise, another abandonment.

I came home and said to my husband, "I think we're done." There didn't seem to be anything more to say after that.

But there was still lots to do. We called an emergency board meeting for that Sunday morning and gathered in the upstairs room to look at the numbers from Tuesday, which put bankruptcy squarely on the table. Were we really and truly finished?

It was hard to imagine how we could carry on. But out of the conversation came a sense that we also couldn't stand to give up without one more try. And in any case, the nine of us on the board couldn't really make that call. The co-op membership as a whole would have to decide. We'd been sounding the alarm for four years, to the point that it sometimes felt like crying wolf, and I cringed inside every time I had to deliver another upbeat-yet-urgent message. But at least we hadn't been hiding the fact that we were on a downward spiral which couldn't continue indefinitely. The indefinite had now become definite, and the members needed to know it.

FIGURE 10. In January 2020, the co-op had finally added signage and a new mural but was on the edge of bankruptcy after several years of struggle.

—Photo: Atlantic Image Creations

So we called another emergency meeting, this time for the whole membership. I started making spreadsheets and infographics detailing where things stood and what it would take to stave off bankruptcy. I'll be honest: there were moments when I felt something like relief at the idea that this might be over, that I could step outside that relentless cycle of surviving two weeks at a time on the margins of a system set up to make it all but impossible for us to persist. I knew even less about taking a business apart than I'd known about running one, and I had no idea what declaring bankruptcy actually involved, other than being quite sure there would be a lot of paperwork and probably lawyers. But I did know that at some point it would be finished, and I could take all the lessons I'd learned through this experience and find some less strenuous way to be a conscientious eater and member of my community and educator about the food system. I'd been starting to think about writing this book, and failure, while certainly not a happy ending, was at least some kind of terminus, a place to reflect from.

At the end of that sad Tuesday morning meeting the management team made a list of all the advisors and funders we wanted to talk to. We were out of ideas, but we weren't out of friends, and we wanted to put our situation in front of people we trusted and see what they thought.

The first person on the list was Dean Cycon at Dean's Beans. Julie and I asked if we could come to see him at the beanery and he made some time for us on his first day back in the office after having had both hips replaced a few weeks earlier.

The conversation didn't start well. We laid out our financial basics and Dean responded the way most people tended to—by making suggestions about what else the store might sell or how we might market ourselves more widely. Julie and I gave each other a despairing look. Why was it so hard to grasp that we actually had a pretty good idea what we needed to do, we just didn't have sufficient resources to do it?

Dean must have seen the dismay on our faces because he asked us to tell him more. We laid it out for him—steep learning curve, hard-won lessons, back bills paid, shelves emptied, options depleted, wall hit. It was my flip chart in capsule form.

When we were done, Dean paused in thought but only for a moment. Then he got out of his chair, stiffly. It was odd to see him moving slowly—normally, like his good friend Karl Bittenbender, he bounded around like a mountain goat. He left the office for a few minutes and then came back to tell us, "We just held a member drive and you now have fifteen new members." Translation: Dean's Beans was buying each of its employees a Quabbin Harvest membership, to be paid for on the spot.

There was more: he'd listened to our assertion that we knew what sold well in the store and were confident that if we could keep those things better stocked we could generate more sales. He offered a credit arrangement for coffee that would help us in the short term without tying us down with too much more longer-term debt. And before we left he put the icing on the cake by offering to underwrite some of his bookkeeper's time to help us unravel the accounting mysteries we were still wrestling with in our financial systems.

None of it would fundamentally turn things around. But it didn't have to. It just opened some breathing room. It was how Dean had been operating for decades in small, mostly Indigenous communities hintered and hindered by the logic of bigness and cheapness. He understood development as something that had to be done from the ground up, starting from where people were and looking for immediate steps that could make things just a little better, things you could build on.

The biggest boost from our visit to Dean was the sense of mutuality, a recognition that we were all in something together, whether that was the North Quabbin or the diffuse, hard-to-pin-down good food movement or some broader vision of a more human-scaled, less rapacious kind of economic system. Those of us trying to keep Quabbin Harvest going were still a bunch of mostly white people in a mostly white area. But being in business with Dean's Beans helped put us into something closer to solidarity with Indigenous farmers and food businesses all around the world who were trying to hold on and prosper on their own terms. This wasn't General Foods demanding the cheapest possible tapioca flour from poorer parts of the world and using it to make the cheapest and most convenient processed foods, with some of the benefits trickling down to places like Orange until they suddenly stopped. It was using a business to strengthen a diffuse network of the smallest of the small and redirect resources where they were needed most. It was the future we'd been trying to work toward, and it was good to be reminded that although it felt distant and untenable in many ways, in other ways it was already happening, just across town and all around the globe.

Some of the other people we wanted to talk with happened to be at a one-day conference I attended in Boston that same week. It was a regional gathering of groups and institutions and people working on food systems issues, held at the top of a Boston skyscraper that towered directly over the downtown church with the Rube Goldberg furnace where my husband and I worked when we lived in the city decades before.

It felt odd to be so far above places we'd once walked on a daily basis, odd to have this bird's-eye view of the neat geometric pathways crisscrossing Boston Common, visible through still-bare trees. It felt odd to have so many pieces of my life and livelihood converging in the same big room—colleagues from my own university, people I'd worked with on consulting projects, acquaintances from other conferences and organizations, people I'd met through the co-op, including some from Mount Grace Land Conservation Trust and the Massachusetts Food Trust Program.

Those were the ones I needed to speak with, and it felt particularly odd to be trying to convey the urgency of what was happening back in Orange in a series of quick hallway conversations, essentially begging for help in the midst of the kind of professional discourse that prevails at conferences—measured in both tone and time, with everything in tidy increments that always start with a cordial introduction and end with a spatter of applause.

It reminded me of an encounter a couple of years earlier with a very small farmer and a very large squash.

The farmer was small in both stature and the scale of the farming she was doing. She was trying to start her own vegetable business, and she came to a meeting of the Greater Quabbin Food Alliance in late 2017 to voice her frustrations with trying to find a local market where she could sell the food she was growing.

The tone of the Food Alliance was not unlike that of the conference in Boston: professional, mannerly, well-organized. There were occasional moments when something more urgent punctured the calm demeanor, usually instigated by farmers or someone pursuing the all-but-impossible goal of making money selling food. Kate Stillman came to one meeting to voice her frustration about how the Healthy Incentives Program was hurting her meat business. Eric Stocker from Squash Trucking occasionally threw some cold water onto proposals for financially unrealistic farm-to-institution or farm-to-supermarket ideas that were floated at meeting after meeting. It was John Moore's blunt statement that the Orange and Athol farmers markets were dying that sparked the creation of a working group to focus on that issue.

Even those discussions, though, stayed within the realm of the polite—except for this one, which felt raw and awkward. The programs always started with a round of quick "lightning talks" and the little farmer was one of those speakers. She told us that selling at farmers markets wasn't compatible with her work schedule but that she had grown a lot of beautiful vegetables and was deeply upset that nobody in the area seemed able to buy them from her.

To underscore the point, she had brought a Blue Hubbard squash with her. The Blue Hubbard is the humpbacked whale of the squash family, knobbly and oversized and awkwardly majestic. This one was about half the size of the little farmer herself. Deb Habib volunteered to hold it while the farmer read a prepared statement, and the two of them performed a kind of slow-motion *pas de deux*, Deb shifting the weight of the giant squash from one arm to the other while the farmer read from the piece of paper she was gripping with shaking hands.

She told us about going to Quabbin Harvest with a big harvest of eggplant only to be told there was no way the co-op could buy or store or sell that much all at once—the exact opposite of the problem of small farmers not being able to supply things in large enough quantities to supermarket chains. The tiny farm and the small store were supposed to help each other, but they couldn't because their capacities weren't anywhere close to being in sync.

As the chair of the co-op's board, I felt her sense of betrayal like a punch in my own gut. She was trying to make sense of the absurd problems of scale and understand why this store that was supposedly all about local food and farms had turned her away. Hadn't she done her part? Why weren't we doing ours?

I couldn't actually see what else the co-op could have done. And you could argue that she *hadn't* done her part by talking to anyone or learning more about Quabbin Harvest as a potential market before she planted her crops. But the raw emotion of her response, the hurt and puzzlement, was hard to hear. She wasn't wrong to be so upset about the irrationality and intractability of the situation we were both in.

I suspect that the look on my face then was precisely what I was seeing on the faces of the people I was button-holing in the hallway during that conference in Boston in early 2020. They were empathetic, distressed even, but what could they do? It was one of those moments when I realized just how far I'd stepped across the line between the world of talk and the challenge of actually trying to keep a food business afloat. Now I was the one who was shaking but compelled to speak, trying to find some kind of register between professional discourse and a howl of anguish, desperate to gain the attention of anyone who might help even though there might not be any logical way for them to do anything, a supplicant from the margins carrying a weight that was too heavy to hold up alone.

Midway through the afternoon there was an unannounced interlude: Naima Penniman, who had spoken earlier in the day, would share a poem. The Penniman sisters, Naima and Leah, are driving forces at Soul Fire Farm, an important node in food-movement conversations about why it's not going to be possible to address what's wrong with the modern food system unless we're willing to take it right down to its foundations and look at the way it's been built over centuries on extractive and unequal and unhealthy relationships to land, to other species, and to each other as humans, especially across the racialized divides and disparities that grew alongside the modern capitalist world itself.

The earlier presentation had laid all of that out in a more measured, conference-appropriate way. But the poem was something different.

Naima Penniman's poems are living things—words on a page can remind you of them, but print flattens and diminishes the incantatory effect of Penniman's voice and presence, which invoke an authority that goes far deeper than the author's own. The Pennimans usually include poetry in their public presentations, and I always find it a powerful moment, a way to say things and stir people beyond what the more linear language of planning and analysis can do.

That day it was exactly what I needed to hear. The language invoked intergenerational memory and connection to the land among people displaced and distanced from farming and boxed out of the routes to prosperity that run from and through centers of modern power. Among such people, Penniman told us, every seed planted, every garden cultivated was "a terrain of remembrance, a vote for survival in an unpromised future." There was a phrase about turning hardship into harvest that resonated with what I'd been learning at the co-op: how you could almost miraculously withstand scarcity if you could find ways to act generously and generatively, out of love rather than fear.

Penniman told us that the present moment of division and calamity was precisely the time when we needed to act most purposefully. "Give what you most deeply desire to give," the poem concluded. "Possibility is as wide as the space we create to hold it."[1]

The poem broke me open. By the end I was—embarrassingly, inappropriately—in tears. I went out into the hallway and got myself back together, but it took a while. I wasn't weeping because our co-op was going to fail but because Penniman's words made me ashamed that we hadn't been able to keep going any longer, that we hadn't been as strong or as tough as all the people who had struggled for generations and centuries with far fewer resources and fewer well-placed friends and less hope of success than we had. I felt wimpy and white and small and wrung dry. But it also felt as though we were in fact giving up too readily, letting the world down just when it really needed us to find some way to keep going.

We heard that message in different ways in the next week. We sent an email to the whole membership about the meeting and the word percolated out quite quickly into the community: Quabbin Harvest was going broke. Julie started fielding distressed phone calls from farmers. "You're my biggest single customer," several told her.

It was a whole new perspective, but it made sense as we thought about it. We'd honored all our back bills to farmers and were paying most of them on delivery now. We were well past the point we'd been at when we had to turn away the little farmer with the truck full of eggplant. Bit by bit, Julie had been rebuilding relationships and finding ways to fit the puzzle of scale together.

And it wasn't just farmers. We were a not-inconsiderable outlet for Dean's Beans coffee and a substantial customer for Marty's Local, which had recently merged with and then replaced Squash Trucking. We bought a cooler's worth of dairy products every Tuesday through the one-man delivery service that brought milk and yogurt from the Connecticut River Valley. We could sell as many eggs as our local suppliers could bring us. The Farm School planned its planting around the summer program that distributed bags of fresh vegetables to low-income seniors. Every Thursday there was a rack of good things from an artisanal bakery on the other side of the Quabbin Reservoir. We were one of their major wholesale customers too.

We were so used to thinking of ourselves as tiny and frail that it was startling to realize how substantial a role we already played within the network of food businesses in the area, a network still full of gaps in capacity and scale. One big addition—like HIP in its heady first year—could throw things out of whack. One loss, especially of an intermediary node like the co-op, could have the same kind of disproportionate effect. As we prepared for the emergency meeting at the end of February, I came to a new appreciation for the multiplicity of interlocking scales inherent in what we call "local food" and an awareness of the ways those different scales could reinforce each other. To build on Naima Penniman's imagery, every seed planted, every node, every rope flung across a chasm, every small venture that could find some kind of handhold and manage to hang on, was important when the rifts were still so wide and the odds so long.

A lot of our vendors and farmers came to the emergency meeting. Some elected officials sent their aides. There were representatives from some of our funders, including the Massachusetts Food Trust Program. The new director of Mount Grace Land Conservation Trust was there. And there were a lot of concerned members.

We decided to hold the meeting in the store itself rather than upstairs in the boardroom. It seemed important for people to be able to look around and be reminded of what we were trying to save. That ability to look around was still hindered by the gigantic bank of mostly empty freezers which divided the floor space, but it felt right to be there, even if it made it hard to talk to everyone at once. With some careful placement of chairs and our most robust "teacher voices" we were able to present our analysis of where we were financially and our projections of what it would take to get us back to a position where we could envision keeping the store going.

People asked questions and offered suggestions. There were blessedly few ideas about new products to sell that might magically turn everything around. By and large, the membership seemed to accept that the store's inventory was on the right track and that the board's analysis of the situation was solid. We'd been staving things off with short-term fixes and it was obvious that we had to get beyond that and put things onto a more stable footing.

In the short term, we couldn't continue without a large and immediate infusion of cash. The Massachusetts Food Trust Program was willing to make a second loan, to match the donations that had been coming in through the Share a Shelf program since the fall. And with a handful of individual donors who had already made pledges, we were on our way toward a first-phase fundraising target. Was there the energy and tolerance for yet another full-fledged emergency campaign? Would members accept that there would be follow-up phases, that we needed to go on raising funds very vigorously right through the rest of the year and well beyond, as well as trying to motivate more people to shop in the store once it was restocked?

What came through in the discussion was a kind of positive negative, a collective digging-in of heels, a larger version of the leadership's own stubborn refusal over the past four years to accept failure. People talked in different ways about what would be lost if the store closed, not just in the present—the outlet for very small farmers who needed wholesale markets, the weekly abundance of the vegetable shares, the delights of Nalini's cooking—but even more for the future.

We weren't all thinking of exactly the same future or feeling the same way about what we thought we were headed toward. If we'd had to come to an agreement on that, we'd probably still be there arguing. For some, the store was a way to hedge against uncertainties to come; for others it was a resource for those already struggling. I thought I heard echoes of past losses in the conversation too, a shared awareness of the unbridgeable distances between board tables where decisions were made and places where their effects were felt, muted comments after the fact ("No true New Englander will like Delaware"). Everyone who spoke, recent settlers in the area and people descended from long-ago ones, those who had come and stayed or left and returned or never left at all, articulated a sense of being part of this place—the region, the town—and wanting to hold onto something we all wanted to see survive. It really came down to just that: we decided together to hold on, no matter what it took.

As far as I know I was the only anthropologist in the store on the night of that meeting in February 2020. But all of us had been doing something fundamentally anthropological in disassembling the taken-for-grantedness of the food system and our own complicity with it, building up a new body of knowledge—awkwardly, slowly, but with growing clarity and complexity, the way anthropologists do—about how we might create something new within the gigantic structures we couldn't yet do without. We had gotten to a point where we could recommit to a shared purpose that was partly about the store and partly about a different vision for the food system and partly about the North Quabbin and partly about each other. It was the answer to my moment of feeling that we were giving up too easily.

It came down to a vote. The board passed a resolution that if we could get 95 percent of the way to our first-phase fundraising goal in the next week, we would take it as a sign that there was enough support to keep going. The meeting broke up in a flurry of conversations and planning. And shopping—people swarmed the shelves, buying up nearly everything that was still left. The recently restocked coffee from Dean's was almost gone by the time we finally closed up at the end of the night. I went home to draft a new email pitch and set up a crowdfunding campaign.

A week later we had reached our goal and were well on the way to restocking the store, just as the future arrived.

Over that week I was watching the news and adjusting my urban anthropology lectures to touch on the news about a novel virus starting to circulate globally. Images of empty streets in locked-down Chinese cities and stories about overflowing hospital wards in Italy were unsettling but still safely distant until they weren't anymore. As the first U.S. deaths from the new COVID-19 virus began to be tallied, everything went from abstract to concrete in a hurry. Instead of inching our way toward spring break we were reconfiguring classes to be taught online as campuses shut down and everyone went home—or as close to home as they could get—and into lockdowns of our own. Everyday life turned on its head or came to a screeching halt.

Except that we all still had to eat. And suddenly a lot of people were getting a crash course in a lot of things they'd been taking for granted about the industrial food system.

News stories about farmers dumping milk and euthanizing pigs showed just how unwieldy and specialized food supply chains had become, unable to downsize or adapt in response to abrupt changes in demand.

When supermarket shelves emptied in the first wave of pandemic-induced panic shopping, the "efficiency" of just-in-time inventory management started to look more like a vulnerability too, a disturbing flaw in our collective ability to provide for ourselves. A lot of people—at least those who had the luxury of working from home or sheltering in place—found comfort in nurturing a sourdough starter or learning a new cooking technique from YouTube. But why did the stores keep running out of bread flour? How could there be a shortage of yeast?

The thick layer of undervalued labor that the whole system had always rested on became more visible to more people: slaughterhouse workers whose already-arduous conditions were worsened by the new risk of disease and pressure to keep the meat industry going at full speed; field crews swathed to the eyeballs in hundred-degree heat as California's Central Valley burned in a now-annual apocalyptic fire season; low-wage grocery store and restaurant workers newly deemed "essential" and joined by a growing legion of precariously employed in-store shoppers and drivers for food delivery services. A lot of the gaps and shortages in food supply turned out not to be about the food itself but about labor and about how desperate you needed to be to risk your actual life for not very much money.

People who had never really had to think about these things were shocked—as Americans have always been—by juxtaposed surplus and need, convenience and violence. There were valiant efforts to adjust, to redirect food to where it was needed, to reconfigure the flows, to "pivot," in the buzzword of the moment. Neighborhood restaurants donated back stock to laid-off employees and started selling quirky selections of groceries pieced together from their own networks of supply, while school systems opened pick-up stations to distribute what would have been free school breakfasts and lunches.[2]

And Quabbin Harvest, which had been so hard to explain and define, so illegible, suddenly made sense to more people in a way that it hadn't before.

Partly it was because we were small and scrappy and used to adapting to crises that we were able to pivot without missing a beat. Julie instituted a remote-ordering and curbside-pickup system within the first days of the shutdown, and it stayed busy and popular for months, attracting new customers as well as serving existing ones.

Partly it was that our more variegated and regional supply chains were better able to withstand shocks than national and global ones. Marty's Local had been extending its reach westward into New York State, and when the big flour and bread companies couldn't meet increased demand with their scaled-down labor forces, Marty's was able to source bread from an eastern New York State bakery that quickly scaled up, along with flour from a mill processing New York–grown wheat. Our main supplier of soap and sanitizer, a small company in Boston, kept us well-stocked when bigger stores were running out. Whole Foods offered to buy up their entire inventory, but the owner said no, preferring his existing network of loyal smaller customers to a one-time windfall. Farmers in the North Quabbin and Connecticut River Valley were just starting to plant when the pandemic hit, and the timing was good for ramped-up production, with fresh local greens hitting the shelves soon after it became clear this was not going to be just a temporary blip.

And everyone wanted those greens. In the early confusion about how the virus was spread and whether there was anything that could be done to ward it off, there was consensus that eating lots of vegetables was probably a smart thing to do. The co-op increased its orders from Marty's Local from once a week to twice, and even so the produce cooler was stripped bare by the time the new stock arrived. It was a bonus that much of it—and more as the growing season got underway—came from closer to home than what people were used to seeing at the supermarket. And it wasn't just about the produce. Amid national news stories about nightmare conditions in industrial slaughterhouses, buying high-quality ground beef and sausages from a small store that sourced locally processed meat from grassfed animals on small area farms felt transparent, ethical, and safer as well.

Beyond the desire for healthy and knowable food, there was a sense, especially in the first months of the pandemic, that everyone should be helping each other. That included finding ways to support shuttered restaurants and struggling neighbors and small independent businesses that kept Main Streets alive. The combination of what Quabbin Harvest sold and what the store was trying to be made us exactly what a lot of people were suddenly looking for. From being a struggling outlier we were now a kind of community anchor. We expanded our HIP enrollments and partnered on other emergency programs that helped get fresh food to people on the economic margins. A local politician underwrote a string of free pop-up fruit-stands on the town commons around her district all summer, sourcing through the co-op. Huge amounts of food—huge compared with where we'd been a mere month before—were moving through the store every week, barely staying long enough for the greens to need sprucing up or to find their way into the dishes Nalini continued to turn out in the kitchen.

For those of us who had spent years painstakingly shifting our shopping habits so we could support the co-op—learning the weekly delivery schedules, tamping down our annoyance when something wasn't in stock, coming to value the store for what it was instead of fixating on what it wasn't—it was amazing to see so many new shoppers falling instantly into those more flexible and accepting patterns. People were grateful when they found what they were looking for, delighted when they discovered something new, remarkably tolerant when Julie explained a gap or delay.

With food provisioning now an open question rather than a certainty, simply having an accessible and forthright person to talk to felt like a boon. It could be a little harder to stay the requisite six feet apart, but our small footprint went the other way too. Smaller stores felt inherently safer than big ones, in ways that were far more than just physical.

I was in the upstairs office working with MaryEllen and the borrowed bookkeeper from Dean's Beans on the first Saturday that our weekly sales went over $9,000. I kept running downstairs to check the total, coming back with breathless updates. In the weeks that followed, sales kept going up and up, to double where we'd been, then even higher. For one giddy month we were actually operating above profitability. And even when things eventually settled back down again, the sales figures were still higher than they'd ever been.

It's not an exaggeration to say that the COVID-19 pandemic saved Quabbin Harvest.

Of course, you could also say that the membership and community had already saved the store with the emergency fundraising campaign. Without that, there would have been almost nothing for people to buy when the panic-buying started and far fewer reasons for shoppers to come back or spread the word. But without the months that followed, without all the closures and anxieties and partial reopenings and ever-changing mandates and the feeling that we all needed to look out for each other in small and large ways, those emergency funds might well have proven to be just one more short-term fix that couldn't be sustained.

As the pandemic went on and sales continued to be robust, we paid off more back bills, removing threats that someone would call in a debt we couldn't pay. And we were able to make one major cost-cutting change: we got rid of the old freezers. Along with its second loan, the Massachusetts Food Trust Program provided another grant, this one to pay for a couple of smaller, more efficient freezer units. Bruce Scherer came in with his tools and took apart the old freezers that had been gobbling up electricity and squatting in the middle of the store like a physical manifestation of the bigness that hampers and hinders small stores. The oversized monster went out the door as pieces of glass and scrap metal. Julie added new shelf space for groceries in its place and we stopped dreading the monthly arrival of the electric bill or the possibility of another breakdown. It was liberating and lightening.

Looking back at the first months of the pandemic, what still astonishes and invigorates me is that so many people—far beyond the farmers market faithful—were able to see so quickly and perceptively into the fissures that opened up in the industrial food system's glossy veneer. It was as though the fundamental problems inherent in that insoluble koan and slick magic trick had always been a kind of public secret that everybody knows and just never talks about until something makes it impossible to ignore. The glaring inequalities—who was at greatest risk of being infected and killed by the COVID-19 virus, who was able to work safely from home, what kinds of preexisting conditions added to vulnerability, who was driving the trucks and processing the meat and doing the personal shopping—all shone a bright light on the interwoven lines of race and class in America, tracing how difference and disparity had been coded into both rural and urban places, and how they continued to work across the increasingly polarized political landscape. The massive resurgence of the Black Lives Matter movement after the police killing of George Floyd in Minneapolis that May, alongside the feverish final months of the 2020 election campaign, prompted a lot of soul-searching about pasts that refused to stay past, worlds that had already ended, possible futures that had been blocked and hindered but that continued to assert themselves around flash-points like the one we were in the middle of.

In the moment, there was a broad wave of support for those who were already building and nurturing alternatives and dismantling taken-for-granted habits and dependencies. We felt it at Quabbin Harvest, and you could see it all around the alternative food sector, especially in the wider public awareness of food projects addressing racial inequity and all that stems from it. Along with efforts to get food to people who needed it during the pandemic, there was suddenly much wider acknowledgment that emergency, in-the-moment food assistance alone wasn't nearly good enough, and discussion of how unequal access to healthy food was linked to poverty, racism, and policies that too often focus only on symptoms and never get to root causes.

Most of the big headlines in 2020—the global pandemic, the unresolved national struggle around race and civil rights, the starkly incompatible visions of America that drove the election campaign and its aftermath—were not centrally about food. But food was connected to and through everything that was happening, all of the histories and legacies that were suddenly more glaringly obvious. The dailyness of eating, its essentialness, its links with health and place and belonging, made food a starting point for a lot of people who were feeling that something had to change. Food, once again, was an obvious place to act from, something to act with and upon.

Decades before avoiding gluten became a trend, I was diagnosed with a wheat allergy. When I finally found a doctor who could make sense of my oddly variegated symptoms, he said something that stuck with me, something I often repeat on the first day of my food classes: "You know, the gut is where we meet the world."

My students tend to have the same reaction I did at the time: first *eww*, and then *woah*. The intimacy of it, the immediacy, can feel both invasive and intriguing. I still struggle with the invasiveness but the fascination has stayed too.

Humans are always connected to the world around us when we eat. But one of the things that anthropology teaches you is the importance of being very specific when you talk about people, cultures, societies, economies, times, places. So I emphasize to my students that *this* world, the one that can be so hard to digest and comprehend, is the industrialized world, pieced together out of fossil fuels and commodity markets and Western scientific knowledge and plantations and assembly lines and the modern hubris of thinking that we'll always be able to invent ourselves out of any problems we might invent ourselves into.

Over the past couple of centuries, this industrialized world has become a kind of carapace that we live under and now mistake for the sky. It encases the entire globe, still expanding and reinforcing itself in some places even as it renders others abject and uninhabitable. And everywhere, everywhere it is brittle, often on the verge of breakdown, requiring massive infusions of capital and political will to maintain its fictions of limitless economic growth and the promise of middle-class prosperity for all. Many of us who have grown up under it start life with an inherently impoverished sense of how things might be different. Whether we inhabit zones of prosperity or of breakdown, we often have very little tolerance for dealing with the big paradoxes we live within, all those questions that resist answers.

And yet, as the early months of the COVID pandemic showed, that tacit awareness of fissures is also present, and people will act on it in immediate and consequential ways, given the right stimulus. The now-regular extreme weather events of the changed climate—yet another "historic drought" in our part of New England last summer, and this year rains washing out roads and flooding farmers' fields, at the same time as we're blanketed with smoke from distant Canadian wildfires—bring more and more people in once-comfortable places to the realization that the status quo is no longer tenable.

Where to go from here remains a big open question. As a teacher and writer, I'm always convinced of the power of learning—good, critical learning—to point us in the right directions, and indeed it is worth noting how many of the voices that have helped broaden our understanding of the problems within the food system belong not to planners or economists or political leaders but to authors and filmmakers and educators, people with the skills to translate across often-incommensurate languages and ways of knowing.[3]

As my students continually remind me, learning is not the same as taking action. But it can help inoculate us against simplistic or short-sighted or too hasty actions and distinguish an actual alternative from a facile or misleading one. And it can suggest ways to align ourselves with projects being built up from different foundations.

These are everywhere, once you know what you're looking for. There are Indigenous food businesses reaching toward both tribal sovereignty and commercial development without trying to reconcile all of the possible contradictions between the two; farmers and scientists re-partnering with the microbes and insects and ruminants with whom our agricultural ecosystems have co-evolved over millennia; labor organizers deftly holding progressive brands to account for inequities in their supply chains; activists and organizers knitting together food and history and science and spirit in projects of regeneration at neighborhood, community, and larger scales; farmers and their allies speaking out against corporate consolidation and the deep distortions of the meat-grain complex and parity pricing, for heaven's sake—that wonky policy point that Americans have avoided talking about for decades and decades; food banks whose leaders are connecting the dots among hunger and the lack of affordable housing or decent entry-level jobs; emerging programs that follow the HIP model by eschewing the cheap food of the subsidized industrial surplus and redirecting subsidy toward smaller farmers growing food in and for the places where they belong; aquaculturalists and fisherfolk and wetland reclamation efforts that approach the earth's waters as a commons filled with fellow-beings, an edge zone where we're learning—in the unbalanced climate that we ourselves have shaped—that we have to pay attention to what water wants and to adapt in ways that modern minds still find largely unimaginable. There are new co-ops being formed all the time, including in Orange where Dean Cycon's retirement in the spring of 2023 opened the way for Dean's Beans to become a worker-owned co-operative. People all around the world—*this* world—are imagining and acting on these ideas in both top-down and grassroots ways, sometimes in tension with one another, sometimes overlapping, dancing with both markets and legislative processes, and finding wiggle room in sometimes unexpected places. These efforts are inescapably political, in the sense of dealing with power and collective decision-making.[4] Working toward them can build and strengthen a body politic as well as requiring it.

The list above isn't my attempt at the kind of blanket hopefulness that tends to show up at the ends of books about the global environmental crisis, the ones Elizabeth Kolbert calls "the additional three pages" explaining why we shouldn't give in to despair while careening into almost unimaginable disaster.[5] Most or all of those projects are gappy, emergent, contested. But one of the many things I've learned as an avocational grocer is that even when we don't know enough about what we're doing or have everything we need, we can still act in ways that are purposeful and generous and real. And if we've started in the right direction—if we can tell a true alternative from a merely cosmetic one, and develop a tolerance for what it means to take some responsibility for keeping it going—then that *is* enough. In some ways, it is everything. Even those of us who have historically felt ourselves to be at the center of the modern world can cultivate the kinds of skills and awareness it has always taken to operate on its margins, where things are forever falling apart and endlessly coming into being. We are all on the edge now. And we all still have to eat.

On a June day in 2021, as we moved into the second year of COVID, I came into the store to find Nalini making yuca fritters. With the days lengthening and more people beginning to be vaccinated against the virus, there was a sense of cautious optimism—premature, it turned out—that we might be moving out of the pandemic. After the grueling

2020 election campaign and its violent aftermath, there seemed to be calm—if not harmony—in the political world at last. It was a hopeful moment, a respite.

Which may have been why I was so struck by the sight of Nalini cooking yuca. I'd spent the spring immersing myself in the histories of Orange and the Minute Tapioca Company, learning how this small town had shaped the global supply chains of a tough and obstinate plant and how that plant had helped some people resist and survive the plantation while enabling others to make fortunes and still others to display their new middle-class prosperity in a manically expanding industrial society. Coming in to Quabbin Harvest to find Nalini peeling and boiling and mashing yuca seemed like a perfect closing of the circle. The waxed yuca roots in the produce cooler, looking like bulky brown carrots, were both a commodity and something Nalini was reclaiming from commodity chains through knowledge and skills formed and shared on the margins of the colonized world.

It was as though a faint breeze had stirred the giant fire curtain behind the stage in the town hall, allowing a glimpse of that unnamed yuca farmer in his field—maybe in Java, maybe Puerto Rico—tending a crop that would end up in Orange and on tables all around the United States as "an almost magically successful dessert ingredient," to quote a 1929 promotional recipe booklet.[6]

The convenience and variety and cheapness that companies like Minute Tapioca wrought are still with us and still accelerating their reach wherever they can. But that farmer is still there too, however veiled and out of view. In a world unsettled by a pandemic and shaken by a changed climate and forced into greater awareness of the disparities and distances on which the whole modern project rests, it felt as though something might finally be changing in a more lasting way. It was, at the very least, one more crack in the facade, letting in a little more light for all of us to see by as we move together into this new world.

NOTES

INTRODUCTION: MAGIC

1. These included Eric Schlosser's *Fast Food Nation: The Dark Side of the All-American Meal* (New York: Houghton Mifflin, 2001, made into a film in 2006); Barbara Kingsolver with Steven L. Hopp and Camille Kingsolver, *Animal/Vegetable/Miracle: A Year of Food Life* (New York: Harper, 2007); Michael Pollan, *The Omnivore's Dilemma: A Natural History of Four Meals* (New York: Penguin, 2006), and his other works; and the films *Supersize Me* (2004), *King Corn* (2007), and *Food Inc.* (2008).
2. "'Plant Yourself in My Neighborhood': An Ethnographic Landscape Study of Farming and Farmers in Columbia County, New York," Martin Van Buren National Historic Site/National Park Service/Northeast Region Ethnography Program, 2012. For an overview of the project, see Cathy Stanton, "Farming in the Sweet Spot: Integrating Interpretation, Preservation, and Food Production at National Parks," *George Wright Forum* 34, no. 3 (December 2017): 275–84, http://www.georgewright.org.
3. INCITE! Women of Color against Violence, *The Revolution Will Not Be Funded: Beyond the Non-Profit Industrial Complex* (Durham, NC: Duke University Press, 2017).
4. Ellen Meiksins Wood, *The Origin of Capitalism: A Longer View* (New York: Verso, 2002).
5. Wendell Berry, "The Pleasures of Eating," in Berry, *What Are People For?* (Berkeley, CA: Counterpoint, 1990), 150.
6. Chris Newman, "Into the Abyss: Why the Local Food Movement Needs to Stop Congratulating Itself," Medium, January 7, 2017, https://medium.com.
7. Michael Carolan, "Adventurous Food Futures: Knowing about Alternatives Is Not Enough, We Need to Feel Them," *Agriculture and Human Values* 33 (2016): 141–52.

CHAPTER 1: SETTLING

1. National Register of Historic Places, Registration Form for Orange Center Historic District, U.S. Department of the Interior, National Park Service, 1988, 8n19, https://catalog.archives.gov. For the history of the New Home Sewing Machine Company, see "The Men behind New Home," *International Sewing Machine Collectors' Society News*, no. 56 (July 1997), https://ismacs.net.
2. Dona Brown, *Back to the Land: The Enduring Dream of Self-Sufficiency in Modern America* (Madison: University of Wisconsin Press, 2011).
3. "Orange Bicentennial: Orange Innovation Center with Noel Vincent," interview by Pat Larson, Athol-Orange Community Television, 2010, http://24.39.25.146.
4. Michael Pollan, "The Food Movement, Rising," *New York Review of Books*, May 20, 2010; Eric Holt-Giménez, "Food Security, Food Justice, or Food Sovereignty?" *Food First Backgrounder* 16, no. 4 (Winter 2010).
5. This approach is supported by two regional land and food planning documents,

Wildlands and Woodlands, Farmlands and Communities (based at Harvard Forest in the North Quabbin town of Petersham; see https://wildlandsandwoodlands.org), and the *New England Food Vision* (based at the University of New Hampshire and currently being updated as part of the six-state "New England Feeding New England" process; see https://nefoodsystemplanners.org).

6. Different places and levels of government offer different legal mechanisms for doing this. Massachusetts's Agricultural Preservation Restriction (APR) program, created in 1977, was the earliest in the United States. See Jen Boudrie, Massachusetts Department of Agricultural Resources, APR Program Guide, n.d., 4, https://www.mass.gov.

7. Ricky Baruch and Deb Habib, *Making Love While Farming: A Field Guide to a Life of Passion and Purpose* (Amherst, MA: Levellers Press, 2019). Their quest for land is described on pages 23–28.

CHAPTER 2: HANDHOLDS

1. On the evolution of the cold chain, see Susanne Freidberg, *Fresh: A Perishable History* (Cambridge, MA: Belknap Press of Harvard University Press, 2009), and Jonathan Rees, *Refrigeration Nation: A History of Ice, Appliances, and Enterprise in America* (Baltimore: Johns Hopkins University Press, 2016).

2. Two nearly identical versions of this story appear in the *Orange [MA] Enterprise and Journal*, November 20, 1925, and "Thank a Sick Sailor," in *The Story of a Pantry Shelf: An Outline of Grocery Specialties* (New York: Butterick, 1925), 160–63.

3. To piece together the Stavers story, I used census records and street directories in Ancestry.com; U.S. Patent Office records; Find-a-Grave.com; the online collections of the Boston Public Library's Leventhal Map Center (especially their wondrous Atlas-cope tool); and the *Harpers Weekly* supplement, December 14, 1872, 985–86, about the Great Fire, which includes a detailed lithograph capturing the damage to the Stavers's boardinghouse. At the Orange end, I also drew on the digital newspaper collections of the Wheeler Memorial Library in Orange, the collection of the Orange Historical Society, and the court records of *Whitman Grocery Company v. Susan Stavers* (1895) in the archives of the Massachusetts Supreme Judicial Court.

4. Michael Holleran, *Boston's Changeful Times: The Origins of Preservation and Planning in America* (Baltimore: Johns Hopkins University Press, 1998), 19.

5. David Mehegan, "Hang on a Minute," *Boston Globe*, January 2, 2008, http://archive.boston.com.

6. "Sweet Cassava," *Orange [MA] Journal*, June 28, 1889.

7. Katherine J. Parkin, *Food Is Love: Advertising and Gender Roles in Modern America* (Philadelphia: University of Pennsylvania Press, 2006); Tracey Deutsch, *Building a Housewife's Paradise: Gender, Politics, and American Grocery Stores in the Twentieth Century* (Chapel Hill: University of North Carolina Press, 2012).

8. Eben Gridley, later the company's president, recalled this at the fiftieth anniversary celebrations in 1947. "Fiftieth Anniversary of Minute Tapioca Manufacture Observed," *Orange Enterprise and Journal*, September 18, 1947.

9. These early struggles are detailed in "'Industry' Carries Article on Local Industry," *Orange Enterprise and Journal*, December 2, 1937, which in turn cited a trade publication called *Industry* that profiled the Minute Tapioca Company that month.

10. "Orange Leaves," *Orange [MA] Enterprise*, April 9, 1895.

11. "Orange Leaves," *Orange Enterprise*, February 19, 1895.

12. Advertisement, *Life Magazine*, Vol. 17, No. 5, December 18, 1944, 57.

13. "Dedication Exercises at the Enlarged Shoe Shop," *Orange Journal*, May 8, 1891.

14. "Minute Tapioca Co. Is Fifty Years Old September 10th," *Orange Enterprise and Journal*, September 7, 1944.

15. Nancy Rubin, *American Empress: The Life and Times of Marjorie Merriweather Post* (1995; reprint Lincoln, NE: iUniverse Star, 2004), 36–37; Mark Pendergrast, *Uncommon Grounds: The History of Coffee and How It Transformed Our World* (2001; reprint New York: Basic Books, 2020), 101–2.

16. Rubin, *American Empress*, 137–44; Freidberg, *Fresh*, 251–53.

17. "Minute Tapioca Company Acquired by Postum Cereal Company," *Orange Enterprise and Journal*, October 1, 1926.

18. "No True New Englander Will Like Delaware," *Orange Enterprise and Journal*, August 8, 1963.

19. "Minute Tapioca Company Acquired by Postum Cereal Company."

20. Megan Poinski, "Why a North Carolina Couple Brought Postum Back," *FoodDive*, November 5, 2018, https://www.fooddive.com.

CHAPTER 3: TARGET MARKET

1. Domenic Poli, "Orange 'Pocket Park' Gets Matching Grant for Renovations," *Greenfield [MA] Recorder*, August 25, 2016.

2. Josée Johnson and Shyon Baumann, *Foodies: Democracy and Distinction in the Gourmet Foodscape* (New York: Routledge, 2009); Julie Guthman, "'If They Only Knew': The Unbearable Whiteness of Alternative Food," in *Cultivating Food Justice: Race, Class, and Sustainability*, ed. Alison Hope Alkon and Julian Agyeman (Cambridge, MA: MIT Press, 2011), 263–81; Alison Hope Alkon, Yuki Kato, and Joshua Sbicca, eds., *A Recipe for Gentrification: Food, Power, and Resistance in the City* (New York: New York University Press, 2020).

3. "Feasibility Study for the Relocation and Expansion of the North Quabbin Community Cooperative," Field to Table, 2012, 16, copy in author's possession.

CHAPTER 4: DECONSTRUCTED BURGER

1. Leonard L. Richards, *Shays's Rebellion: The American Revolution's Final Battle* (Philadelphia: University of Pennsylvania Press, 2002).

2. On how the taken-for-granted patterns of supermarket marketing and shopping came into being, see Rachel Bowlby, *Carried Away: The Invention of Modern Shopping* (New York: Columbia University Press, 2001); Tracey Deutsch, *Building a Housewife's Paradise: Gender, Politics, and American Grocery Stores in the Twentieth Century* (Chapel Hill: University of North Carolina Press, 2012); Paul B. Ellickson, "The Evolution of the Supermarket Industry: From A&P to Walmart," in *Handbook on the Economics of Retail and Distribution*, ed. Emet Basker (Cheltenham, U.K.: Edward Elgar, 2016), 368–91; Shane Hamilton, *Supermarket USA: Food and Power in the Cold War Farms Race* (New Haven, CT: Yale University Press, 2018); and Benjamin Lorr, *The Secret Life of Groceries: The Dark Miracle of the American Supermarket* (New York: Avery, 2020).

3. Ellickson, "The Evolution of the Supermarket Industry," 4.

4. Daniel Scroop, "The Anti-Chain Store Movement and the Politics of Consumption," *American Quarterly* 60, no. 4 (December 2008): 925–49.

5. In *A Theory of Shopping* (Ithaca, NY: Cornell University Press, 1998), anthropologist Daniel Miller investigates how we "shop our feelings" (including our feelings for others).

6. "Know your farmer, know your food" was an Obama-era local-food promotion campaign created by then-Deputy Secretary of Agriculture Kathleen Merrigan. This focus

on transparency in sourcing has been championed by popular food writers like Michael Pollan and questioned by some others as too limited. See, for example, Julie Guthman, "Can't Stomach It: How Michael Pollan et al. Made Me Want to Eat Cheetos," *Gastronomica: The Journal of Food and Culture* 7, no. 2 (2007): 75–79.

7. Julie Guthman, "'If They Only Knew': The Unbearable Whiteness of Alternative Food," in *Cultivating Food Justice: Race, Class, and Sustainability,* ed. Alison Hope Alkon and Julian Agyeman (Cambridge, MA: MIT Press, 2011), 263–81.

8. Branden Born and Mark Purcell, "Avoiding the Local Trap: Scale and Food Systems in Planning Research," *Journal of Planning Education and Research* 26 (2006): 195–207; Margaret Gray, *Labor and the Locavore: The Making of a Comprehensive Food Ethic* (Berkeley: University of California Press, 2013).

9. On what some have called "fairwashing," see Daniel Jaffee, *Brewing Justice: Fair Trade Coffee, Sustainability, and Survival* (Berkeley: University of California Press, 2014), 268.

10. The same principle and some of the same laws also applied to ale, a more perishable staple drink that was widely consumed in England before brewing beer with hops became common. See Judith M. Bennett, *Women in the Medieval English Countryside* (Oxford: Oxford University Press, 2004), 120. For more on the assize of bread (and ale), see Alan S. C. Ross, "The Assize of Bread," *Economic History Review* 9, no. 2 (1956): 332–42; Howard Rock, *Artisans of the New Republic: The Tradesmen of New York City in the Age of Jefferson* (New York: New York University Press, 1987), chap. 7; James Davis, "Baking for the Common Good: A Reassessment of the Assize of Bread in Medieval England," *Economic History Review* 57, no. 3 (2004): 465–502; and James W. Ely, "Economic Liberties and the Original Meaning of the Constitution," *San Diego Law Review* 45 (2008): 681–85.

11. Quoted in Joy Santlofer, *Food City: Four Centuries of Food-Making in New York* (New York: Norton, 2016), 53.

12. R. J. Van der Spek, Jan Luiten van Zanden, and Bas van Leeuwen, eds., *A History of Market Performance: From Ancient Babylonia to the Modern World* (London: Routledge, 2014). Sometimes intentionally, sometimes inadvertently, anthropologists have gathered a great deal of data about people encountering capitalist markets for the first time, which shows that capitalism's logic and the effects it has on social relationships often strike neophytes as immoral, occult, even cannibalistic. See, for example, the work of Jean Comaroff, John Comaroff, Peter Geschiere, and Michael Taussig, among many others. There are a lot of opinions about how to interpret these responses, but David Graeber was probably right when he said that anthropologists' trove of information shows not only what kinds of other economic systems might be possible but how they are actually being pursued in the world right now. "The West may have introduced some new possibilities," he wrote in 2004, "but it hasn't canceled any of the old ones out." Graeber, *Fragments of an Anarchist Anthropology* (Chicago: Prickly Paradigm Press, 2004), 50.

13. Davis, "Baking for the Common Good."

CHAPTER 5: (SOME) PEOPLE BEFORE PROFITS

1. Daniel Korschun and Grant Welker, *We Are Market Basket: The Story of the Unlikely Grassroots Movement That Saved a Beloved Business* (New York: American Management Association, 2015), xiv, 2.

2. Supermarkets' share of the grocery business expanded from 35 percent in 1948 to nearly 50 percent by 1963. See Harvey Levenstein, *Paradox of Plenty: A Social History of Eating in Modern America* (New York: Oxford University Press, 1993), 113.

3. Korschun and Welker, *We Are Market Basket,* 8.

4. In 2014 an experienced Market Basket cashier could make $40,000 a year with benefits, nearly twice the national average. Sally Kohn, "How Market Basket Workers Are Fighting Greed," CNN, August 21, 2014, https://www.cnn.com.

5. I. M. Baker, "Steps to Success in Self-Service Store," *Chain Store Age*, January 1941, quoted in Benjamin Lorr, *The Secret Life of Groceries: The Dark Miracle of the American Supermarket* (New York: Avery, 2020), 33.

6. "How Do Grocery Stores Make Money When Their Profit Margins Are So Low?" Marketplace, May 13, 2022, https://www.marketplace.org; Barbara Bean-Mellinger, "What Is the Profit Margin for a Supermarket?" *Chron*, November 14, 2018, https://smallbusiness.chron.com.

7. On the "fixed stomach" problem, see Levenstein, *Paradox of Plenty*, 108.

8. Curt Nickish, "The Mystery of Market Basket's Missing Website, and the Lone Shopper Who Filled the Void," WBUR, July 13, 2014, https://www.wbur.org; Brian J. White, "Welcome to 1997: Market Basket (Finally) Has a Website," *Boston Globe*, October 25, 2017. On Market Basket strategies in general, see Korschun and Welker, *We Are Market Basket*, 22–25. They discuss bonuses on page 62, eschewing business schools on page 81, grooming code and uniforms on page 80, and the website saga on page 87.

9. Korschun and Welker, *We Are Market Basket*, 154–55.

10. Shane Hamilton, *Supermarket USA: Food and Power in the Cold War Farms Race* (New Haven, CT: Yale University Press, 2018), esp. chap. 1, "Machines for Selling."

11. Korschun and Welker, *We Are Market Basket*, 23, 22. There's always been a debate in the grocery sector about whether slotting fees are good or bad. See Phil Edwards, "The Hidden War over Grocery Shelf Space," Vox, November 22, 2016, https://www.vox.com.

12. Korschun and Welker, *We Are Market Basket*, 62, 93, 81.

13. Steve Bailey, "Demoulas Redux," *Boston Globe*, June 23, 2004: "My solution: meat cleavers in Aisle 9. Arthur S. Demoulas vs. his cousin Arthur T. Demoulas, winner take all. Messy for sure, but quicker and more economical. And it has a finality the courts will never offer this mad bunch." Back-to-back *Boston Globe* profiles of both Arthurs during the 2014 uprising attempted to take a balanced view. See Shirley Leung, "Some See Kinder, Gentler Side of Arthur S. Demoulas," *Boston Globe*, August 22, 2014, and Callum Borchers, "Arthur T. Demoulas' Personal Touch Can Cut Both Ways," *Boston Globe*, August 23, 2014.

14. Korschun and Welker, *We Are Market Basket*, 97; Casey Ross, "Close Look at a Decade of Demoulas Fighting," *Boston Globe*, August 15, 2014. Walmart stopped its employee profit-sharing program in 2010 but kept giving quarterly bonuses until 2021. "Wal-Mart to End Profit-Sharing in Benefits Switch," Reuters, October 8, 2010, https://www.reuters.com; Melissa Repko, "Walmart Ends Quarterly Bonuses for Store Associates, as It Raises Employees' Hourly Pay," CNBC, September 9, 2021, https://www.cnbc.com.

15. Korschun and Welker, *We Are Market Basket*, 38, 101–3, 108, 112; Jim Dudlicek, "Delhaize Reportedly Eyeing Market Basket," *Progressive Grocer*, August 7, 2014, https://progressivegrocer.com; David Welch and Tom Moroney, "At Least 12 Buyers Eye Market Basket," Bloomberg News, August 16, 2014, https://www.telegram.com.

16. Curt Nickish, "Market Basket Shows Power of Organized Labor without Unions," WBUR, September 3, 2014, https://www.wbur.org.

17. Korschun and Welker, *We Are Market Basket*, xi–xii.

18. Korschun and Welker, *We Are Market Basket*, 54.

19. Melanie DuPuis, *Dangerous Digestion: The Politics of American Dietary Advice* (Berkeley: University of California Press, 2015), esp. chaps. 3–4.

20. Quoted in Lorr, *The Secret Life of Groceries*, 31.

21. Toby Sterling and Robert-Jan Bartunek, "Ahold, Delhaize in $28 Billion Merger Focused on U.S. East Coast," *Reuters*, June 24, 2015, https://www.reuters.com.

22. Income and wealth disparities have widened significantly over the past four decades, roughly the era of what we call "economic globalization" and "neoliberal" economic policies in the United States and many other places. As the Pew Research Center concluded in a white paper shortly before the start of the COVID-19 pandemic on "Trends in Income and Wealth Inequality," "income inequality in the U.S. has increased since 1980 and is greater than in peer countries." Juliana Menasce Horowitz, Ruth Igielnik, and Rakesh Kochhar, "Trends in Income and Wealth Inequality," Pew Research Center, January 9, 2020, https://www.pewresearch.org.

23. Chris Faraone, "The Last Stand for the Middle Class Is Taking Place in a Parking Lot in Massachusetts," *Esquire*, July 29, 2014, https://www.esquire.com.

24. Casey Ross, "1 Year Later: Bitter Family Dispute Didn't Stifle Growth at Market Basket," *Boston Globe*, June 28, 2015.

25. Casey Ross, "Grateful Demoulas Focuses on What Awaits," *Boston Globe*, September 12, 2014.

26. Ross, "1 Year Later."

CHAPTER 6: AFTER THE PLANTATION

1. Daniel Korschun and Grant Welker, *We Are Market Basket: The Story of the Unlikely Grassroots Movement That Saved a Beloved Business* (New York: American Management Association, 2015), 191.

2. Casey Ross, "1 Year Later: Bitter Family Dispute Didn't Stifle Growth at Market Basket," *Boston Globe*, June 28, 2015.

3. Steven G. Rabe, *U.S. Intervention in British Guiana: A Cold War Story* (Chapel Hill: University of North Carolina Press, 2005), 4.

4. Sugar cane was first domesticated in New Guinea and spread westward through Asia, the Middle East, and Europe. Crystalline sugar (what we now think of as "table sugar") was first produced in northern India, as recorded in ancient texts there. See Sidney Mintz, *Sweetness and Power: The Place of Sugar in Modern History* (New York: Penguin, 1985), 32. In *A Billion Black Anthropocenes or None* (Minneapolis: University of Minnesota Press, 2018), 33–39, Kathryn Yusoff draws on the thinking of Jamaican anticolonial writer Sylvia Wynter to suggest that the enslavement of Africans on that first Portuguese plantation in 1452 was one possible origin point for the "Anthropocene."

5. Natalie Hopkinson, "The Booker Prize's Bad (Guyanese) History," *New York Times*, October 17, 2017, https://www.nytimes.com; Michael McNay, "Berger Turns Tables on Booker," *Guardian (London)*, November 23, 1972, https://www.theguardian.com.

6. Maxine Berg, "Skill, Craft and Histories of Industrialisation in Europe and Asia," *Transactions of the Royal Historical Society* 24 (2014): 127–48, doi:10.1017/S0080440114000061; Stephen Broadberry and Bishnupriya Gupta, "Cotton Textiles and the Great Divergence: Lancashire, India and Shifting Competitive Advantage, 1600–1850," International Macroeconomics and Economic History Initiative Discussion Paper series, no. 5183, Center for Economic Policy Research, 2005, https://cepr.org. And there's a good (if non-peer-reviewed) account of this by the blogger LK, "The Early British Industrial Revolution and Infant Industry Protectionism: The Case of Cotton Textiles," Social Democracy for the 21st Century: A Realist Alternative to the Modern Left, June 22, 2020, http://socialdemocracy21stcentury.blogspot.com.

7. For a more direct analysis of how the plantation as an institution depended on the

"underdevelopment" of certain places and kinds of people, see the work of Sidney Mintz's contemporary the economist George Beckford and others who have built on his "plantation economy thesis." See, for example, Beckford, *Persistent Poverty: Underdevelopment in Plantation Economies of the Third World* (1972; reprint Kingston, Jamaica: Canoe Press, 1999); Lloyd Best and Kari Levitt, *Essays on the Theory of Plantation Economy: A Historical and Institutional Approach to Caribbean Economic Development* (Mona, Jamaica: University of the West Indies, 2009); and Katherine McKittrick, "Plantation Futures," *small axe* 42 (November 2013): 1–15.

8. In *The Botany of Desire: A Plant's Eye View of the World* (New York: Random House, 2001), Michael Pollan popularized the emerging sense that plants have domesticated people as much as the other way around. Anna Tsing's "Unruly Edges: Mushrooms as Companion Species," *Environmental Humanities* 1 (2012): 141–54, makes a broad anthropological and historical case for the same idea, which is also pursued in the works of other environmental anthropologists and historians.

9. Hopkinson, "The Booker Prize's Bad (Guyanese) History"; Eric Foner, *Nothing but Freedom: Emancipation and Its Legacy* (Baton Rouge: Louisiana State University Press, 1983), 22. This represented about half of the people who went from India to the Caribbean during the indenture period, according to Lomarsh Roopnarine in *The Indian Caribbean: Migration and Identity in the Diaspora* (Jackson: University Press of Mississippi, 2018), 13. Trinidad and Suriname were the other main destinations for indentured workers.

10. Rabe, *U.S. Intervention in British Guiana*.

11. Sidney Mintz, *Tasting Food, Tasting Freedom: Excursions into Eating, Culture, and the Past* (Boston: Beacon Press, 1996), 41. See also Sylvia Wynter, "Novel and History, Plot and Plantation," *Savacou* 5 (June 1971): 95–102; Foner, *Nothing but Freedom*, 18–22, 55; Lynsey Ann Bates, "Surplus and Access: Provisioning and Market Participation by Enslaved Laborers on Jamaican Sugar Estates" (PhD diss., University of Pennsylvania, 2015); and Marietta Morrissey, *Slave Women in the New World: Gender Stratification in the Caribbean* (Lawrence: University Press of Kansas, 2021), esp. chap. 4 on "Household Economies."

12. Kenneth M. Olsen, "SNPs, SSRs and Inferences on Cassava's Origin," *Plant Molecular Biology* 56 (2004): 523.

13. John A. Dixon, "Cassava in Indonesia: Its Economic Role and Use as Food," *Contemporary Southeast Asia* 3, no. 4 (March 1982): 363.

14. James Scott, *Against the Grain: A Deep History of the Earliest States* (New Haven, CT: Yale University Press, 2017), 21.

15. Kelly Wisecup, "Foodways and Resistance: Cassava, Poison, and Natural Histories in the Early Americas," in *Dethroning the Deceitful Pork Chop: Rethinking African American Foodways from Slavery to Obama*, ed. Jennifer Jensen Wallach (Fayetteville: University of Arkansas Press, 2015), 10–11.

16. Janette Bulkan, "The Place of Bitter Cassava in the Social Organization and Belief Systems of Two Indigenous Peoples of Guyana," *Culture, Agriculture, Food and Environment* 41, no. 2 (2019): 117–28. On the names of different landraces, see page 121.

17. Harvey Washington Wiley, the USDA chemist who later became the first head of the U.S. Food and Drug Administration, made a study of cassava in 1894 and concluded that it would be a viable commercial crop in parts of Florida, Alabama, Mississippi, Louisiana, and Texas. See Wiley, *Sweet Cassava: Its Culture, Properties and Uses* (Washington, DC: Government Printing Office, 1894), and Wiley, *The Manufacture of Starch from Potatoes and Cassava* (Washington, DC: Government Printing Office, 1900).

18. "Fiftieth Anniversary of Minute Tapioca Manufacture Observed," *Orange [MA] Enterprise and Journal*, September 18, 1947.

19. Dixon, "Cassava in Indonesia," 361.

20. Between the world wars, there was as much land devoted to growing cassava in Indonesia as in the rest of the world combined. While much of this was for domestic consumption, exports also rose substantially in this period. Pierre van der Eng, "Cassava in Indonesia: A Historical Re-Appraisal of an Enigmatic Food Crop," *Southeast Asian Studies* 36, no. 1 (1998): 5. In Orange, which had helped spur this shift toward exports, the local paper noted, "Since 1914 practically all high quality tapioca flour has come from Java." "Minute Tapioca Co. Is Fifty Years Old September 10th," *Orange Enterprise and Journal*, September 7, 1944.

21. "A Peculiar Coincident," *Orange Enterprise and Journal*, September 13, 1912.

22. "It is planned to raise enough tapioca for the needs of the company's growing business, although roots may have to be bought for a time from the natives. The natives use the tapioca roots to bake and eat, grind up and make cakes of, and also for all laundry starch." "A Peculiar Coincident."

23. "Concerning Tapioca Production," *Orange Enterprise and Journal*, October 10, 1913. On the centrality of cheapness in the modern industrialized food system (and world), see Raj Patel and Jason W. Moore, *A History of the World in Seven Cheap Things: A Guide to Capitalism, Nature, and the Future of the Planet* (Berkeley: University of California Press, 2018).

24. "25 Years Ago," *Orange Enterprise and Journal*, November 16, 1944.

25. "Fiftieth Anniversary of Minute Tapioca." This is from Gridley's speech at Minute Tapioca's delayed fiftieth anniversary celebration, described in more detail in chapter 8.

26. You can find a good introduction to this body of thought and scholarship in "The Plantationocene Series: Plantation Worlds, Past and Present" from *Edge Effects*, a digital magazine about environmental issues based at the University of Wisconsin–Madison, https://edgeeffects.net/plantationocene-series-plantation-worlds/.

27. "Reflections on the Plantationocene: A Conversation with Donna Haraway and Anna Tsing," *Edge Effects*, June 18, 2019, https://edgeeffects.net. On the development of farm as factory, see Deborah Fitzgerald, *Every Farm a Factory: The Industrial Ideal in American Agriculture* (New Haven, CT: Yale University Press, 2003), and Paul K. Conkin, *A Revolution Down on the Farm: The Transformation of American Agriculture since 1929* (Lexington: University Press of Kentucky, 2008). Two episodes of Sarah Taber's *Farm to Taber* podcast featuring Caitlin Rosenthal, entitled "Factories Didn't Ruin Farms, Farms Ruined Factories," also explore these histories and connections.

28. Dean Cycon, *Javatrekker: Dispatches from the World of Fair Trade Coffee* (White River Junction, VT: Chelsea Green, 2007), 10. Other quotes, unless attributed, are from a 2021 interview that I conducted with Dean Cycon.

29. In 2015 there were more than 23,000 Starbucks stores worldwide. By 2023 that had risen to more than 35,000. "Number of Starbucks Stores Worldwide from 2003 to 2022," Statista, 2023, https://www.statista.com. In 2018 Starbucks sold its packaged coffee division to Nestlé in order to concentrate on its cafés, so the Starbucks products on supermarket shelves are actually Nestlé.

30. Cycon, *Javatrekker*, xi. Janina Grabs and Stefano Ponte have tracked these trends in the coffee industry over the past four decades in "The Evolution of Power in the Global Coffee Value Chain and Production Network," *Journal of Economic Geography* 19, no. 4 (July 2019): 803–28. The essays in Sarah Lyon and Mark Moberg, eds., *Fair Trade and Social Justice: Global Ethnographies* (New York: New York University Press,

2010), explore these trends in both general and place-specific ways, while Paige Welt's *From Modern Production to Imagined Primitive: The Social World of Coffee from Papua New Guinea* (Durham, NC: Duke University Press, 2012), looks in depth at one iconic coffee-producing region. Also see Daniel Jaffee, *Brewing Justice: Fair Trade Coffee, Sustainability, and Survival* (Berkeley: University of California Press, 2014).

31. The major umbrella organization was originally called Fairtrade Labelling Organizations International when it was created in 1997. It's now Fairtrade International. The mechanics and history of the fair-trade movement are recounted in Gavin Fridell, *Fair Trade Coffee: The Prospects and Pitfalls of Market-Driven Social Justice* (Toronto: University of Toronto Press, 2007), and in Lyon and Moberg, *Fair Trade and Social Justice*.

32. This organization "fight[s] to protect nature for people" and works "to spotlight and secure the critical benefits that nature provides to humanity," a human-centered vision of the natural world that exemplifies the merely surface-level environmental commitments of much of the corporate sector. "About Conservation International," Conservation International, https://www.conservation.org.

33. Brian MacQuarrie, "Bitter Feelings over Coffee Bean Prices," *Boston Globe*, November 18, 2003, http://archive.boston.com; Rob Walker, "The Joys and Perils of Attack Marketing," *Inc*, April 1, 2004, https://www.inc.com.

34. Joe Fassler, "You Can't Compost Your Food Waste and Eat It Too," *The Counter*, January 3, 2017, https://thecounter.org.

35. Dean Cycon, "My New Life as a Pirate," Dean's Beans Blog, March 31, 2005, https://deansbeans.com.

36. Dean Cycon, "Johnny Depp, Fair Trade and Me—A Cautionary Tale," Dean's Beans Blog, August 13, 2011, https://deansbeans.com.

37. Cycon, *Javatrekker*, 202, 228.

38. A few of the best-known projects are Soul Fire Farm in Grafton, New York; Cooperation Jackson in Jackson, Mississippi; the Detroit Black Community Food Security Network; and the Southeastern African American Farmers' Organic Network. For some of the scholarly work that addresses plantation legacies and race specifically, see McKittrick, "Plantation Futures," and Janae Davis, Alex A. Moulton, Levi Van Sant, and Brian Williams, "Anthropocene, Capitalocene, . . . Plantationocene? A Manifesto for Ecological Justice in an Age of Global Crises," *Geography Compass* 13, no. 11 (2019).

CHAPTER 7: HINTERED LANDS

1. Saskia Sassen, "At the Systemic Edge: Expulsions," *European Review* 24, no. 1 (2016): 89–104.

2. Ricky Baruch and Deb Habib, *Making Love While Farming: A Field Guide to a Life of Passion and Purpose* (Amherst, MA: Levellers Press, 2019), 69–70.

3. Sidney Mintz, *Sweetness and Power: The Place of Sugar in Modern History* (New York: Penguin, 1986).

4. The classic anthropological texts on this include Bronislaw Malinowski's *Argonauts of the Western Pacific* (1922), and Marcel Mauss's *The Gift: Forms and Functions of Exchange in Archaic Societies* (1925). Both have been roundly and rightly critiqued for being embedded in colonialist ways of thinking about and studying human societies and economic life, but they also stand as evidence of economic thinking that differs strikingly from the assumptions of modern Western capitalism.

5. The USDA counted fewer than 2,000 U.S. farmers' markets in 1994 and nearly 8,300 in 2014, according to a widely used chart. U.S. Department of Agriculture, Economic

Research Service, "Number of U.S. Farmers' Markets Continues to Rise," August 4, 2014, https://www.ers.usda.gov. On the saturation question, see Tom Laskawy, "Too Many Markets or Not Enough Farmers?" *Grist*, August 23, 2011, https://grist.org, and Jodi Helmer, "Why Are So Many Farmers Markets Failing? Because the Market Is Saturated," *Salt*, NPR, March 17, 2019, https://www.npr.org. The Farmers Market Coalition, a farmer-centered group, posted lengthy and thoughtful follow-ups to the widely read 2019 NPR story; see Dar Wolnik, "Are There Too Many Farmers Markets? Notes from the Market Field, Part 1," Farmers Market Coalition, May 8, 2019, https://farmersmarketcoalition.org.

6. The phrase has been applied to many human-made "natural" preserves. The Quabbin reference comes mainly from a 1990 book by Thomas Conuel with photographer Les Campbell, *Quabbin: The Accidental Wilderness* (Amherst: University of Massachusetts Press, 1990).

7. Dona Brown, *Inventing New England: Regional Tourism in the Nineteenth Century* (Washington, DC: Smithsonian Institution Press, 1995), esp. chap. 5, "'That Dream of Home': Northern New England and the Farm Vacation Industry, 1890–1900."

8. Brian MacQuarrie, "Long Hunts for Help Add to Addicts' Struggles," *Boston Globe*, May 27, 2014.

9. Baruch and Habib, *Making Love While Farming*, 66.

10. Baruch and Habib, *Making Love While Farming*, 70.

11. Hands across the Hills, https://www.handsacrossthehills.org. On New Englanders' long history of cultural interventions in Appalachia, see David E. Whisnant, *All That Is Native and Fine: The Politics of Culture in an American Region* (1983; reprint Chapel Hill: University of North Carolina Press, 2009). J. D. Vance's 2016 memoir, *Hillbilly Elegy: A Memoir of a Family and Culture in Crisis* (New York: Harper, 2016), became a bestseller largely because it seemed to explain the resentment that fueled Trump's rise; it also spawned a counter-literature by people from the region who insisted on a more complex account of Appalachia's hintering and struggles. See, for example, Elizabeth Catte, *What You Are Getting Wrong about Appalachia* (Cleveland: Belt, 2018), and Anthony Harkins and Meredith McCarroll, eds., *Appalachian Reckoning: A Region Responds to* Hillbilly Elegy (Morgantown: West Virginia University Press, 2019). Historian Steven Stoll's *Ramp Hollow: The Ordeal of Appalachia* (New York: Hill and Wang, 2017), explores generational poverty in Appalachia as part of the far broader struggle of small farmers (often termed "peasants" and "smallholders") to hold onto their land and find a way to subsist within inhospitable, often industrialized landscapes.

CHAPTER 8: THE C-WORD

1. Quoted in Cathy Stanton, *The Lowell Experiment: Public History in a Postindustrial City* (Amherst: University of Massachusetts Press, 2006), 145.

2. Ben Hewitt, *The Town That Food Saved: How One Community Found Vitality in Local Food* (New York: Rodale, 2010), 86–97, 91, 92, 95 (quotations).

3. Some thinkers and activists have talked about the benefits of breadth and ambiguity in food movement thinking in order to enable the inclusion of diverse actors. See Eric Holt-Giménez and Yi Wang, "Reform or Transformation: The Pivotal Role of Food Justice in the U.S. Food Movement," *Race/Ethnicity: Multidisciplinary Global Contexts* 5, no. 1 (Autumn 2011): 83–102, esp. 94; Sam Grey and Raj Patel, "Food Sovereignty as Decolonization: Some Contributions from Indigenous Movements to Food System and Development Politics," *Agriculture and Human Values* 32 (2015): 431–44, esp.

433–34; and Felipe Roa-Clavijo, *The Politics of Food Provisioning in Colombia: Agrarian Movements and Negotiations with the State* (New York: Routledge, 2021).

4. Two essays that clearly set out these options and their implications for making change in the food system are Jack Kloppenburg Jr., John Hendrickson, and G. W. Stevenson, "Coming in to the Foodshed," in *Rooted in the Land: Essays on Community and Place*, ed. William Vitek and Wes Jackson (New Haven, CT: Yale University Press, 1996), 113–12, and Eric Holt-Giménez, "Food Security, Food Justice, or Food Sovereignty?" *Food First Backgrounder* 16, no. 4 (Winter 2010).

5. It was a 2012 study by Dana Gunders of the Natural Resources Defense Council that moved this onto the national radar as an issue. Gunders, *Wasted: How America Is Losing Up to 40 Percent of Its Food from Farm to Fork to Landfill*, National Resources Defense Council, 2012, updated 2017, https://www.nrdc.org.

6. In 2021 the UN Food and Agriculture Organization tracked food supply (i.e., how many food calories are actually available at the retail level) for all regions of the world from 1961 to 2018 and found that by 1970, every region met the baseline of about two thousand calories a day that is widely considered adequate for adult nutrition. Most were above that level even fifty years ago; by 2018 every region was well above it. United Nations Food and Agriculture Organization, "Food Balances (2010–)," https://www.fao.org. Also see Frances Moore Lappé and Joseph Collins, *World Hunger: 10 Myths* (New York: Grove Press, 2015), esp. "Myth 1: Too Little Food, Too Many People"; Eric Holt-Giménez, *Can We Feed the World without Destroying It?* (Cambridge, UK: Polity, 2019), esp. chap. 2, "Hunger in a World of Plenty"; and Marion Nestle, *Let's Ask Marion: What You Need to Know about the Politics of Food, Nutrition, and Health* (Berkeley: University of California Press, 2020), esp. chap. 13, "Can We Feed the World Well?" Holt-Giménez writes about "the myth of scarcity" that is used to drive the search for ever-higher yields and production levels. Nestle calls this "the Big Excuse," Jonathan Latham and others have termed it "the Golden Fact." See Jonathan Latham, "How the Great Food War Will Be Won," *Independent Science News for Food and Agriculture*, January 12, 2015, https://www.independentsciencenews.org.

7. Beyond my very simplistic description here, you can read about the economic effects of overproduction and the idea of parity pricing in the essays published online as part of the Disparity to Parity to Solidarity project, especially Kathryn Anderson, "Supply Management, Parity Prices, and Ecological Thinking as the Foundation for a Practical Agriculture System," Disparity to Parity to Solidarity, https://disparitytoparity.org.

8. Deborah Fitzgerald, *Every Farm a Factory: The Industrial Ideal in American Agriculture* (New Haven, CT: Yale University Press, 2003); Paul K. Conkin, *A Revolution Down on the Farm: The Transformation of American Agriculture since 1929* (Lexington: University Press of Kentucky, 2008); R. Douglas Hurt, *Problems of Plenty: The American Farmer in the Twentieth Century* (Chicago: Ivan R. Dee, 2003).

9. Shane Hamilton, *Supermarket USA: Food and Power in the Cold War Farms Race* (New Haven, CT: Yale University Press, 2018), 35–36.

10. Hamilton, *Supermarket USA*, 35–38.

11. "Food Dollar Series," Economic Research Service, USDA, https://www.ers.usda.gov.

12. Janet Poppendieck, *Sweet Charity: Emergency Food and the End of Entitlement* (New York: Penguin, 1998), 42.

13. "Budget Summary," USDA, 2022, https://www.usda.gov.

14. There's been a recent spate of books critiquing the status quo in the emergency food assistance sector, including Andrew Fisher, *Big Hunger: The Unholy Alliance between Corporate America and Anti-Hunger Groups* (Cambridge, MA: MIT Press, 2018); Graham

Riches, *Food Bank Nations: Poverty, Corporate Charity and the Right to Food* (New York: Routledge, 2018); Rebecca de Souza, *Feeding the Other: Whiteness, Privilege, and Neoliberal Stigma in Food Pantries* (Cambridge, MA: MIT Press, 2019); and Maggie Dickinson, *Feeding the Crisis: Care and Abandonment in America's Food Safety Net* (Berkeley: University of California Press, 2019). A decade earlier, food writer and activist Mark Winne explored the challenges of connecting up fresh and local food with people receiving food assistance; see Winne, *Closing the Food Gap: Resetting the Table in the Land of Plenty* (Boston: Beacon Press, 2009).

15. Bart Barnes, "Gus Schumacher, a Force in the Farm-to-Table Movement, Dies at 77," *Washington Post*, September 27, 2017, https://www.washingtonpost.com. The online biographies of Massachusetts's agricultural commissioners give some sense of the evolution of this and other policies in the state. Massachusetts Department of Agricultural Resources, "MDAR History and Commissioners," https://www.mass.gov.

16. My firsthand experiences with HIP were supplemented with interviews with Jeff Cole and Winton Pitcoff of the Massachusetts Food System Collaborative and Frank Nocito Martinez, formerly of the Department of Transitional Assistance. Also see Susan Bartlett et al., "Evaluation of the Healthy Incentives Pilot (HIP): Final Report," U.S. Department of Agriculture, Food and Nutrition Service, September 2014, https://www.fns.usda.gov. A 2022 report from the Massachusetts Food System Collaborative chronicles the bumpy start and eventual entrenching of the program in the state budget. See Becca Miller, "Healthy Families, Sustainable Farms: Lessons Learned from the Campaign for Healthy Incentives Program Funding," Massachusetts Food System Collaborative, May 2022, https://mafoodsystem.org.

17. See Harvey Levenstein, *Revolution at the Table: The Transformation of the American Diet* (Berkeley: University of California Press, 2003), esp. chap. 4, "The New England Kitchen and the Failure to Reform Working-Class Eating Habits," and Melanie DuPuis, *Dangerous Digestion: The Politics of American Dietary Advice* (Berkeley: University of California Press, 2015).

18. Barnes, "Gus Schumacher, a Force in the Farm-to-Table Movement."

19. Kate Stillman, "'HIP' Benefits Hurt Local Meat Sales," *Sustainable Dish* (podcast), episode 35, December 12, 2017, https://sustainabledish.com.

20. "Fiftieth Anniversary," *Orange [MA] Enterprise and Journal*, September 18, 1947. Accounts of the anniversary event, including excerpts from the speeches, are from this article unless otherwise noted.

21. David Bird, "Clarence Francis, 97, Is Dead; Ex-General Foods Chairman," *New York Times*, December 25, 1985.

22. "Our History," Ingredion, March 2018, https://www.ingredion.com.

23. Center for Sustainable Systems, University of Michigan, "U.S. Food System Factsheet," pub. no. CSS01-06, 2023, https://css.umich.edu.

24. See Dale Allen Pfeiffer, *Eating Fossil Fuels: Oil, Food, and the Coming Crisis in Agriculture* (Gabriola Island, BC: New Society, 2006); Patrick Canning et al., "Energy Use in the U.S. Food System," USDA ERA Economic Research Report no. 94 (March 2010), https://www.ers.usda.gov; and Center for Sustainable Systems, "U.S. Food System Factsheet."

25. Quoted in Nancy Rubin, *American Empress: The Life and Times of Marjorie Merriweather Post* (1995; reprint Lincoln, NE: iUniverse Star, 2004), 97–98.

26. Steve Striffler, *Chicken: The Dangerous Transformation of America's Favorite Food* (New Haven, CT: Yale University Press, 2005); Elanor Starmer and Timothy A. Wise, "Living High on the Hog: Factory Farms, Federal Policy, and the Structural Transformation of Swine Production," Global Development and Environment Institute Working Paper no. 07-04, Tufts University (December 2007), https://sites.tufts.edu; Hamilton,

Supermarket USA, 22; Joshua Specht, *Red Meat Republic: A Hoof-to-Table History of How Beef Changed America* (Princeton, NJ: Princeton University Press, 2019); Alex Blanchette, *Porkopolis: American Animality, Standardized Life, and the Factory Farm* (Durham, NC: Duke University Press, 2020).

27. A letter from President Dwight Eisenhower to Francis about this, dated September 9, 1954, can be found at the American Presidency Project: https://www.presidency.ucsb.edu. On the Food for Peace program, see Hamilton, *Supermarket USA*, esp. chap. 6, "Food Power and the Global Supermarket," and Kristin Ahlberg, *Transplanting the Great Society: Lyndon Johnson and Food for Peace* (Columbia: University of Missouri Press, 2008).

28. "Says Food Will Rise a Bit, Then Decline," *New York Times*, March 29, 1947.

29. "Local Industries Looking Forward to Busy 1947," *Orange Enterprise and Journal*, January 9, 1947.

30. Binyamin Applebaum, *The Economists' Hour: False Prophets, Free Markets, and the Fracture of Society* (Boston: Little, Brown, 2019); Elizabeth Popp Berman, *Thinking Like an Economist: How Efficiency Replaced Equality in U.S. Public Policy* (Princeton, NJ: Princeton University Press, 2022.)

31. "Rodney Hunt Spurns Orange," *Greenfield [MA] Recorder*, November 16, 2015, https://www.recorder.com.

CHAPTER 9: MARGINS

1. Greg Patmore and Nikola Balnave, *A Global History of Co-Operative Business* (New York: Routledge, 2018), sets out the history of co-operatives from a Eurocentric perspective. In *From Mutual Aid to the Welfare State: Fraternal Societies and Social Services, 1890–1967* (Chapel Hill: University of North Carolina Press, 2000), David T. Beito shows how immigrants to the United States mobilized their communities' resources for mutual assistance, a pattern that continues into the present. Jessica Gordon Nembhard traces the history of Black co-ops in *Collective Courage: A History of African American Cooperative Economic Thought and Practice* (Philadelphia: Pennsylvania State University Press, 2014), and the chapters in *Indigenous Food Sovereignty in the United States: Restoring Cultural Knowledge, Protecting Environments, and Regaining Health*, ed. Devon A. Mihuesuah and Elizabeth Hoover (Norman: University of Oklahoma Press, 2019), highlight Indigenous food sovereignty projects that are mutualistic and co-operative in intent if not always in name. Kali Akuno and Ajamu Nangwaya, eds., *Jackson Rising: The Struggle for Economic Democracy and Black Self-Determination in Jackson, Mississippi* (Montreal: Daraja Press, 2017), is a detailed insider account of the extensive co-operative network in one southern U.S. city and region.

2. Julie Guthman has written about the rise of the organic sector in *Agrarian Dreams: The Paradox of Organic Farming in California* (Berkeley: University of California Press, 2004), a critique that Michael Pollan amplified in *The Omnivore's Dilemma: A Natural History of Four Meals* (New York: Penguin, 2006), esp. chap. 9, "Big Organic." Others have also explored the complicated relationship between "natural foods" and capitalism. For example, see Josée Johnson et al., "Lost in the Supermarket: The Corporate-Organic Foodscape and the Struggle for Food Democracy," *Antipode* 41, no. 3 (2009): 509–32; Laura J. Miller, *Building Nature's Market: The Business and Politics of Natural Foods* (Chicago: University of Chicago Press, 2017); and Maria McGrath, *Food for Dissent: Natural Foods and the Consumer Counterculture since the 1960s* (Amherst: University of Massachusetts Press, 2019).

3. Maura Judkis, "The Days of 'Whole Paycheck' Are Over. Here's How the Amazon–Whole Foods Deal Affects You," *Washington Post*, August 24, 2017, https://www.washing

tonpost.com; Eugene Kim, "Whole Foods CEO Says Amazon Helped His Company Escape 'Whole Paycheck' Trap," CNBC, September 28, 2017, https://www.cnbc.com; Kelly Tyko, "Bye-Bye, 'Whole Paycheck'? Amazon's Whole Foods Market Cutting Prices Starting Wednesday," *USA Today*, April 1, 2019, https://www.usatoday.com.

4. Joe Fassler and Kate Cox, "Cattle Operation May Have Caused E. Coli Outbreak Linked to Romaine, FDA Says," *The Counter*, August 6, 2018, https://thecounter.org; Dan Charles, "What Sparked an E. Coli Outbreak in Lettuce? Scientists Trace a Surprising Source," Morning Edition, NPR, August 29, 2018, www.npr.org.

5. bell hooks, "Marginality as Site of Resistance," in *Out There: Marginalization and Contemporary Cultures*, ed. Russell Ferguson et al. (Cambridge, MA: MIT Press, 1989), 341–43.

6. This is the vision that animates Cooperation Jackson, an extensive network of cooperative ventures in the historically hintered, majority-Black state of Mississippi. The paucity and depletion of resources there, writes one of the leaders of the project, "creates a degree of 'breathing room' on the margins and within the cracks of the capitalist system that a project like ours can maneuver and experiment within in the quest to build a viable anti-capitalist alternative." Kali Akuno, "Build and Fight: The Program and Strategy of Cooperation Jackson," in Akuno and Nangwaya, *Jackson Rising*, 10.

7. Becca Miller, "Healthy Families, Sustainable Farms: Lessons Learned from the Campaign for Healthy Incentives Program Funding," Massachusetts Food System Collaborative, May 2022, https://mafoodsystem.org.

8. Since 2012 the corporation had acquired ten other businesses in whole or in part, mostly in the organic and natural foods sector. Patrick Rehkamp, "What Does United Natural Foods See in Supervalu?" *St. Paul [MN] Business Journal*, July 26, 2018, https://www.bizjournals.com.

9. Rehkamp, "What Does United Natural Foods See in Supervalu?"

CHAPTER 10: SIGNS

1. Many co-ops struggle with this dilemma of what to call themselves. See Jon Steinman, *Grocery Story: The Promise of Food Co-Ops in the Age of Grocery Giants* (Gabriola Island, BC: New Society, 2019), 224.

2. John T. Edge, "A Chili Sauce to Crow About," *New York Times*, May 19, 2009; "Sriracha: How a Sauce Won Over the US," BBC, December 20, 2013, https://www.bbc.com; "David Tran: How a Vietnamese Refugee Founded a Multi-Million Dollar Sriracha Empire," Next Shark, https://nextshark.com. On the troubling segregation of certain foods to the ethnic or international category, see Krishnendu Ray, *The Ethnic Restaurateur* (New York: Bloomsbury, 2016); Sam Worley, "The End of the Ethnic Food Aisle," *Epicurious*, May 17, 2017, https://www.epicurious.com; and Priya Krishna, "Why Do American Grocery Stores Still Have an Ethnic Aisle?" *New York Times*, August 10, 2021, https://www.nytimes.com.

3. The 2018 film *Forgotten Farms* includes a segment where people who should know try to explain how the federal price of milk is determined. No one succeeds.

4. Steinman, *Grocery Story*, 107.

5. Steinman, *Grocery Story*, 235.

6. For some of the older foundations of this recent work, see Rachel Bowlby, *Carried Away: The Invention of Modern Shopping* (New York: Columbia University Press, 2002), and Tracey Deutsch, *Building a Housewife's Paradise: Gender, Politics, and American Grocery Stores in the Twentieth Century* (Chapel Hill: University of North Carolina Press, 2010). Some of the newer work comes from the policy and advocacy world, including a debate about how to address so-called food deserts (for example, "Grocery Goliaths:

How Food Monopolies Impact Consumers," Food and Water Watch, December 2013). Ashanté Reese's *Black Food Geographies: Race, Self-Reliance, and Food Access in Washington, DC* (Chapel Hill: University of North Carolina Press, 2019), explores neighborhood-level struggles for food provisioning in the wake of supermarket disinvestment. Other smart explorations and exposés of the supermarket over the past decade include Shane Hamilton, *Supermarket USA: Food and Power in the Cold War Farms Race* (New Haven, CT: Yale University Press, 2018), and Benjamin Lorr, *The Secret Life of Groceries: The Dark Miracle of the American Supermarket* (New York: Avery, 2020).

7. Sandra E. Garcia, "Stop & Shop Strike Ends with Union Claiming Victory on Pay and Health Care," *New York Times*, April 22, 2019, https://www.nytimes.com; Jim Shay, "Timeline of Stop & Shop Strike," AP News, April 22, 2019, https://apnews.com.

8. Joshua Solomon, "With Stop & Shop Strike Over, Now What?" *Greenfield [MA] Recorder*, April 22, 2019, https://www.recorder.com.

CHAPTER 11: FUTURES

1. The performance is recorded on the conference video at about the 3:28:00 mark. "Food, Farms, Fisheries and Forests: Diet, Climate, Conservation, and a Healthy Future for New England," American Farmland Trust, February 19, 2020, https://farmland.org.

2. "Innovations in School Food during COVID-19," Food Policy Center, Hunter College, January 19, 2021, https://www.nycfoodpolicy.org; Brenna Houck, "America's Restaurants Are Closing. What's Happening to the Food?" *Eater*, March 17, 2020, https://www.eater.com.

3. Wendell Berry, Robin Wall Kimmerer, Anna Lappé, Raj Patel, Leah Penniman, Michael Pollan, and Eric Schlosser are just a few of the better-known of these voices, along with Bill McKibben in the adjacent field of energy activism.

4. On Indigenous food projects, see the White Earth Reservation's wild rice business in Minnesota and the Oglala Lakota's Native American Natural Foods, which makes tanka bar from buffalo meat as part of an effort to rebuild a buffalo-centered food economy on the Pine Ridge Reservation in South Dakota. On regenerative, polycultural, agro-ecological approaches to farming, see the Land Institute in Kansas, Singing Frogs Farm in California, and Timeless Natural Food in Montana (the latter grows legume crops that pull nitrogen from the air to fertilize the plants and maintain soil fertility, reducing or eliminating farmers' dependence on synthetic fertilizers). On labor organizing, see the worker-driven social responsibility campaigns at organizations like Migrant Justice and the Coalition of Imokalee Workers. On community organizing and the networks such projects are often part of, see the Detroit Black Community Food Security Network, the Sweet Water Foundation in Chicago, and the HEAL Food Alliance. On farmers and others organizing against the power of the "feed-meat complex," see the Food Not Feed campaign at Farm Action and other efforts to shape the 2023 U.S. farm bill to reduce the emphasis on commodity grains. On projects in support of parity pricing for farmers, see the Disparity to Parity to Solidarity Project based at the National Family Farm Coalition and American University. On radical and critical food assistance efforts, see WhyHunger in New York City and Food Not Bombs all over the world, as well as emerging discussions within the mainstream food banking sector as detailed by Andrew Fisher in the epilogue of *Big Hunger: The Unholy Alliance between Corporate America and Anti-Hunger Groups* (Cambridge, MA: MIT Press, 2018). And on aquaculture projects that decenter human control of ecosystems, see the Slow Water movement in the United Kingdom, as documented in Erica Gies, *Water Always Wins: Thriving in an Age of Drought and Deluge* (Chicago: University of Chicago Press, 2022),

as well as material from groups like the North Atlantic Marine Alliance, Connecticut-based GreenWave, and the Indigenous Aquaculture Collaborative.

5. Elizabeth Kolbert, *Under a White Sky: The Nature of the Future* (New York: Crown, 2021), 204.

6. Minute Tapioca Company, *30 New Recipes from the $20,000 Cookbook* (Orange, MA: Minute Tapioca Company, 1929), 13, copy in author's possession.

CATHY STANTON is distinguished senior lecturer at Tufts University, where she teaches classes in anthropology and environmental studies with a particular focus on food studies. She has published widely on public history and heritage, including her book *The Lowell Experiment: Public History in a Postindustrial City* (University of Massachusetts Press, 2006), which won the National Council on Public History's Book Award in 2007. With Michelle Moon, she co-authored *Public History and the Food Movement: Adding the Missing Ingredient* (Routledge, 2018). Born in Canada, she has resided in Massachusetts for forty years and currently lives with her husband in a small town in the central part of the state.